This pioneering analysis examines the foundations of environmental racism and how marginalized communities became dumping grounds for waste and toxic material, while also demonstrating how these communities have long engaged in activism, resistance, and advocacy for protection. Thoroughly researched and eloquently told, Packing Them In remains a relevant and essential contribution to environmental history and urban studies.

-Lisa Mighetto, Executive Director, American Society for Environmental History

Packing Them In is a classic historical and archeological study of environmental racism in the United States. Where so few studies have attempted to examine environmental racism in the workplace, Sylvia Washington makes her study personal. We come to feel the experiences of Chicago's poor, working class people in neighborhoods like Back of the Yards and Bronzeville. Well done!

-Martin V. Melosi, Hugh Roy and Lillie Cranz Cullen University Professor of History, University of Houston, and author of The Sanitary City

Sylvia Hood Washington broke new ground with this innovative study that pushes the narratives of environmental injustice and resistance to it much earlier than the late 1970s. Packing Them In challenged environmental historians to place race and racism at the core of their scholarship. Theoretically rich and deeply researched, this study explores Chicago's South Side to reveal processes of racialization that redefined Eastern European immigrants as white and thus able to move beyond environmental exposures that continued to plague non-whites. Yet African Americans actively resisted injustices, protesting the placement of toxic industries in their neighborhoods as well as their segregation into unhealthy, dilapidated housing. Trained as both engineer and historian, Washington brings unique talents to a story that has become essential reading in fields ranging from environmental history to urban planning. It is a masterful accomplishment.

-Kathleen A. Brosnan, Travis Chair of Modern History, University of Oklahoma

Packing Them In

*An Archaeology of Environmental Racism
in Chicago, 1865–1954*

Sylvia Hood Washington

PACKING THEM IN
AN ARCHAEOLOGY OF ENVIRONMENTAL
RACISM IN CHICAGO, 1865–1954

iUniverse books may be ordered through booksellers or by contacting:

iUniverse
1663 Liberty Drive
Bloomington, IN 47403
www.iuniverse.com
1-800-Authors (1-800-288-4677)

Because of the dynamic nature of the Internet, any web addresses or links contained in this book may have changed since publication and may no longer be valid. The views expressed in this work are solely those of the author and do not necessarily reflect the views of the publisher, and the publisher hereby disclaims any responsibility for them.

Any people depicted in stock imagery provided by Thinkstock are models, and such images are being used for illustrative purposes only. Certain stock imagery © Thinkstock.

ISBN: 978-1-5320-2615-7 (sc)
ISBN: 978-1-5320-2616-4 (e)

Print information available on the last page.

iUniverse rev. date: 06/23/2017

Contents

Preface

This book began in the early 1990s as I listened to my students of various racial and ethnic backgrounds discuss and debate the notion of "environmental racism." Even though over ten years had passed since the birth of the modern Environmental Justice Movement in the early 1980s, many of them were unfamiliar with both the phrase and its implicit connotations. At the heart of their discussions and debate was a claim that many racial and ethnic groups in the United States and across the world, regardless of color, have experienced some type of environmental disenfranchisement because of who they were or how they were identified in a particular society. Black Nigerians in power environmentally disenfranchise other black Nigerians who aren't in power. Likewise, my memories of the environmental marginalization of my own African American neighborhood in Cleveland, Ohio, which was aided and abetted by African American political leadership during the Civil Rights movement, reinforce the premise of this book: that "environmental racism" is not and has never been simply a problem of white versus black or colored versus noncolored. My argument for this study is that environmental racism existed more than two hundred years before the phrase was coined and the phenomenon recognized in the early 1980s with the birth of the modern

Environmental Justice Movement. The phenomenon is best understood in American history as the marginalization of nonwhite communities versus white communities, and since the very notion of "whiteness" has been fluid, so has been the pathology of environmental racism. If policy makers, urban planners, and environmental scholars and activists want to find solutions to environmental inequalities that exist within a geographical space, they must and should reconcile themselves to the historical pattern and practice of racial marginalization that has characterized that space.

I have written this book to elucidate historical patterns of racial and ethnic marginalization of groups and their concomitant environmental marginalization in one of the most polluted geographies in America, Chicago. The phrase *packing them in* refers to the way in which these populations were forced to exist in deadly high densities because of how they were perceived from both an environmental and social perspective by the larger body politic. This book also shows that each of these community's abilities to escape or find relief from environmental racism was tied to how and when it was allowed to become more white and/or less of a social or environmental threat to the larger community.

Acknowledgments

There are many to whom I am grateful for encouraging me and supporting me in my research endeavors to complete this work over the last ten years. My husband and friend of several decades, Gary Washington, a Harvard-trained policy planner and sociologist, has had a tremendous impact on the direction and scope of my work. His planning and policy perspectives were and still are critical to framing my research in this area. I appreciate the encouragement of my dissertation committee at Case Western Reserve University to pursue this topic as well as their final comments on the subject.

I am also extremely grateful to the senior environmental historians who graciously read and critiqued my manuscript once it started to evolve from the dissertation phase into a book. I sincerely appreciate the input of Jeffrey Stine, past president of the American Society of Environmental History, who was extremely helpful with both written and verbal critiques of the manuscript. Likewise, the written and verbal comments from Andrew Hurley, of the University of St. Louis, literally reshaped the structure and form of the book's argument. The honest input and encouragement of John McNeill, of Georgetown University, made the overall book a more lucid and complete environmental justice history. I am also very grateful for the time that senior African American historian Christopher Robin Reed spent in reviewing and critiquing this book in its eleventh hour from a different but just as relevant perspective. I appreciate the time and effort of individuals at the Center for American Places. Their solicitation of peer reviews and their own critique of my dissertation in the early period were critical in shaping the final outline of the book. I am indebted to the many colleagues who gave me honest and critical advice that in the end helped shape the book, but I am especially grateful to Michelle Murphy, University of Toronto, and Northwestern scholars Henry Binford and Allan Schnaiberg.

This book could not have been completed without the research support of Northwestern University's history department, especially Sarah Maza, and the university's reference librarians. I am grateful to senior archivist Michael Flug of the Vivian G. Harsh Research Collection of Afro American History and Literature of the Chicago Public Library, who led me to archival material that had eluded me in previous and frustrated searches. Thanks are due to archivists at the Harold Washington Library in Chicago, and to the research staff at the Chicago Historical Society and the Newberry Library. I am also extremely grateful to the Chicago Urban League's Vice President of Research, Paul Sweet, who personally assisted me in finding relevant archival material from the organization's on-site archives and gaining access to relevant archival material at the University of Illinois, Chicago, Special Collections; to the Illinois Regional Archives Depository; and to the Metropolitan Sanitary District Archives staff.

Last but not least is my gratitude and appreciation for the patience, cooperation, and support of both my daughters, Sarah and Lauren, who shared their mom with her research and writing efforts.

Introduction

Each individual has his own place; and each place its own individual.
—Michel Foucault, *Discipline and Punish: The Birth of a Prison*

I have been conscious, at times, of writing against the prevailing orthodoxies. . . . Each of these orthodoxies has a certain validity . . . they tend to obscure the agency of working people, the degree to which they contributed, by conscious efforts to the making of history.
—E. P. Thompson, *The Making of the English Working Class*

Why do a disproportionate percentage of poor, working class, and minority communities continue to suffer from environmental inequalities more than twenty years after the modern Environmental Justice Movement? Those currently involved in discussions about the existence of environmental inequalities tied to race or class prefer to use the phrase "environmental justice" rather than the potentially defensive phrase of "environmental racism."[1]

In accordance with philosopher and historian Michel Foucault, I have called the history of environmental injustice discussed in this book the "archaeology" of environmental racism. It is my goal in this book to explain why "environmental racism" is a more accurate description of the past and present phenomena even for "white" communities who suffer from environmental inequalities in the United States. Race, racism, and "whiteness" have been fluid and changing concepts in the United States since its inception, a fact that has been well established by such scholars as David Roediger, Matthew Frye Jacobson, and Ian F. Haney Lopez.[2] Environmental racism is a misunderstood concept in desperate need of explanation from a historical perspective because who becomes a victim of racism is contingent upon the changing notions of race. Environmental racism today is a phenomenon improperly portrayed as a struggle between "blacks" and "whites" in America. Neither blacks nor whites are part of a monolithic community and neither have been perceived as such in the course of their history in the United States. History reveals that environmental racism has been experienced for decades by people or communities who today are classified as white. Their environmental marginalization occurred because at some point in time they were either considered not white or not part of the mainstream white community; subsequently, they were environmentally disenfranchised. These people typically belonged to what today are defined as various ethnic groups, including Irish, Polish, Jewish, Italian, and Appalachian communities. These ethnic groups were rarely, if ever, classified as black; therefore, the argument that African Americans, Hispanics, Native Americans, and Asians are the chief targets of environmental inequalities because they are not white needs to be reexamined. The primary historical difference (from an environmental perspective) between people of color (especially African Americans) and white ethnic groups is that their environmentally marginalized geographical spaces were constructed by more rigid and longer lasting race-based legal decisions and public policies that were sanctioned and endorsed by government at all levels.[3]

Public policies, laws, and private practices that controlled or influenced where people lived and worked in the United States were tainted by notions of race (or who was nonwhite) for over three hundred years. As a result, these policies and practices played a major role in the development of environmental inequalities in poor and working class communities of particular racial or ethnic background in the United States. This became even more prevalent after the Industrial Revolution and the urbanization of cities in the nineteenth century. The current body of environmental histories and studies explicitly and implicitly argues that the ability to minimize or even thwart environmental assaults upon communities became most effective in the latter half of the twentieth century primarily among middle class whites, and brought "lessons learned from previous movements: a knowledge of how the system works, access to a certain amount of scientific expertise, an understanding of how to use the media, and an ability to raise enough funds to maintain viable, albeit lean, organizations."[4] This book challenges this widely accepted belief by showing that minority and poor ethnic white communities also have a history of effective environmental activism that predates the modern Environmental Justice Movement that began in the 1980s and the white, middle class environmental movement that began in the 1970s.

The underlying premise of this book is that poor, foreign, and racial groups have been and are easily constructed as "others"––lepers lying outside the body politic of the larger society––and that this construction is directly related to environmental racism. I use Michel Foucault's concept of "others" in this study to refer to a large array of environmentally marginalized groups within a society because it overcomes the simplistic dichotomy of white versus black. This construction is facilitated by differences in language or dialect, culture, and socially constructed and ever-changing categories of race and ethnicity. The construction of the other is on a cellular level but can, within the larger society, result in the further conceptualization as a "social body" requiring discipline, enclosures, and management by a majority. The twentieth century's Jim Crow laws, restrictive covenants, racial zoning ordinances, and immigration restriction policies are examples of this type of construction and environmental discipline. These groups identified as "others" were, and still are, forced to live in geographical spaces (communities) within the society that are or are becoming environmentally compromised because of their "otherness." Their communities become dumping grounds where waste and toxic material are disproportionately located; apparently, they are the proper place for everything deemed to be undesirable (people and waste). These communities become the ultimate sink for the larger body politic. Historically, "normal and healthy" people did not choose to live in the geographical locations of the leper colony. They sought to maximize the distance between themselves and the lepers.

Similarly, leper colonies were not given the same care and maintenance provided to nonleper colonies. I believe this phenomenon holds true for both social and political lepers; an environmental history of these groups will validate that assumption.

In support of the arguments in this work, Mary Poovey's seminal history, *The Making of a Social Body*,[5] provides an excellent analysis of the emergence of public health policies based upon "otherness" in nineteenth-century Britain. She argues that these policies could only emerge by defining poor communities in nineteenth-century England, and eventually Great Britain, as being a "social body" separate from the body politic. This cultural phenomenon was greatly facilitated by public health policies implemented by Great Britain's famous nineteenth-century sanitarian, Edwin Chadwick, to ameliorate waterborne diseases from urban sewage. Chadwick, a former barrister and self-taught sanitarian, became one of the most influential public health figures in Anglo societies in the late nineteenth and early twentieth centuries.[6]

Poovey points out that England's poor had to be constructed as a social body outside the defined body politic so that they could emerge as Foucault's symbolic "leper" and therefore justifiably be isolated and removed from the larger body. In this way they could be easily individualized (on a macromolecular level) and subsequently identified as "docile bodies" subject to forms of "discipline" that would be of benefit to the society at large.[7] In this case the discipline would be sanitary education and changes in architectural space in order to optimize water quality and therefore minimize the spread of typhoid and other waterborne diseases. Poovey's example of sanitation policies is kindred to the environmental policies under study in my research because the sanitation problem of Britain was worst in poor and immigrant communities. These groups would bear an inequitable share of health problems emanating from environmental pollution as result of rapid industrialization and expansion in a limited urban space.

Like Poovey's poor in Great Britain, Eastern European immigrants and African American migrants in Chicago were constructed as "others" who were not envisioned as being part of the larger body politic. From 1865 to 1940, the immigrants (mostly white) working in the Chicago packing houses voluntarily formed extremely dense residential communities in the same or closely proximate environs of the Chicago stockyards. This area was highly polluted because of legal and illegal waste disposal practices by industrialists, politicians, landlords, and the city itself. Southern African Americans who came to the area between 1915 and 1954 voluntarily moved (and were later forced) into Chicago's Black Belt (and eventually Bronzeville). Bronzeville was the name that black Chicagoans used to refer to their primary geographic space of occupation on the city's South Side.[8]

Both groups were packed into highly degraded environmental spaces because of legal, extralegal, and illegal waste management practices as well as housing policies that were based upon racist and ethnocentric planning policies. Many African American migrants lived in the notorious kitchenette apartments that were firetraps and breeding grounds for tuberculosis and rats. There may have been some Eastern Europeans who lived in kitchenette apartments but these spaces were primarily occupied by black Chicagoan migrants coming into the city during the second migration period. Both groups waged battles to create what today are called "sustainable" living spaces. They fought to maintain, preserve, or restore the environmental integrity of their new homes and immediate environs.

Another objective of this book is to show that environmentally marginalized groups in the United States have a history of environmental activism that predates the historical emergence of the postmodern Environmental Justice Movement launched in 1982 in Warren County, North Carolina, by African Americans who fought unsuccessfully to prevent the disposal of hazardous soil in their communities. Critical to this thematic argument is that the term *environmental racism* actually embraces what I have termed *environmental ethnocentrism*. Written histories to date have focused on either individualized or cellular ethnic community development or labor histories. In each case the immigrants, migrants, or minorities have been portrayed as being either unaware of the hazards emanating from environmental pollution and its concomitant diseases; less caring because of a trade-off with higher needs (economic advancement or security); or impotent in ameliorating their situation because of their social and political rank.

These people were aware of pollution and its potential impact on their neighborhoods and––most importantly––their health. They made many attempts to prevent or stop the environmental degradation of their neighborhoods. Although the communities are each examined for different time spans––Back of the Yards from 1865 to the 1930s and Bronzeville from 1865 to 1954––it is clearly evident that each disenfranchised or marginalized societal group (African American migrants and white ethnic immigrants) made active political and legal attempts to ameliorate environmentally oppressive conditions.

The premise of this book reflects my experiences as an African American woman with firsthand exposure to environmental racism. As a historian, I am keenly aware that facts and reality can be distorted by memory over time, but the oral history tradition among people of African descent and other cultures around the world has been and continues to be a powerful tool for transferring the history of their communities across generations as well as a means of obtaining the full and complete history of a geographical and cultural space or place. As the 2002 national project director of a historic environmental justice and health project funded by the United States Conference of Catholic Bishops and the Knights of Peter Claver, Inc. (the oldest and largest black Catholic lay organization in the United States), I have had the opportunity to hear the environmental memories of hundreds of black people across the country. Their experiences and memories reinforced my own memories as an African American who grew up in a middle class but racially segregated African American neighborhood during the 1960s and 1970s in Cleveland, Ohio. This neighborhood was on the very outskirts of Cleveland and contiguous to Eastern European immigrant (or first generation) neighborhoods. Our neighborhoods shared common environmental spaces that were routinely polluted by the illegal dumping of residential and industrial trash until the 1980s. The African Americans in my community fought against environmental inequalities in an era that predated the modern Environmental Justice Movement. They organized, took political action, and influenced (as much as they could) the environmental conditions of their neighborhood and eventually proved instrumental in preventing another mayoral term for Carl B. Stokes, the first African American mayor of Cleveland, Ohio. The African American citizens of my community believed that this African American mayor was engaged in promoting and executing environmentally racist policies. He, in turn, felt that they were environmental racists who were acting to block the acquisition of sustainable living spaces by less fortunate African Americans who had been spatially confined to the inner city.

This book was also inspired by my professional experiences as an environmental scientist and engineer in the power industry. My relationships with first and second generation Eastern European engineers in the power industry gave me the opportunity to hear their memories about their families' historical environmental struggles for sustainable communities and healthy work environments in urban America. In the early 1980s, when I was working as the plant environmental engineer at the Cleveland Electric Illuminating Company's Lake Shore coal-fired power plant situated on Lake Erie, I heard a recitation of environmental memories similar to mine from a young Slovenian engineer whom I will call "Joe." Joe's family had immigrated to the United States in the 1960s. As a child he came to the United States to live with an extended family who was residing in Cleveland's notorious Flats neighborhood, situated near the city's steel mill industry. Many of Joe's relatives had suffered the physical indignities of living and working in Cleveland's steel mills and had lost limbs and suffered overall poor health because of their working conditions prior to the institution and enforcement of Occupational Safety and Health Administration (OSHA) standards. Joe told me about his uncles who fell victim to molten steel or highly pressurized steam only to return home to crowded and unsanitary housing. Joe shared his family "environmental" stories with me because he wanted me to understand that Eastern European immigrants had also been environmentally marginalized because of their race or ethnicity. They struggled to escape their environmental disenfranchisement both on the job and in the neighborhood through hard work and education to provide them with the economic means for escaping to suburban green space.

Unfortunately, these same techniques were, for decades, useless for African American migrants and their offspring (unless they could racially "pass for white") because of the visual marker of race creating a more insidious stigma of "environmental otherness."

Environmental histories have been written by lay people, nonhistorians, and other social scientists, including such environmental sociologists as Robert Bullard in *Dumping in Dixie*[9] or David Pellow in *Garbage Wars*.[10] Their main emphasis, however, is not in rendering a historical narrative about people, place, and environment so much as making a contemporary analysis of the state and future of the postmodern Environmental Justice Movement. Environmental histories written by professional historians to date have attempted to illustrate the full impacts (both positive and negative) of technologies and technological processes on modern and postmodern societies as a result of the interplay between social, cultural, and political forces. What I have noticed, however, in a large number of these histories is that there is a pervasive silence about the reactions and actions of those who seem to suffer the most and disproportionately from negative environmental impacts: the working class poor and ethnic and minority groups. The vast majority of these histories (with the exception of Andrew Hurley's *Environmental Inequalities*) seem to have an implicit underlying assumption that communities that become environmentally disenfranchised are historically helpless and ignorant victims who have suffered from environmental policies because they did not understand or did not attempt to influence them until the Environmental Justice Movement began in Warren County, North Carolina.

Environmental history in the United States has an environmental "veil" with respect to elucidating the historical perspectives of socially marginalized communities who have experienced environmental inequalities from their own perspectives. This book and my current research is an attempt to lift that veil so that readers can see as well as hear the environmental history of these communities from the perspectives of those who have been environmentally disenfranchised.

This book humbly reflects the beginning of my own research efforts to deconstruct the prevalent historical myth of centuries-long environmental illiteracy, complacency, and inactivity among ethnic and African American communities experiencing both environmental racism and ethnocentrism because they were willing to trade their health and the health of their families for work.

A few key environmental history studies greatly shaped my desire to pursue this type of historical research. They are Andrew Hurley's *Environmental Inequalities*, Ted Steinberg's *Nature Incorporated: Industrialization and the Waters of New England*, Jeffrey Stine's *Mixing the Waters*, and Joel Tarr's *The Search for the Ultimate Sink: Urban Pollution in Historical Perspective.* Each of these works addressed the interaction of social, political, technological, and cultural decisions that have influenced the environmental integrity of a region or a particular city. All of these histories and most of their contemporary studies have, in my opinion, primarily produced "top down" environmental histories from the perspectives of those in power––be it political, social, or economic––or those who had access to power. Steinberg's and Stine's histories each allude (in varying degrees) to the environmental impacts on the working class and socially disenfranchised groups in American history but never really develop the historical perspective of "environmental others" about the radical changes in their environmental space, which were, for the most part, negative. Jobs were created for the masses from these changes but their living spaces became highly polluted and unsustainable from a public health perspective.

Nature Incorporated and *Mixing the Waters* both provide richly detailed descriptions of the technocrats and other players who were key to implementing the major technological changes that transformed the environment and ecosystems within a given region. The reader walks away from this literature with a clear understanding that environmental change brought about by technology cannot be decoupled from a small minority of persons who wield and have access to the majority of power and critical decision makers within a society. It is also clear in these historical narratives that the masses have very little influence or power in making technological decisions or in preventing technological decisions made by a ruling class. For instance, in *Mixing the Waters*, Stine provides two explanations of why the efforts of the environmentalists opposed to the construction of the Tennessee-Tombigbee waterway failed, both explanations attributing the failue to the inability of the group to form consensus with other groups (the minority groups and the railroad companies) who questioned the project. Stine points out:

> One of the most outspoken black leaders . . . questioned the environmentalists' motives and asserted that the black communities affected by the waterway stood to benefit from the creation of thousands of jobs. . . . He charged the national environmental groups with caring more about wildlife than the desperate needs of suffering poor people. . . . Environmentalists . . . warned the community activists not

to be misled by the promise of abundant employment opportunities . . .
and speculated that there might be a net loss of jobs if the waterway
brought an end to . . . local employers.[11]

In Steinberg's *Nature Incorporated*, the reader is provided more detail
(from a social-historical point of view) into the lives and philosophies of
the dominant group (the Boston Associates) that gained control over the
New England waterways as well as the opposition forces.

> The Boston Associates was not a formal organization but a network of
> individuals and families joined by bonds of marriage, friendship, and . . .
> finance. . . . They were prominent in banking, insurance, philanthropy,
> and politics.[12]

Steinberg describes the associates as individuals who sought to control
their environment and the economy, and he concludes that their opponents
seeking to dismantle their hold on the waterways of the New England
waterways achieved very little success. The Boston Associates' opponents
(like those opposed to the Tennessee-Tombigbee Waterway Development
Authority [TTWDA] in *Mixing the Waters*) were not as cohesive or as
powerful. In describing an uprising against the efforts of the Boston
Associates in New Hampshire, Steinberg points out that the leaders of
the riot were

> two people out for revenge, urging on a small group of men most of who
> were economically marginal . . . frustrated . . . by the broader economic
> transformation of the region that did not benefit everyone equally.[13]

The rioters, like most of the opposition in Steinberg's study, fail to achieve
their objectives because they did not possess the political, social, and
economic power to stop the associates. Steinberg's book does fail to provide
any substantial discussion about the views of the marginalized group
regarding the radical environmental transformation of both their living
and working space as a result of the incorporation of nature.

Very few environmental histories written by environmental historians
deal extensively with the community response (from the community's
perspective) to pollution. Andrew Hurley's *Environmental Inequalities:*

Class, Race, and Industrial Pollution in Gary, Indiana, 1945–1980 is, to date, the only formal environmental history that directly addresses environmental inequalities.[14] Hurley's monograph illustrates how African Americans and middle class white women organized themselves in Gary, Indiana, to halt industrialization and suburbanization efforts that would have had a negative impact on their community. Hurley places a strong emphasis on the direct and indirect power wielded by middle class white housewives and provides very little information on the working class minority community. Harold Platt at Loyola University has also dealt with community activism and environmental inequalities. Platt has presented several papers on the role of Jane Addams, founder of Chicago's Hull House Settlement, in advocating optimum environmental conditions for immigrants and the working class who lived near the settlement house.[15] None of these histories has been written from the perspective of the working class, minority, or ethnic community.

Finally, an important historical work that ideologically shapes and influences both this book and my research is E. P. Thompson's *The Making of the English Working Class*.[16] In his preface, Thompson states that some histories "tend to obscure the agency of working people, the degree to which they contribute, by conscious efforts, to the making of history." It was my intent in writing this book to produce a history that reveals the agency, actions, and influences of working class, ethnic, and minority groups, and women, on their own environmental history. This desire to write this type of history is in response to environmental historian Martin Melosi's critique in his essay "Urban Pollution: Historical Perspective Needed." He argues that other avenues that should be explored in the environmental field are the urban environment and the political, socioeconomic, and cultural groups that shaped and influenced the implementation of environmental laws and culture in this system. Melosi points out, "There is . . . a substantial need for historical studies that discuss the role of specific groups and individuals as pollution fighters. Very little has been written about urban-based reform groups who fought for changes in legislation to improve the environment of cities. Little, too, has been written about professional groups who were engaged in environmental reform."[17]

This book relies on traditional sources of information but also includes oral and autobiographical information because very little historical information has been recorded about the experiences of socially marginalized groups from their own perspectives. I view this work as a natural and progressive scholarly step in the current field of environmental history (as opposed to environmental sociology), a new type of environmental history about how disenfranchised people impacted by inequitable environmental policies utilized political mechanisms that they tried and sometimes failed to control or influence. Environmental disenfranchisement does not arise simply from the incorporation of nature but rather from the social construction of citizens as "others," which disentitles them to an equal opportunity to have a choice to live in a healthy and clean environment. In *The Search for the Ultimate Sink: Urban Pollution in Historical Perspective*, Joel Tarr points out that "many who advocated urban decentralization were as motivated by considerations of social control as by a desire to enable men to live more comfortable or healthy lives. City slums crowded with immigrants usually had high crime rates and poor sanitary conditions, and middle- and upper-class citizens worried about the threat of violence and disease posed by congested working-class areas."[18] However, Tarr fails to articulate the historical fact that these congested areas had become "the ultimate sink" because their occupants had become environmentally disenfranchised.

I structure the present work into three parts. Part I, Historical and Philosophical Foundations of Environmental Racism and Environmental Justice, includes chapter 1, "Social Darwinism, Scientific Racism, and the Birth of the Environmental Leper," and chapter 2, "An Archaeology of the Modern Environmental Justice Movement." Chapter 1 discusses the historical and philosophical foundations for the emergence of environmental racism and ethnocentrism in twentieth-century America. I elucidate the historical and philosophical connection between social Darwinism, eugenics, scientific racism, and the emergence of environmental racism. The goal of this chapter is to show how the creation of environmental "others" was a function of how they were imagined and perceived as contributing to or detracting from the environmental health of modern society and the larger body politic; and how these perceptions were legitimized by science. Chapter 2 provides a history of national environmental movements or movements that had environmental objectives by marginalized communities in response to environmental inequalities in their communities. The goal of this chapter is to show that environmental activism and concerns among the socially and racially marginalized in this country existed prior to today's environmental movement, which began in 1982.

Part II, Packing Them In, focuses on an early environmental justice history of European immigrants living in the neighborhood known as Back of the Yards, which was adjacent to the Chicago stockyards. Chapter 3, "Justice in the Jungle," elucidates the history of environmental activism in response to environmental degradation (and consequential public health problems) on the part of the immigrants (and their descendants) living near Back of the Yards, as well as that of their supporters and advocates. The goal of this chapter is not to determine whether the immigrants won or lost an environmental battle but to establish the fact that they cared about the environmental integrity of their community and took measures to resolve environmental issues that affected their own health and the health of their community decades before today's Environmental Justice Movement.

Chapter 4, "Engineering and Environmental Inequality," specifically elucidates the history of the environmental space where the immigrants came to live and how it came to be polluted as a result of political and technological decisions made by the local, state, and federal governments and city and regional planners. The west end of the Chicago River, which ran through these neighborhoods, became severely polluted and came to be known as Bubbly Creek. This chapter also provides a history of the actions that residents of this area took to resolve the pollution produced by the stockyard industries.

Part III, Broken Promises, provides a case history of early environmental justice struggles by African Americans in Chicago in the first half of the twentieth century, during the first two great migration periods, when the use of restrictive covenants was still legal. Chapter 5, "Planning and Environmental Inequalities," shows how planning, real estate policies, and violent aggressions by neighborhood community groups (bolstered by eugenics philosophies and scientific racism) were critical to the formation and maintenance of environmentally marginalized spaces for African Americans (especially migrants) who were living in Chicago. All of these forces resulted in African Americans being packed into the Black Belt and eventually into Bronzeville, creating blighted urban spaces that had severe public and environmental health impacts on this marginalized community. Chapter 6, "'We Fight Blight': Block Beautiful and the Urban Conservation Movement in Chicago's Black Belt, 1915–1954," provides an account of an early environmental justice struggle led by African Americans that sought to create sustainable communities for its members despite racial discrimination and rampant environmental disenfranchisement. The Urban Conservation Movement, built upon an earlier Block Movement, was the first such movement led by African American institutions like the *Chicago Defender* and the Chicago Urban League.

An early environmental justice history of Chicago's marginalized communities is critical to understanding why the problem still exists. This thematic point is the foundation of the book's epilogue, "Raisins in the Sun." The epilogue provides an environmental history of the Altgeld Gardens community and its environmental justice organization, People for Community Recovery. The objective of this final section of the book is to provide an understanding of the complexity of resolving environmental justice struggles for marginalized communities, especially since this particular community was supposed to be the answer to urban blight and environmental marginalization faced by African Americans in Chicago beginning in the mid-1940s. In the end it gained worldwide recognition as the worst environmental living space in Chicago because of the highly polluted geographical space upon which the community was built in an attempt to preserve the long-standing policies of racial segregation in housing in Chicago.

Notes

1. Sylvia Hood Washington, "Environmental Justice Movement," in *Encyclopedia of American Social Movements* (2005). By the mid- to late 1980s, this phenomenon of environmental disenfranchisement would be labeled *environmental racism* or *environmental (in)justice*, first by Benjamin Chavis of the United Church of Christ and subsequently by the United States Environmental Protection Agency.

2. David R. Roediger, *The Wages of Whiteness: Race and the Making of the American Working Class* (New York and London: Verso, 1991); Ian F. Haney Lopez, *White by Law: The Legal Construction of Race* (New York: New York University Press, 1996); and Matthew Frye Jacobson, *Whiteness of a Different Color: European Immigrants and the Alchemy of Race* (Cambridge: Harvard University Press, 1998).

All three of these scholars have shown how the notion of who is white in America has been a dynamic and ever-changing idea with legal and social impacts.

3. To elucidate marginalized environmentalism in this work, I have analyzed the historical records of the communities, employing the ideological frameworks of Foucault's paradigm on power relations and its implementation through discipline. Foucault's symbolic concepts of "leper" and the "docile body" especially within the context of the Panopticon model can be utilized to understand race- (and ethnicity-) based segregationist policies and the penalties imposed upon those who attempted to circumvent them.

4. The following works elucidate more completely the role of class and environmental activism: Barbara K. Roades and Rice Odell, comp., *A Dictionary of Environmental Quotations* (Baltimore and London: Johns Hopkins University Press, 1992), 90; Adam Rome, *The Bulldozer in the Countryside* (New York: Cambridge University Press, 2001); and Hal K. Rotham, *Greening of a Nation? Environmentalism in the United States since 1945* (Fort Worth: Harcourt Brace, 1998).

5. Mary Poovey, *The Making of a Social Body: British Cultural Formation 1830–1864* (Chicago: University of Chicago Press, 1995).

6. Martin V. Melosi, *The Sanitary City: Urban Infrastructure in America from Colonial Times to the Present* (Baltimore: Johns Hopkins University Press, 2000), 44–45.

7. The term *macromolecular* refers to an examination of the subject on a large scale as opposed to a micro or small scale. A society consisting of millions or thousands of people can be envisioned as a singular body consisting of many segments (arm, leg, or brain) of the society, which then can be analyzed for their effectiveness or detriment to the body at large. The construction of a social body evolves when a part of the larger body is perceived as being the cause of many of society's ills, such as poverty, crime, and epidemics. The only way to ameliorate the problem would be to isolate this segment and develop policies that would eliminate the problem. In Poovey's study, England was beset with epidemics, crime, and poverty, which the larger body felt was due to the immigration of Irish and others who were different from themselves. This perception led to their spatial segregation and stigmatization, and ushered in public policies such as the use of poorhouses to deal with them as an entity outside of the mainstream.

8. Maren Stange, *Bronzeville: Black Chicago in Pictures 1941–1943* (New York: The New Press, 2003), xiii. The name, originally coined by the black newspaper, *Chicago Defender*, both literally and figuratively referred to a "city within a city" and the largest black city in the 1940s, stretching seven miles long and one half mile wide from 22nd to 63rd Streets between Wentworth and Cottage Grove.

9. Robert Bullard, *Dumping in Dixie: Race, Class and Environmental Inequality* (Boulder, CO: Westview, 1990).

10. David Pellow, *Garbage Wars: The Struggle for Environmental Justice in Chicago* (Cambridge: MIT Press, 2002).

11. Jeffrey Stine, *Mixing the Waters: Environment, Politics, and the Building of the Tennessee-Tombigbee Waterway* (Akron, OH: University of Akron Press), 180–81.

12. Theodore Steinberg, *Nature Incorporated: Industrialization and the Waters of New England* (Amherst: University of Massachusetts Press, 1991), 53.

13. Steinberg, *Nature Incorporated*, 53.

14. Andrew Hurley, *Environmental Inequalities: Class, Race, and Industrial Pollution in Gary, Indiana, 1945–1980* (Chapel Hill: University of North Carolina Press, 1995).

15. Harold L. Platt, "Jane Addams and the Ward Boss Revisited: Class, Politics and Public Health in Chicago, 1890–1930," *Environmental History* 5, no. 2 (April 2000): 194–222.

16. E. P. Thompson, *The Making of the English Working Class* (New York: Vintage Books, 1966).

17. Martin Melosi, *Garbage in the Cities* (Chicago: Dorsey Press, 1981).

18. Joel A. Tarr, *The Search for the Ultimate Sink: Urban Pollution in Historical Perspective* (Akron, OH: University of Akron Press, 1996), 318.

PART ONE

HISTORICAL AND PHILOSOPHICAL FOUNDATIONS OF ENVIRONMENTAL RACISM AND ENVIRONMENTAL JUSTICE

CHAPTER ONE

Social Darwinism, Scientific Racism, and Birth of the Environmental Leper

Racism is fundamentally a theory of history. . . . It is a theory of who is who, of who belongs and who does not, of who deserves what and who is capable of what. By looking at racial categories and their fluidity over time we glimpse the competing theories of history which inform the society and define its internal struggles.

——Matthew Frye Jacobson, *Whiteness of a Different Color*

We see the appearance of a State racism: a racism that society will direct against itself, against its own elements and its own products. This is the internal racism of permanent purification, and it will become one of the basic dimensions of social normalization.

——Michel Foucault, *Society Must Be Defended*

A mere surface examination of the communities suffering from environmental racism will reveal that they are the same communities who have lamented for generations that they have been systematically disenfranchised in all realms of society since they have stood on the shores of the United States. They are communities of color (African

American, Native American, Hispanic, and Asian) and they are poor whites (of "native" and immigrant stock) who packed themselves into urban and rural settings that became environmentally marginalized with the rise of industrialization in the late nineteenth and twentieth centuries. Some environmental scholars, and especially those tied to the modern Environmental Justice Movement like Robert Bullard, Beverly Wright, and Bunyan Bryant, have argued that the environmental disenfranchisement of these communities stems from environmental racism, a term that for many lay people only connotes civil and social inequality and disenfranchisement as a function of race (primarily white versus nonwhite). This chapter seeks to respond to other environmental scholars in fields varying from economics to geology who have vehemently opposed the notion and/or existence of environmental racism. Donald Coursey, an economist at the University of Chicago, has articulated that today's environmentally marginalized groups voluntarily moved into neighborhoods that already had heavy industries and were heavily polluted before their arrival.[1] Coursey and other scholars argue that environmentally marginalized groups are only marginalized because they choose to be. Other environmental economists have argued that these communities have become the geographical places that bear the environmental costs in the cost-benefit analysis equation for modern and postmodern industrialized societies simply by chance. All of these scholarly discussions fail to recognize or acknowledge that the geographical and spatial restrictions placed on people of color and ethnic groups by residential bombings, restrictive covenants, redlining, and both private and public housing policies were organic societal techniques of discipline that led to forced segregation and eventually environmentally compromised and unsustainable communities for more than two-thirds of the twentieth century.

Urban historians, sociologists, and African American scholars have produced a voluminous amount of work that documents the austere and sometimes violent spatial, and hence environmental, segregation of African Americans after they came "up from slavery" and migrated into America's northern industrial cities. Examples include W. E. B. Dubois's *Philadelphia Negro*; Allan Spear's *Black Chicago: The Making of a Negro Ghetto Metropolis*; Thomas Sugrue's *The Origins of the Urban Crisis: Race and Inequality in Post-war Detroit*; Douglas S. Massey and

Nancy Denton's *American Apartheid: Segregation and the Making of the Underclass*; and Thomas Philpott's *The Slum and the Ghetto: Neighborhood Deterioration and Middle-Class Reform, Chicago, 1880–1930*.[2] No serious attempt at understanding the continued existence of environmentally unequal geographic spaces should dismiss these historical facts––it is how individuals are constructed and perceived by the larger body politic that will heavily determine the environmental space they occupy and their access to an environmentally sustainable community.

Historically, however, the notion of race has never been a static concept in this country. It has been rapidly evolving since the end of the nineteenth century. Scholars like John Higham, David Roediger, Matthew Frye Jacobson, and Ian F. Haney Lopez, discussed below, have thoroughly elucidated the historical fact that many who are considered "white" today were not considered "white" in the last half of the nineteenth century and the first quarter of the twentieth century. Even if they were considered white by some, they were classified as racially inferior whites. These classifications as inferior whites or nonwhites resulted in the first examples of environmental racism. They were prevented from occupying sustainable geographical spaces (forced into living in ghettos) and, if they were even allowed to work, they were forced into life-threatening jobs. In the packing house industry, trimming room work was specifically reserved for new immigrants. These trimming rooms were cold storage areas kept at near-freezing temperatures with cold dripping water running along the walls and "damp ice-cold floors."[3] Many non-Western and racially marginalized immigrant groups would eventually become barred or limited from migrating into the United States.

The connection between racism, "white" otherness, and geographical constriction has been clearly shown in labor historian David R. Roediger's *The Wages of Whiteness: Race and the Making of the American Working Class*, which focused on Irish immigrants. Roediger points out that the Irish did not ease into "whiteness." They were initially classified by the U.S. Census Bureau as distinct from other native "whites" and foreigners. They were considered by influential social scientists like Herbert Spencer and Madison Grant and prominent newspapers like the *New York Times* to be on a similar level of the racial evolutionary scale as blacks. This racial conceptualization of the Celt was belied by the "Nativist folk wisdom that held that an Irishman was a 'nigger' inside out."[4] The racism exhibited toward the Irish by native whites resulted in their sharing the same type of jobs in the domestic service and transportation industries as African Americans, and "living side by side [with them] in the teeming slums of American cities."[5]

In his work *White by Law: The Legal Construction of Race*, Ian F. Haney Lopez points out that both a scientific and common law understanding of racial distinctiveness eventually led to federal laws in the United States restricting immigration to the United States on the basis of race for nearly one hundred years, roughly from the Chinese exclusion laws of the 1880s until the end of the national origins quotas in 1965. Between 1882 and 1917, Congress passed race-based restrictions on Chinese laborers. The first restriction came in 1882, with the passage of the Chinese Exclusion Act, which resulted in a ten-year suspension on the immigration of Chinese labor immigration. This act was extended in 1884 and barred the laborers' immigration indefinitely; finally, in 1917, an "Asiatic barred zone" was created, which excluded all Asian people.[6] In addition to the race-based legal restriction of Chinese immigrants, in 1921 the U.S. government implemented a temporary quota system that severely restricted the immigration of "racially undesirable southern and eastern Europeans."[7] The temporary 1921 immigration restriction on eastern and southern Europeans eventually evolved into the 1924 National Origin Act.[8] This bar on "other" Europeans was soon followed by the government's failed attempt to bar all black immigrants and immigrants of African descent and its successful efforts to cause "approximately 500,000 people [to be] forcibly returned to Mexico during the Depression, more than half of them U.S. citizens."[9] These government attempts were partially successful in their race-based immigrant policies; they were able to bar Asian immigrants but not immigrants of African descent. They were also able to successfully force Mexican immigrants (who were not considered at this time to be white) back to their native country.

All of these disciplinary and segregating actions toward scientifically constructed racialized "others" resulted in them being forced into less-than-optimal environmental spaces. All of these immigrants were not banned, but those who were able to remain in (or enter) the United States ended up living in areas like Chicago's Back of the Yards, whose abysmal living conditions were made famous by Upton Sinclair's *The Jungle* in 1906. From an environmental perspective, these "others" were being forced into less technologically developed societies, even as the United States was emerging as one of the leading modern industrialized societies. This was also the same time period in which the United States was creating a highly developed sanitary infrastructure and public health system for its rapidly expanding and industrialized cities to protect its citizenry from mortal epidemics like cholera, dysentery, and typhoid fever. The ouster of these "others" occurred during what environmental historian Martin Melosi has referred to as the "Bacteriological Revolution of 1880 to 1945"––a period that saw the development of modern sanitary services, when "water supply, wastewater, and solid-waste systems of this period were designed to provide permanent relief from threats to health."[10]

Although divergent in their explanations of how "whiteness" and concomitant "white privilege" emerged between 1840 and 1924, none of the aforementioned scholars have explicitly and specifically addressed the power and knowledge relationship between the social construction of "whiteness" and the access (or lack of access) to environmentally sustainable space as a function of race. Most of the scholarship in this area has tended to focus on the political and economic ramifications of being classified as nonwhite or inferior white. This chapter focuses on the void in the discussion on the history of environmental impacts (and specifically environmental racism) as a result of being nonwhite or an inferior white as defined by biologists, anthropologists, and social scientists.

The phrase *environmental racism* in its purest manifestation and conceptualization derives from the Foucauldian power and knowledge relationship. The contemporary linguistic use of the term today, however, creates confusion. Environmental racism in the postmodern United States has come to imply the social and political disenfranchisement of blacks. In reality, however, the phenomenon actually embraces environmental disenfranchisement based upon multiple race categories (including whites), class, and ethnicity. Environmental scholars and future environmental policy makers need to reconcile the existence of environmental inequality with the historical fact that the communities who are today bearing the disproportionate costs of environmental pollution have or had a history of being constructed as racially inferior (whether they were white or non-white) in this country for several centuries, which resulted in their being forced into unsustainable living spaces. The construction of varying degrees of racial inferiority, regardless of color, was supported and validated initially by European and American scientists who referred to themselves as Social Darwinists and eugenicists at the end of the nineteenth century and the first three decades of the twentieth century. These scientists and social scientists developed a paradigm of race and concomitant rights to American enfranchisement that became the operative and core episteme for determining the types of citizenry that would be entitled to salient "green space" into the twenty-first century.

The vestiges of the historic national embrace of racial inferiority are the foundation for today's environmental inequality in marginalized communities. These communities are ones whose residents have suffered and continue to suffer disproportionately from environmental illnesses (like asthma, lead poisoning, miscarriages, and chemically induced mental and learning disorders) because their geographic spaces have been highly degraded and even poisoned from both legal and illegal waste management practices.[11] The environmental integrity of these communities has also been tainted by the industrial, commercial, and retail operations legally and illegally allowed to exist in the same environmental spaces. No one seeks out these communities as ideal living spaces. Those living in these areas have had little luck escaping from them because of the body politic's historic view of them—as undesirable people fit only to live in undesirable places. People who have been constructed by a larger body politic as being threats to the larger social body are usually the ones who end up living in these spaces: nonwhites, the homeless, poor people, and the unemployed.[12]

So what was the role of the power and knowledge relationship between the tenets of Social Darwinism, scientific racism, and eugenics at the end of the nineteenth century and during the first decades of the twentieth century in defining the relationship between government, the environment, and race?

Social Darwinism, Eugenics, and the Birth of "Environmental Others"

In his seminal work, *Race: The History of an Idea in America*, Thomas Gossett summarized the basic tenets of Social Darwinism: first, that societies and their institutions slowly evolve; second, that no society could change beyond the point where evolution had brought it and that any attempt to change it would produce disastrous results; and third, that heredity (in this case, race) was the primary factor in determining how far a society had and would evolve.[13] For Social Darwinists, "the idea of natural selection was translated into a struggle between individual members of a society, between members of classes of a society, between different nations and between men." Far from being evil, this natural conflict was "nature's indispensable method for producing superior men, superior nations and superior races."[14]

The chief and most influential person in the theoretical development of Social Darwinism during this time was the nineteenth-century British philosopher, sociologist, and scientist Herbert Spencer (1820–1903). Spencer's "reputation at the time rivaled that of Charles Darwin. Spencer was best known for developing and applying evolutionary theory to philosophy, psychology and the study of society—what he called his 'synthetic philosophy.'"[15] It was Spencer who coined the two terms associated with human evolution, "the struggle for existence" and "the survival of the fittest."[16] He also developed the paradigm of the slow evolution of society akin to biological evolution that should not be artificially interfered with. The environmental consequences for the "unfit" are apparent when one takes into account that Spencer was an avid proponent of laissez-faire who was opposed to sanitation laws, public education, free libraries, and the licensing of medical doctors and nurses. Spencer's ideal society was one that had no social legislation, no regulation of industry, and no assisted relief for the poor. It would be a society that would allow natural selection to occur by doing nothing for primitive and lesser people. He was also a strong advocate of the eugenic effects of war, which acted to eliminate inferior people.[17] Spencer heavily influenced the field of American sociology and "most of the people who took up the study of sociology in this country between 1870 and 1890 were drawn to the subject by Spencer's writings."[18] Spencer's chief

American disciple was the highly influential Yale University professor of political science and sociologist William Graham Sumner. Sumner was also an adamant supporter of laissez-faire who opposed public education, poor laws, and labor laws regulating hours and working conditions in factories. The environmental consequences of laissez-faire and Social Darwinist thought would be that those already marked as being outside the pale of the social body were not to be assisted by the government. If the unfit could not remedy the environmental problems of their marginalized geographic spaces themselves, they would suffer the natural consequences of their condition: disease, mortality, and eventual extinction. This mentality would explain why sanitary infrastructures built at the turn of the century usually benefited primarily the native "white" communities.

Racist, nativist thought during this time period was also boosted by the emergence of the eugenics movement led by British psychologist and anthropologist Sir Francis Galton, a cousin of Charles Darwin. It was Galton who would coin the terms *eugenics* and *nature and nurture* and develop the first intelligence tests. Galton believed that there was "not merely grades of men within races but also grades of races . . . and that primitive races (and not just nonwhites) were inferior."[19] Unlike Social Darwinists, eugenicists believed in government intervention that would act to discourage the reproduction and proliferation of inferior races within the body politic and social body of a state. American eugenicist G. Stanley Hall ridiculed reform but advocated government support of the sterilization and segregation of the unfit.[20] Both Social Darwinists and eugenicists felt that the poor's environmental conditions stemmed from their own inferiority. This sentiment was shared by his historical contemporary, Stanford University president David Starr Jordan, who stated that "poverty, dirt and crime are due to poor human material."[21]

In *Whiteness of a Different Color*, historian Matthew Frye Jacobson points out that racial categorization in the nineteenth and twentieth centuries was based on the development of "otherness" (abnormality) as it related to the normal and superior true American, the Anglo Saxon. Jacobson points out in his history of racial evolution that the "period of mass European immigration from the 1840s to the restrictive legislation of 1924 [Johnson-Reed Act, also known as the National Origins Act] witnessed a fracturing of whiteness into a hierarchy of plural and scientifically determined white races."[22] Jacobson's conclusions are consistent with those of the seminal immigration historian, John Higham, in *Strangers in the Land: Patterns of American Nativism, 1860–1925.*[23] The thrust of Higham's work was that Anglo Saxon nativism in the last decade of the nineteenth century was compounded by imperialism and an emerging ideology of scientific racism. This thought was embraced by such influential upper class "Yankee" intellectuals in the American mainstream as Kentucky-born Harvard geologist Nathaniel S. Shaler, who was head of the Lawrence Scientific School; Harvard-educated political scientist and statesman Henry Cabot Lodge; and Massachusetts Institute of Technology economist Francis A. Walker. Higham points out that, by the mid-1890s, both Shaler and Lodge arrived at the same conclusion. "Instead of indicting the immigrants as a whole . . . [they] now drew a sharp racial contrast between northwestern and southeastern Europeans, maintaining that the new 'non-Aryan' peoples were wholly different from earlier immigrants and innately impossible to Americanize."[24] For Higham, Lodge was the most extreme and influential of the three intellectuals, someone who was "exceptional both in his direct contact with European race-thinking and in the degree to which he embraced an ideal of race purity." It was Lodge who tried to persuade his fellow U.S. statesmen about the perils of non-Aryan immigration. Lodge based his logic on the racist ideologies of such European scholars as Gustave Le Bon, who argued that crossbreeding among races (ethnic groups) would prevent a nation from achieving its full destiny.[25]

Francis Walker, a superintendent of the U.S. Census in 1870, was more concerned about the birthrate of foreigners in the country and the concomitant potential for biological defeat of native Aryan stock. Higham points out that it was Walker who counteracted the positivist Darwinian notion by "declaring that natural selection was now working in reverse due to the cheapness and ease of steam transportation, the fittest now stay at home; the unfit migrate."[26] Walker's "scientific naturalism" argued that the rapid birthrate of unfit, non-Aryan immigrants would lead to the extinction of the native Aryan stock.

Lodge, Walker, and Shaler all influenced the nativist and racist immigration policies that emerged during this time frame. Their views represent the power/knowledge relationship articulated by Foucault in describing how power is exerted in a modern society based upon race. In 1976 Foucault postulated that "the discourse of race struggle . . . will become the discourse of a centered, centralizing power. It will become the discourse of a battle that has to be waged not between races, but by a race that is portrayed as the one true race, the race that holds power and is entitled to define the norm, and against those who pose a threat to the biological heritage."[27] All three of these intellectuals' ideologies are consistent with the Foucauldian notion that government was responsible for protecting the larger body from biological threats, which, in this case, were "other whites" who needed to be separated and quarantined from the large native "white" body. As a result, non-Aryan immigrant stock would end up voluntarily (by self-discipline) and involuntarily occupying environmentally compromised geographic spaces (i.e., slums and ghettos) in American cities because of the nativist and racist hostilities from native "white" Americans.

Historian John S. Haller Jr. concurs with the historians cited above.[28] For Haller, the men responsible for transferring these early notions of scientific racism were Herbert Spencer, John Wesley Powell, Edward Drinker Cope, Frederick Hoffman, Joseph Le Conte, and Nathaniel S. Shaler. The majority of these men were highly respected scientists, intellectuals whose publicly articulated ideologies about race deeply influenced the social construction of "others" within American society who would come to be socially, politically, and environmentally disenfranchised because they were thought to be outside the pale of the American social body. These "others" were the same non-Aryan people described above; the majority were of African descent. The "scientific" ideologies of these men also contributed to race-based restrictive immigration laws and nationally embraced segregation policies. Most of these men were Spencerian Social Darwinists or neo-Lamarckians who believed that environmental influences as a means to uplift a race were not beneficial for non-Aryan people. Haller's study also supports Foucault's thesis that power and knowledge are codependent and mutually generative. In this case, "science became an instrument which verified the presumptive inferiority of the Negro and rationalized the politics of disenfranchisement and segregation into a social-scientific terminology that satisfied the troubled conscience of the middle-class."[29]

The Lamarckian racial view of University of Pennsylvania paleontologist

Edward Drinker Cope was similar to that of Shaler and American-trained physician and evolutionary idealist Joseph Le Conte. Le Conte was of French-Huguenot descent, the son of scientist Louis Le Conte, a student of Louis Agassiz, and an avid disciple of Herbert Spencer. Le Conte believed that the "negro race had evolved as far as possible under slavery" and that whites would need to maintain some type of control over the negro because of his "inability to care for himself in freedom and because race struggle and the increased energy of civilization appeared to threaten his survival."[30] This ideology would dominate national thoughts about the assimilative capacity of blacks in the larger social body into the twenty-first century. Despite being freed from slavery, African Americans have carried the racial stigmas originally articulated by these scientifically endorsed ideologies the longest.

Even today, blacks, as the penultimate social "others," continue to suffer disproportionately from environmental policies. As pointed out by scholars David Roediger and Matthew Frye Jacobson, previously defined non-Aryan European immigrants would eventually became absorbed into the larger "white" social body and cease to be thought of as "others" by the late 1920s; at the very least, they ceased being thought of as separate racial groups. Their ability to access sustainable living space was a direct benefit of this development. This has not been the case for blacks. A significant part of this chapter, therefore, concentrates on blacks' history as the ultimate environmental lepers in modern and postmodern society. The discussion uses the most racially segregated city in America, Chicago, as its historical reference point for discussion because its past and recent racial and environmental history provides an ideal Foucauldian paradigm of power and knowledge relationships. Despite the midcentury Civil Rights Movement and the Environmental Justice Movement, the majority of Chicago blacks still live in highly racially segregated communities that carry a disproportionate amount of environmental waste disposal facilities. Environmental sociologist Robert D. Bullard has indicated that 92 percent of Chicago's 1.1 million blacks live in racially segregated communities.[31] Chicago is also the home of one of the most egregious environmental toxic communities in the United States, Altgeld Gardens. The Gardens has over "50 active or closed commercial hazardous waste landfills, 100 factories (including seven chemical plants and five steel mills) and 103 abandoned waste dumps."[32] It is also inhabited by a large African American population.

Blacks, the "Interminable Environmental Others"

Urban black communities that formed in the North during the two great migration periods had sought out a Mecca and a Promised Land articulated by industrial boosters, the black media, and black social and political organizations. Their presence created concerns among the Northern white body politic, who regarded them as a black plague and black menace. In response, these communities were forced to settle into highly segregated and environmentally degraded environments near industrial facilities. These factors, coupled with little or no sanitary infrastructures, created a public health problem for black migrating communities. For the more conservative members of American society, this was perceived as a solution to the larger public health problem.

The perception and treatment of blacks under segregationist policies fits Mary Poovey's thesis of the construction of social bodies by those in power in order to isolate a segment of the larger society with the ultimate objectives of managing, manipulating, or controlling them. Poovey argues in *The Making of a Social Body: British Cultural Formation* that Victorian British society developed the cultural concept of the social body to refer to its isolated poor citizenry. According to Poovey, this development "allowed social analysts to treat one segment of the population as a special problem at the same time that they could gesture toward the mutual interests that (theoretically) united all parts of the whole." This cultural development led to the concept of pauperism. According to Poovey, pauperism was a "moral and physical designation, which encompassed all of the components eventually relegated to the social domain; criminal tendencies, bodily health, environmental conditions, education, and religion."

More so than the Victorian English poor, African Americans living in Chicago throughout the migration period were highly visible and thought of as being a "diseased" segment of the larger social body and body politic. The aggressive actions by the larger white social body to keep them essentially spatially and environmentally quarantined would lead to violence in the form of race riots and bombings, and, eventually, to de facto segregation. This perception of blacks as the ultimate social undesirables and "others" can be seen in the following contemporary news headlines, which addressed the black migration into Chicago during the first Great Migration:

HALF A MILLION DARKIES FROM DIXIE SWARM TO THE NORTH TO BETTER THEMSELVES

RUSH OF NEGROES TO CITY STARTS HEALTH INQUIRY
Philadelphia Warns of Peril, Health; Police Heads to Act

NEGROES ARRIVE BY THOUSANDS––PERIL TO HEALTH
Big Influx of Laborers Offers Vital Housing Problem to City

DEFENSE BOARD WARNED AGAINST NEGRO INFLUX
Investigators See Peril Such as Resulted in East St. Louis

NEGRO INFLUX BRINGS DISEASE
Health Commissioner Orders Vaccination of Arrivals to Check Small Pox

Darwinism and Public Health Implications for Blacks

In the wake of emancipation, blacks would face the insidious impacts of scientific racism articulated by Social Darwinists who helped facilitate the acceptance of scientific racism. The publication of Darwin's *Origin of Species* in 1859 reenergized racist philosophies about black inferiority and support of social, political, and economic disenfranchisement. There was wide acceptance of Darwinist-based ideologies such as that of Herbert Spencer, who advanced the notion that blacks, nonwhites, and other whites belonged to "unfit" races that would not survive in the emerging modern society. For several decades following emancipation, there was a prevalent ideology among both Northern and Southern whites that blacks, after having made their artificial exodus from slavery, were doomed to extinction because of their intellectual inferiority and their physical constitution. This point of the widely held societal view of impending black extinction is made in George M. Fredrickson's study, *The Black Image in the White Mind: The Debate of Afro-American Character and Destiny, 1897–1914.*[33] Fredrickson points out that even Reconstructionists like novelist and freedman bureaucrat from 1866 to 1868 John W. Deforest publicly articulated the view that "the Negro . . . no matter how well educated, is not the mental equal of the European and will surely pass into sure and deserved oblivion."[34] This perception of the impending demise of African Americans was shared by Europeans like geologist Auguste Legel who, although in favor of constitutional amendments guaranteeing black equality, felt that "the days of the black race are numbered and fatal laws condemn it to die out, or rather be transformed."[35] French journalist Georges Clemenceau wrote in 1869 that the black man would never be able to successfully compete with the white man and that he was "fated to be the victim of that natural selection which is constantly operating under our eyes in spite of everything, and he must eventually go under, in the more or less distant future."[36]

The 1870 U.S. Census, the first after emancipation, provided support to some in the belief of impending extinction for blacks because it supposedly showed that the population rate for blacks had declined since slavery and was only fifty percent of the rate for whites. This prediction of impending extinction would be overturned by the 1880 census, which showed that the population rate for Southern blacks was much larger than that of their white counterparts. The results and interpretations of the census data varied from 1870 to the turn of the century, but all in all the concept of impending black extinction remained at the forefront of the discussion among scientists, medical doctors, politicians, novelists, and journalists. German-born insurance statistician Frederick L. Hoffman's 1896 book, *Race Traits and Tendencies of the American Negro*, had enormous influence in convincing white insurance companies of the folly of providing insurance coverage to blacks. Hoffman's book was written in the tone of the prevailing Social Darwinist philosophy. He argued that black extinction was taking place because of race traits and tendencies that resulted in the proliferation of disease among blacks that had little or nothing to do with environmental factors but was due in large part to their own indigenous immorality. According to Hoffman, the "Negro" had begun to degenerate after emancipation, and the "tendency of [the] race has been downward and . . . will lead to a still greater mortality, a lesser degree of economic and social efficiency, a lower standard of nurture and a diminishing excess of births over deaths . . . and in the end cause the extinction of the race."[37] Hoffman's work was strongly supported by University of Virginia medical professor and chairman of the faculty Dr. Paul R. Barringer. In his book, *The American Negro: His Past and Future*, Barringer made the Social Darwinist argument that any social problems that the "Negro" was encountering were rooted in his own biological inferiority and were an indication that he was, in actuality, reverting to his natural, primitive, savage state. The dogma on biological destiny elucidated by Hoffman and Barringer's works was soon joined by historian Joseph A. Tillangast in his study *The Negro in Africa and America*. The argument set forth in Tillangast's book was that blacks had evolved in the hot climates of Africa with a long history of cannibalism, ignorance, and immorality. According to Tillangast, the New World would deal a mortal blow to this community because of the coldness of the climate and the structure and demands of a more advanced and civilized society. Public health for the "Negro" was oxymoronic under the paradigm of Social Darwinism, since the best public policy was no policy, a concept that cooperated with nature's tendency to eliminate the unfit.

Black Migration: A Public Health Menace

The obvious failure of the hypotheses elucidated by Social Darwinists regarding the "natural" fate of the emancipated black population was materialized and symbolized by the black migrations that occurred during the first half of the twentieth century. In his study on the black migration to Chicago, urban historian James R. Grossman points out that "approximately one-half million black southerners . . . started life anew in northern cities during 1916–19, and nearly one million more followed in the 1920s. New York's black population grew from 91,709 in 1910 to 152,467 in 1920; Chicago's from 44,103 to 152,467; Detroit's small black community of 5,741 in 1910 mushroomed to 40,838 in a decade."[38] Lured by wartime jobs made more abundant by the loss of immigrants, African American men and eventually African American families poured into industrial cities like Chicago. African American historian Arvarh E. Strickland's history of the Chicago Urban League points out that Chicago's black population would be further expanded by 65,000 as a result of wartime jobs by 1944.[39] Still reproducing and healthy enough to move about, black migrating populations to mostly white and Northern cities resulted in the perception and subsequently societal articulation of a "Negro problem" in modern America. This problem was for many (both black and white) a real and imagined public health dilemma for America's industrial and urban cities (like New York, Philadelphia, Detroit, and Chicago) that had to be dealt with since it was continually being exacerbated by the labor demands of both wartime and peacetime industries. The penalty for the failed hypotheses, however, was borne by blacks, especially black migrants, who packed the urban centers of America. This penalty was largely environmental as we understand the term today: high levels of diseases and death from politically and socially constructed unsustainable communities. Like immigrants, blacks were socially constructed to be "environmental lepers" and perceived as lethal environmental blights upon the urban domain to be constricted and restricted to marginalized living spaces for the benefit of society's "fittest."

In the wake of the "surviving unfit," universities, philanthropists, religious institutions, settlement workers, Progressives, and politicians all sought out a solution to this impending American public health menace. The first "scientific study" of the problem was conducted in Philadelphia in 1896 by the African American scholar and political activist W. E. B. Dubois. The study was commissioned by Susan Wharton, leader of the Philadelphia College Settlement (which was a member of the College Settlement Association), and Charles C. Harrison, her neighbor and acting provost of the University of Pennsylvania. The College Settlement Association had already demonstrated its belief in the primary need for research and had funded women college graduates to conduct research on public health problems in cities.[40] In their study of Dubois's research, Michael B. Katz and Thomas J. Sugrue remind us that it reflected the fact that the college women involved in the settlement movement believed that "social reconstruction" was hinged upon hard facts.[41] "Documenting conditions among the urban poor would awaken the conscience of the rich and provide data for social and political reform."[42]

Historian David Levering Lewis makes the point that Wharton and Harrison of the College Settlement Association, "like many Progressives (especially older ones), were prey to eugenic nightmares about 'native stock' and the better classes being swamped by fecund, dysgenic aliens. The conservative College Settlement Association gentry thought of poverty in epidemiological terms, as a virus to be quarantined—'a hopeless element in the social wreckage.'"[43]

Settlement Houses, Social Darwinism, and the Response to Black "Others"

The historical evidence about settlement houses supports the claim that the policy of a majority of these organizations during this time was the intentional segregation of white immigrants and black migrants. As explained in the contemporary report "Churches and Voluntary Associations in the Chicago Negro Community," none of the white settlement houses were identified as being instrumental in the acculturation and assimilation of blacks.[44] Likewise, no description of white settlement house involvement with black migrants was found in any of the contemporary annual reports of the Chicago Urban League.[45] In its first report, the league stated that "the problem of the Negro in Chicago is, on the whole, one with the problem of the immigrant. Work and wages, health and housing, the difficulties of adjustment of an essentially rural population to the conditions of a city environment, and to modern life—these are the matters of most immediate concern to him and to us."[46] The report also made it clear that, although white social agencies had had experience dealing with migrant-related needs because of their dealings with immigrants, the "regular welfare agencies of the city find themselves,—since Negroes are rarely represented on their boards or in their administration,— somewhat at a loss in dealing with the colored people."[47]

Thomas Lee Philpott's work *The Slum and the Ghetto* is one of the few histories that deals with the intentional segregation policies of the settlement houses. Philpott argues that both public and private institutions sanctioned these segregationist policies.[48] In 1930, the Joint Committee on the Survey of Agencies Serving the Negro Community "did not expect settlement houses in neighborhoods bordering on black districts or containing Negro enclaves to open their doors to blacks." According to the committee, the "whole aim" of neighborhood work was "the bringing together of persons in voluntary social groups."[49]

A prevailing argument among historians and scholars that the immigrants naturally did not want, on a voluntary basis, to interact with black migrants is addressed by Philpott, who offers the counterargument that immigrant attitudes were heavily influenced and shaped by the personal ideologies of the settlement leadership.[50] Philpott claims that Dr. Graham Taylor, one of the foremost settlement leaders at the time and founder of the Chicago Commons settlement, wielded great influence in the settlement movement and strongly advocated segregationist views. According to Philpott:[51]

> Graham Taylor, editor of the *Commons* and founder of the Chicago Commons, was pained at the prospects of a black influx into Northern cities. Like Jane Addams, he professed to believe that "all foreign born" brought "rich and varied" cultures from the Old World to the New. . . . Nowhere, however, did he praise the heritage of Negroes and he never talked of assimilating them.

Dr. Taylor, writing in the *Chicago Daily News* on January 13, 1917, stated, "Not only for the safety and progress of the city as a whole, this [Chicago Urban] League should rally to its equipment and direction, its growth and efficiency, both personal and financial resources adequate to this end."[52]

Taylor wrote both a personal letter and an article in a public newspaper within a month of the 1919 Chicago race riot that clearly demonstrated his belief in racial segregation. In one of his weekly articles for the *Chicago Daily News*, "Chicago May Help Save Race Situation," Taylor states, "Segregation by statute or ordinance could not be upheld by any courts, because it would be class legislation and against constitutional rights. But what could not be enforced by law can be accomplished by mutual understanding."[53] The day before this article ran, Taylor sent a letter to Mr. James Basiger discussing the development of housing for blacks by the Chicago Housing Authority.[54] Taylor makes it clear in the letter that housing construction for blacks should only proceed by ensuring or maximizing their segregation from white neighborhoods. He states, "I do not know what to say about devoting the first building venture of the Chicago Housing Association to Negroes. They certainly need it most, but perhaps later attempts to build for white tenants would for awhile be suspected of being an effort to scatter the Negro population—which of course ought to be done without mixing the races more than is necessary."[55]

Taylor's belief in segregation would explain his support of separate social service agencies for blacks, especially black migrants. In his newspaper articles and his published works he makes it very clear that it was the responsibility of black agencies or agencies devoted to understanding interracial problems to assimilate black migrants:

> The relation between the two races is slowly improving under the growing urge of self-respecting Negro citizens, who are discontented with the political prestige given the vicious element that exploit their own people and are exploited by politicians for personal and factional gains. The high civic and economic ideals of the Urban League win influential leadership and publicity. The Interracial Commission of the Chicago Federation of Churches, on which prominent representatives of the churches of both races serve, is valuably promoting better understanding by the conferences . . . and exchange of pulpits annually on Sunday devoted to race relationship.[56]

Graham Taylor was candid in openly and publicly supporting the efforts of separate black and integrated organizations like the Chicago Urban League and the National Association for the Advancement of Colored People (NAACP) that were established to deal with the problems of a segregated black society. He felt that the effort to assimilate blacks migrating into Chicago should

> be made by the agency best qualified to undertake this task. It is the National League on Urban Conditions Among Negroes. This league consists of able representatives of both races, who have organized to secure the co-operation of all agencies to promote the improvement of Negro life and labor, to protect their women and children, to fit their workers for efficient work, to train and enlist Negro social workers for boys' and girls' clubs, neighborhood centers, probation work, playground direction and for the prevention and relief of dependency, to investigate conditions of city life as a basis for practical work to improve the urban conditions of Negro populations.[57]

The goals and functions of the Chicago Urban League to assimilate migrating blacks were almost identical to those of the settlement houses in assimilating ethnic immigrants. The implicit or explicit acceptance of racial segregation policies by the settlement houses is evidence that while white immigrants were beginning to be accepted as legitimate members of the dominant white social body, black migrants who had been in America for generations were still outside the pale of this social body. They were to be quarantined from societal organizations that were substantially more experienced in assimilating and settling newcomers into the city of Chicago.

The following statement was made by Jane Addams, founder of Chicago's Hull House (an immigrant settlement house) and considered to be one of the most influential Progressive-era social reformers in the United States.[58] Her statement provides some indication about settlement house views regarding the justification for continuing the physical separation of blacks from the larger "white" social body and from the newly assimilating ethnic groups in the urban environment. A close examination of her statement reveals the basic ideological principles of Social Darwinist thought:

> Whatever may be the practical solution it is still true that a complete segregation of the Negro in definite parts of the city, tends itself to put him outside the immediate action of that imperceptible but powerful social control which influences the rest of the population. Those inherited resources of civilization which are embodied in custom and kindly intercourse, make more for social restraint than does legal enactment. One could easily illustrate this lack of inherited control by comparing the experience of a group of colored girls with those of a group of Italian immigrants. . . . Italian fathers consider it a point of honor that their daughters shall not be alone upon the street after dark. . . . The fathers of colored girls, on the other hand, are quite without those traditions, and fail to give their daughters the resulting protection. . . . The Italian parents represent the social traditions which have been worked out during centuries . . . it is largely through a modification of these customs and manners that alien groups are assimilated into

American life. . . . The civilizations in Africa are even older than those in Italy . . . but were broken up during the period of chattel slavery. . . . It was inevitable that the traditions were lost and that customs had to be built up anew. . . . Every chance meeting between representatives of the two races is easily characterized by insolence or arrogance. To the friction of city life and the complications of modern intercourse is added this primitive race animosity.[59]

Addams's statement implies that racial integration in settlement work was severely hampered by what she perceived as long-term and naturally evolved gross cultural and social disparities.

According to Philpott, the *Settlement Journal* provided very little coverage on the "Negro problem" and, when it did, it emphasized the defects of blacks and the point that assimilation was for whites only.[60] The chief objective of settlement workers in multiethnic immigrant communities was to bring "white" ethnic groups into "harmonious relationships" and to never exclude members of an ethnic group, regardless of pressures from other ethnic groups. These same settlement works, however, "could not cope with the segregation of blacks; they reinforced it."[61]

The "Canaryville" papers of the University of Chicago Settlement House's first director, social reformer and activist Mary McDowell, and her contemporary biography written by Howard Wilson in 1928, provide evidence that part of the assimilation process for white "ethnics" was the absorption of the prevailing racial disdain toward blacks. It is more than likely that this process played a major role in circumscribing the black migrant's inclusion in public outreach services that could have ameliorated their environmental plight. Wilson points out that, during the 1919 race riot, McDowell gained firsthand knowledge of "race prejudice and animosity at its worst. One day a settlement worker came into her Settlement living room to tell how the members of a white gang were stationed at the gateway into the yards, each man with a club, and each beating a colored man on his way home from work at the close of the day."[62]

Environmental Impacts of Social Darwinism on Urban Blacks

In conducting his research on the Philadelphia Negro, Dubois found a heavily segregated and underemployed black population that was wasting away from disease because "Negroes are, as a mass, ignorant of the laws of health." The public health issues (such as pneumonia, consumption, and tuberculosis) faced by blacks in Chicago were parallel to those Dubois observed among blacks living in Philadelphia's Seventh Ward. Dubois observed that these conditions were deeply connected to the type of living conditions the migrants faced in the city after migration: "If one goes through the streets of the Seventh Ward and picks out those streets and houses which on account of their poor condition, lack of repair, absence of conveniences and limited share of air and light, contain the worst dwellings, one finds that the great majority of such streets and houses are occupied by Negroes."[63]

Like the migrant blacks in Philadelphia, the blacks migrating to Chicago were constricted to living in an environmentally marginalized area known as the Black Belt. The Black Belt was a highly circumscribed geographical area that was "dilapidated, decaying and overcrowded, and its landlords were obdurate in their refusal to make needed repairs. It was also a breeder of disease and the city's officially sanctioned receptacle for vice."[64] Although in 1925 the Chicago Health Department could boast about the city's overall low mortality rate—the lowest of any city in the world with a population over one million—the health statistics didn't hold up for its black residents. The death rate for blacks in Chicago was twice that of whites. "The stillbirth rate was also twice as high; the death rate from tuberculosis and syphilis was six times as high; and from pneumonia and nephritis it was well over three times as high."[65] Like those of the Philadelphia Negroes, black Chicagoans' health problems were directly related to the living conditions imposed upon them by unyielding segregationist policies.

Dubois believed that Negro diseases were largely genetic but could have been greatly ameliorated by government intervention. He felt that the failure of the city of Philadelphia to act demanded action by the black community itself for relief. He stated,

There cannot be much doubt, when former social conditions are studied, but that hereditary disease plays a large part in the low vitality of Negroes today and the health of the past has to some extent been exaggerated. All these considerations should lead to concerted efforts to root out disease. The city itself has much to do in this respect. For so large and progressive a city its general system of drainage is very bad; its water is wretched, and in many other respects the city and the whole State are "woefully and discreditably behind almost all the other states in Christendom." The main movement for reform must come from the Negroes themselves and should start with a crusade for fresh air, cleanliness, healthily located homes and proper food. All this might not settle the question of Negro health, but it would be a long step toward it.[66]

Dubois's conclusion that blacks should take action themselves to build healthier communities reverberated among institutions dedicated to solving the "Negro problem." In fact, it inspired the Urban League Movement to play a major role in addressing public health problems facing migrating and urbanized black populations across the country, especially in Chicago.

A number of historians have written about the 1919 Chicago race riot and have emphasized the competition for labor as a primary cause. This reasoning is ahistorical and logically flawed because it fails to account for the level of violence directed toward black migrants and the virulent racism permeating American society at the time. William Tuttle's historical account of the race riot provides enormous evidence that reveals blacks were socially constructed by a multitude of diverse white ethnic groups as being outside of their communities during this time period, which led to the development of the black ghetto. He writes,

The labor unrest affected numberless others––anyone depending on consumers for his income. The economic basis of discontent was thus present in Chicago. Compounded by Chicago's vast, heterogeneous population, individual discontent was potential mass violence; and the focus of violence was facilitated by the distinguishing physical characteristic of the black people––the skin which to so many white people meant evil, danger, even a threat to their existence.[67]

The existence of this negative stereotyping of black Chicagoans to the point of their exclusion from other communities is supported by other historians and studies of race relations in Chicago. In *Black Metropolis*, author St. Claire Drake points out that "Negroes, regardless of their affluence or respectability, wear the badge of color. They are expected to stay in the black belt."[68] Drake also points out that there was a mutual friction between blacks and foreigners and that "the foreign born were not slow to adopt the prevailing stereotypes about Negroes. 'Foreigners learn how to cuss, count, and say "nigger" as soon as they get over here,' grumbled the Negroes."[69]

The conclusion that factors race as a key prerequisite for blacks' status as outsiders in Chicago is also drawn by Harold G. Gosnell in *Negro Politicians: The Rise of Negro Politics in Chicago*. Although blacks in Chicago had played a significant role in the city's political games, they were never able to obtain the rewards that were usually bestowed upon white ethnic groups who were just as critical in these games. Gosnell points out that the "'Black Belt' had not been given the important patronage position on the organization slates that would go to another racial minority group of the same size but whose visibility was much less. The German-born groups soon lose their foreign language habits and accents and are merged in the general body politic."[70] He concludes his study with the following assessment:

> In the last analysis the peculiar difficulties that confronted the Negroes in their struggle for political power can in some way be related to the factor of color. If the group was not conspicuous, if the identifying mark of color was not present, then individual members would be able to compete with members of other groups on a more or less equal basis. Many foreign-born white persons have come to the United States without wealth, without social prestige, and with little educational equipment and they have achieved positions of economic, social and political power. The ruling elite in America has accepted the leaders of immigrant groups with comparatively little hesitation. Negroes have been handicapped from the start [because] Negroes had to face the obstacle of color.[71]

A confirmation of the rigid construction of blacks as the most undesirable of "others" would exhibit itself in the violent attempts to keep them out of the white neighborhoods adjacent to the Black Belt as the Belt began to rapidly grow in population around World War I. This population growth necessitated an expansion of the geographical boundaries of the Belt into what were considered white communities, including Packingtown, Hyde Park, and the Kenwood communities. Additionally, there was a shortage in housing as a result of the cessation of building operations during World War I. By 1918, "ugly interracial competition for homes broke out, as enterprising realtors touched off artificial panics with rumors that the 'blacks' were invading. Many whites soon blamed blacks for the perplexities of property values, the scarcity of housing and urban decay."[72] Drake concurs with this development of panicking responses in white neighborhoods at the possibility of blacks moving into these neighborhoods and points out that:

> several property owners' associations that had been originally organized for neighborhood improvement now began to focus their attention upon keeping Negroes out. They sponsored numerous mass meetings to arouse citizens to the peril of "invasion." They published scathing denunciations of Negroes branding them arrogant, ignorant, diseased, bumptious, destructive of property and generally undesirable.[73]

The final solution to the "invasion" for some whites may have been the bombing of black-owned properties adjacent to white areas. The first bombing occurred in July 1917. There was then "an eighth-month hiatus, during which the black expansion continued, and the bombers returned in earnest. From March 1918 to the outbreak of the riot, twenty-five bombs rocked the homes of blacks and the offices of real estate agents."[74] Within ten years, a less deadly and more effective barrier arose with the emergence of the restrictive covenant in Chicago during the late 1920s. Historian Christopher Robert Reed points out that the covenant was part of a popular public policy developed specifically for racial exclusion, which "benefited real estate interests and satisfied white neighborhoods which sought racial exclusivity."[75]

Throughout the literature, the construction of blacks as undesirable others was advanced and exacerbated by their negative portrayal in the white daily newspapers. The Chicago Commission's race relations study contained an entire chapter devoted to the study of the press in 1918 and

1919 as an "instrument in opinion making as it pertained to race relations." The report stated:

> Race relations are at all times dependent upon the public opinion of the community and that . . . careful handling of this kind of news is a question of great concern and has been the subject of much comment and criticism both by Negroes and whites. These criticisms are frequent and vehement. Negroes in Chicago almost without exception point to the Chicago Press as the responsible agent for many of their present difficulties. Throughout the country it is pointed out by both whites and Negroes that the policies of newspapers on racial matters have made relations more difficult, at times fostering new antagonism and enmities and even precipitating riots by inflaming the public against Negroes.[76]

The commission studied the "three Chicago white daily papers with the largest circulation and the three Negro weekly papers most widely read . . . to provide an adequate basis for a test of news handling, and for measuring the effect on the public of accounts of racial happenings."[77] The white newspapers studied were the *Chicago Tribune*, the *Chicago Daily News*, and the *Chicago Herald-Examiner*. The black newspapers included in the study were the *Chicago Defender*, the *Chicago Whip*, and the *Chicago Searchlight*. The commission included as part of its study select headlines from the various newspapers, which they felt exemplified the white press's influence on negative race opinions:

ST. LOUIS VOTES TODAY ON NEGRO SEGREGATION

SEGREGATION OF NEGROES SOUGHT BY REALTY MEN
Plan Legislation to Keep Colored People from White Areas

URGE RACE SEGREGATION LAW
Members of Real Estate Board to Move to Save South Side

RACE SEGREGATION IS RENT BOOSTERS' AIM
Owners Hope to Prevent Encroachments of Either Colored or White Citizens

NEGRO ROBBERS ATTACK WOMAN NEAR HER HOME.
Tear Open Her Waist in Search for Money, but Fail to Find $6
Which She Had

NEGRO SLAYER ESCAPES FROM JAIL

NEGRO STANDS WITH KNIFE OVER SLEEPER IN PARK

CORONER CLEARS POLICEMAN FOR KILLING NEGRO[78]

A search of the archives of the *Chicago Tribune* for news coverage of blacks during the same time frame revealed findings consistent with those found in the report. Samples of the types of articles found in the research are: "Four Lynched in Mississippi: Two Are Women"; "Negroes Charge Injustice By U.S. in Chicago Jobs"; "Patients Removed from Negro Hospital"; "Arkansas Mob Lynches Negro Slayer of Police"; and "Society Formed to Get Jobs for Negro Fighters."[79] The substance of these articles was consistent with the commission report's observation of *Chicago Tribune* articles about blacks; they were depicted as either violent, depraved, or socially and politically disruptive. The commission stated that the "*Chicago Tribune* published, in 1918, 145 articles, which because of their emphasis on crime, clashes and . . . efforts to 'invade white neighborhoods' definitely placed Negroes in an unfavorable light."[80] The final conclusion of the report was that

> much of the current literature and pseudo-scientific treatises concerning Negroes are responsible for such prevailing misconceptions as: that Negroes have inferior mentality; that Negroes have inferior morality; that Negroes are given to emotionalism; that Negroes have an innate tendency to commit crimes, especially sex crimes. . . . We urge especially upon white persons to exert their efforts toward discrediting stories and standing beliefs concerning Negroes which have no basis in fact but which constantly serve to keep alive a spirit of mutual fear, distrust and opposition.[81]

A perusal of the Chicago Commission study following the 1919 race riot finds many examples of the period's negative racial pubic opinions and views that had been created in the media during this time period that were a source of grave concern for black Chicagoans. These same concerns by blacks about social inequalities and negative public opinion also reverberate throughout the contemporary issues of the leading black newspaper at that time, the *Chicago Defender*. The front pages of the *Defender* for the time periods before and after the 1919 race riot always included some type of cartoon commentary or article on the ills and injustices of racism, segregation, and lynching. Four *Defender* cartoons that appeared in 1919 are good representatives of this artwork: "The Only Cure," "Birds of a Feather," "Historical Inevitables," and "A Tip from One Who Knows."

"The Only Cure" portrayed a person who looks like a working class or poor white male (wearing the sign "Riot Ring Leaders") grabbing an equally poor (and tied up) black man as he readies him for a public lynching. The picture also showed scraps of paper scattered at both men's feet containing the words "law," "order," and "justice."[82] "Birds of a Feather" is a picture of four ugly vultures or buzzards sitting on the same branch of what appears to be a lifeless tree (it has no leaves). The buzzards each have a label: "The Lyncher," "The Bolsheviks," "Bomber of Our Homes," and "Segregator." The birds look more repulsive than threatening and the message is that they are blights or unfortunate natural contributors of social death and disease.[83] The third cartoon is one of the most poignant and socially straightforward pieces of artwork. "Historical Inevitables" consists of six panels that illustrate the causes for the falls of Rome and Greece.[84] The captions under each panel explain that the demise of these civilizations took place because they "oppressed and mistreated her subjects" or because they "were an overbearing government . . . after years of tyrannical existence." The final panel shows the United States, with the caption reading, "Our country, maliciously guilty of injustice to twelve million of her citizens. . . . Is nearing the rocks upon which other nations have gone down." The message is clear: the black community felt that the United States had taken a self-destructive path by systematically disenfranchising its non-white citizens and that this course of action would result in the country's demise. Finally, "A Tip from One Who Knows" portrays a Southern U.S. official or bureaucrat who represents "The White

South" reading a proclamation that states, "This being a white man's country, 'We Are Supreme,' and the Negro has no rights that we should respect."[85] This bureaucratic figure is shown with the figure of Germany's ex-Kaiser leaning over his shoulder and touching his elbow with cautionary advice: "That supremacy stuff doesn't pay, old man . . . I tried it once myself." Both figures are shown standing on top of the world, which has the smoke of bombs (warfare) covering the globe. This artwork shows that the *Defender* wanted to make it clear to its readers that the racist policies and beliefs of the South as it pertained to blacks were on par with and as repulsive as those of racist and nativist Germany and would cause the demise of the United States.

By the 1920s, Chicago's major social body was "white" and had expanded to include both native whites and white immigrant groups from all over Europe. These groups would benefit environmentally, politically, and socially from this development. Blacks, however, would still be considered a threat to this larger social body. This fact is supported by the 1922 Chicago Commission on Race Relations report. The conclusion of this report also supports arguments that blacks were perceived by each other as well as by the body of diverse white ethnic groups as being an "other" and not really part of American citizenry. The report stated:

> The practice of "keeping the Negro in his place" or any modification of it in northern communities has isolated Negroes from all other members of the community. Though in the midst of an advanced social system and surrounded by cultural influences, they have hardly been more than exposed to them. Of full and free participation they know little. The pressure of the dominant white group in practically every ordinary experience has kept the attention and interests of Negroes centered upon themselves and made them race conscious.[86]

Notes

1. Donald Coursey, "Environmental Racism in the City of Chicago." Paper presented at Irving B. Harris School of Public Policy, University of Chicago, October 1994.

2. W. E. B. Dubois, *The Philadelphia Negro* (Philadelphia: University of Pennsylvania Press, 1996).

3. Mary McDowell, "Our Proxies in Industry," Chicago Historical Society, Mary McDowell Collection, Box 3, Folder 15, 4.

4. David R. Roediger, *The Wages of Whiteness: Race and the Making of the American Working Class* (New York and London: Verso, 1991), 133.

5. Roediger, *Wages of Whiteness*, 133–34.

6. Ian F. Haney Lopez, *White by Law: The Legal Construction of Race* (New York: New York University Press, 1996), 37.

7. Lopez, *White by Law*, 38.

8. A detailed analysis of immigration restrictions can be found in Lopez, *White by Law*, 37; John Higham's *Strangers in the Land: Patterns of American Nativism, 1860–1925* (New York: Atheneum, 1970); and in any of Oscar Handlin's treatises on immigration in America.

9. Lopez, *White by Law*, 38.

10. Martin V. Melosi, *The Sanitary City: Urban Infrastructure in America from Colonial Times to the Present* (Baltimore: Johns Hopkins University Press, 2000), 13.

11. The edited collection by Robert D. Bullard, *Confronting Environmental Racism* (Boston: South End Press, 1993), provides an excellent synopsis of the relationship between toxic substances and the health of minorities.

12. Michel Foucault, *Power/Knowledge: Selected Interviews and Other Writings, 1972–1977*, ed. Colin Gordon, trans. Colin Gordon, Leo Marshall, John Mepham, and Kate Soper (New York: Pantheon Books, 1980).

13. Thomas S. Gossett, *Race: The History of an Idea in America* (Dallas: Southern Methodist University Press, 1963), 144.

14. Gossett, *Race*, 145.

15. William Sweet, "Herbert Spencer," *The Internet Encyclopedia of Philosophy*, 2001.

16. Gossett, *Race*, 146.

17. Gossett, *Race*, 146.

18. Gossett, *Race*, 153.

19. Gossett, *Race*, 156.

20. Gossett, *Race*, 159.

21. Gossett, *Race*, 159.

22. Matthew Frye Jacobson, *Whiteness of a Different Color: European Immigrants and the Alchemy of Roce* (Cambridge: Harvard University Press, 1998), 7.

23. John Higham, *Strangers in the Land: Patterns of American Nativism, 1860–1925* (New York: Atheneum, 1970).

24. Higham, *Strangers in the Land*, 141.

25. Higham, *Strangers in the Land*, 141.

26. Higham, *Strangers in the Land*, 143.

27. Michel Foucault, *Society Must Be Defended, Lectures at the College de France, 1975–76*, ed. Mauro Bertani and Alessandro Fontana, trans. David Macey (New York: Picador, 1997), 61.

28. John S. Haller Jr., *Outcasts from Evolution: Scientific Attitudes of Racial Inferiority, 1859–1900* (Urbana: University of Illinois Press, 1971).

29. Haller, *Outcasts from Evolution*, x.

30. Haller, *Outcasts from Evolution*, 159.

31. Robert D. Bullard, *Unequal Protection: Environmental Justice and Communities of Color* (San Francisco: Sierra Club Books, 1994), 13–15.

32. For more details please read Bullard, *Unequal Protection*, 13–15, and David Pellow, *Garbage Wars and Environmental Justice Struggles in Chicago* (Cambridge: MIT Press, 2002).

33. George M. Fredrickson, *The Black Image in the White Mind: The Debate of Afro-American Character and Destiny, 1897–1914* (Hanover, NH: Wesleyan University Press, 1971).

34. Fredrickson, *The Black Image in the White Mind*, 238.

35. Fredrickson, *The Black Image in the White Mind*, 237.

36. Fredrickson, *The Black Image in the White Mind*, 237-38.

37. Fredrickson, *The Black Image in the White Mind*, 251.

38. James R. Grossman, *Land of Hope: Chicago, Black Southerners and the Great Migration* (Chicago: University of Chicago Press, 1991), 3–4.

39. Arvarh E. Strickland, *History of the Chicago Urban League* (Columbia: University of Missouri Press, 1966, 2001), 138.

40. Katherine Pearson Woods's Boston study, "Diseases and Accidents Incident to Occupations," and Ada S. Woolfold's New York study, "The Obstacles to Sanitary Living among the Poor."

41. Michael B. Katz and Thomas J. Sugrue, eds., *W. E. B. Dubois, Race and the City: The Philadelphia Negro and its Legacy* (Philadelphia: University of Pennsylvania Press, 1998), 16.

42. Katz and Sugrue, *W. E. B. Dubois*, 15.

43. Dubois, *Philadelphia Negro*, xiv.

44. "Churches and Voluntary Associations in the Chicago Negro Community," Chicago Historical Society Archives, Chicago, Illinois.

45. "The Chicago Urban League Annual Report, 1916–1936, Two Decades of Service," Chicago Urban League Files, Chicago Historical Society. The Chicago Urban League evolved in response to the problems and needs that accompanied the massive migration of blacks into Chicago around World War I.

46. "First Annual Report of the Chicago League on Urban Conditions in Chicago, Oct. 31, 1917," Chicago Urban League Files, Chicago Historical Society, 3.

47. "First Annual Report of the Chicago League," 4.

48. Thomas Lee Philpott, *The Slum and the Ghetto: Neighborhood Deterioration and Middle-Class Reform, Chicago 1880–1930* (New York: Oxford University Press, 1978), 313.

49. Philpott, *The Slum and the Ghetto,* 309.

50. Philpott, *The Slum and the Ghetto,* 309.

51. Philpott, *The Slum and the Ghetto,* 293.

52. Graham Taylor Papers, Newberry Library, Chicago, Illinois.

53. Graham Taylor Papers and the *Daily News* column, July 1914–1925, Newberry Library.

54. The Graham Taylor Papers do not provide any professional or social information on Mr. Basiger.

55. A letter from Graham Taylor to Mr. James F. Basiger, August 8, 1919, Graham Taylor Papers, Newberry Library.

56. Graham Taylor, *Pioneering on Social Frontiers* (Chicago: University of Chicago Press, 1930), 243.

57. January 13, 1913, *Daily News* column, Graham Taylor Papers, Newberry Library.

58. Victoria Bissel Brown, "Jane Addams," in Rima Lunin Schultz and Adele Hast, eds., *Women Building Chicago, 1790–1990: A Biographical Dictionary* (Bloomington: Indiana University Press, 2001), 14–22.

59. Jane Addams, *The Second Twenty Years at Hull House* (New York: Macmillan Company, 1910), 396–98.

60. Philpott, *The Slum and the Ghetto,* 295.

61. Philpott, *The Slum and the Ghetto,* 341.

62. Howard Wilson, *Mary McDowell, Neighbor* (Chicago: University of Chicago Press, 1928), 175.

63. Dubois, *Philadelphia Negro,* 160.

64. William M. Tuttle Jr., *Race Riot: Chicago in the Red Summer of 1919* (Chicago: University of Illinois Press, 1970, 1996), 164.

65. Tuttle, *Race Riot,* 164.

66. Dubois, *Philadelphia Negro,* 162–63.

67. Tuttle, *Race Riot,* 142.

68. St. Claire Drake and Horace R. Cayton, *Black Metropolis: A Study of Negro Life in a Northern City* (New York: Harcourt Brace, 1945), 206.

69. Drake and Cayton, *Black Metropolis,* 57.

70. Harold G. Gosnell, *Negro Politicians: The Rise of Negro Politics in Chicago* (Chicago: University of Chicago Press, 1935, 1967), 91.

71. Gosnell, *Negro Politicians,* 358.

72. Tuttle, *Race Riot,* 169.

73. Drake, *Black Metropolis,* 178.

74. Tuttle, *Race Riot*, 175, and Chicago Commission Report, and *Chicago Defender*.

75. Christopher Robert Reed, *The Chicago NAACP and the Rise of Black Professional Leadership, 1910–1966* (Bloomington: Indiana University Press, 2000), 62.

76. Chicago Commission on Race Relations, *The Negro in Chicago: A Study of Race Relations and a Race Riot in 1919* (Chicago: University of Chicago Press, 1922), 520.

77. Chicago Commission, *The Negro in Chicago*, 523.

78. Chicago Commission, *The Negro in Chicago*, 525–29.

79. *Chicago Tribune* articles: Dec. 21, 1918, Dec. 19, 1918, Dec. 20, 1918, Jan. 16, 1919.

80. Chicago Commission, *The Negro in Chicago*, 532.

81. Chicago Commission, *The Negro in Chicago*, 594.

82. "The Only Cure," *Chicago Defender*, August 9, 1919.

83. "Birds of a Feather," *Chicago Defender*, July 12, 1919.

84. "Historical Inevitables," *Chicago Defender*, October 4, 1919.

85. "A Tip from One Who Knows," *Chicago Defender*, 1919.

86. Chicago Commission, *The Negro in Chicago*, 475.

CHAPTER TWO

An Archaeology of the Modern Environmental Justice Movement

To leave the Negro helpless and without a ballot today is to leave him, not to the guidance of the best but rather to the exploitation and debauchment of the worst.

—W. E. B. Dubois, *The Souls of Black Folks*

I believe it is the duty of the Negro—as the greater part of the race is already doing—to deport himself modestly in regard to political claims, depending upon the slow but sure influences that proceed from the possession of property, intelligence, and high character for the full recognition of his political rights. I think that the according of the full exercise of political rights is going to be a matter of natural, slow growth, not an over-night, gourd-vine affair.

—Booker T. Washington, *Up from Slavery*

Whether intentional or unintentional, the political capitulation and impotency of early civil rights leaders like Booker T. Washington and W. E. B. Dubois to segregationist policies, in the first half of the twentieth century, was critical to establishing the foundation for environmental racism in the twentieth and twenty-first centuries in African American communities. Even after these early civil rights leaders and advocates had left the national scene, the die had been cast and the efforts of succeeding generations of civil rights leaders like Martin Luther King Jr. would prove almost ineffectual in launching environmental movements that could create sustainable living spaces for the majority of racially segregated African American communities in the United States. The struggle for environmental justice, especially for African Americans, thus reflects the historical power relations that have existed between groups classified as environmental "others" and the larger body politic as well as the consequential development of separate spaces for these groups stemming from this labeling. For African Americans, this cycle of environmental disenfranchisement has been exacerbated by the political ideologies and impotencies of their civil rights leaders.

By the close of the nineteenth century, blacks were disenfranchised in all spheres (socially, politically, and economically) in the aftermath of various Supreme Court decisions—key among them was the *Plessy v. Ferguson* case, which led to Jim Crow laws and de facto segregation in the North.[1] This legal social disenfranchisement created civil rights controversies within the African American community. The disparate approaches and internal civil rights controversies within the African American community and among its leadership was critical to the development of past and future environmental power relations that resulted in historical and contemporary environmental inequalities in their geographic spaces. These internal controversies were initially embodied and determined by the national debate between W. E. B. Dubois and Booker T. Washington, who found themselves vehemently at odds on the question of whether African Americans should demand social and political equality at the turn of the twentieth century. An important ideological question in these debates was that of self-segregation for African Americans, initially advocated by Booker T. Washington and eventually by W. E. B. Dubois.

The complicity of both Dubois and Washington in publicly supporting the self-segregation (albeit for opposing reasons) of their own black communities, combined with their public and published statements regarding the social and political ineptness of the African American social body, supported power relations that contributed to the development and continuation of segregated geographical places and spaces that eventually became the physical zones inequitably targeted for environmental waste in the twentieth and twenty-first centuries.

Washington, the preeminent black leader at the turn of the century, was an accommodationist who was politically and financially supported by the top white industrialists of his time. The most prominent among them, and the one who gave Washington the most money, was Andrew Carnegie, who was a firm believer in Social Darwinism.[2] Washington, the founder and first president of Tuskegee (Normal and Industrial) Institute, also believed in certain tenets of Social Darwinism and eugenics.[3] Washington attended the First National Conference on Race Betterment, held in Battle Creek, Michigan, in 1914. The conference drew various naturalists and eugenicists from across the country, the majority of whom supported the theories of Herbert Spencer. Washington would plead at this conference for environmental changes "if the American Negro is to become a fully integrated member of the American society."[4]

As the unrivaled black political leader at the turn of the twentieth century, Washington publicly promoted African American acceptance of voluntary racial segregation (while privately he was opposed to legalized racial segregation), articulated notions of black inferiority, and emphasized industrial and agricultural education over higher education for the black masses.[5] In his biography of Washington, *Booker T. Washington: The Wizard of Tuskegee, 1901–1915*, Louis R. Harlan points out that even as Washington's public career began to wind down, he maintained his public ambiguity about racial segregation by continuing to "advocate . . . the same self-segregation that he and his colleagues at Tuskegee Institute had been practicing in their all-black school for more than thirty years."[6] In his famous Atlanta Exposition Address, which served as the impetus for his eventual political leadership, Washington argued, "In all things that are purely social we [blacks] can be as separate as the fingers, yet one as the hand in all things essential to mutual progress."[7] Washington publicly admonished black attempts to participate in what he believed was a more advanced white society and firmly believed that "it is at the bottom of life we must begin, and not at the top."[8] Louis R. Harlan points out that "the burden of his compromises and accommodations to a repressive system of white supremacy often vitiated his efforts to advance the interests of blacks, and indeed the history of his years of black leadership in America illustrates the impossibility of reforming a system while at the same time accommodating to its institutions and spirit."[9] Washington's abdication of social equality and promotion of separateness mirrored the belief of many of his white supporters, who fervently believed in racial zoning and racial planning to create legally separate societies for at least the first half of the twentieth century.

Washington's stance for racial separateness occurred concomitantly with the development of the segregation ordinance movement, which had begun in 1910 when African American migrants began their northern migration into urban centers. As geographer David Delaney points out, "The segregation ordinance movement was a grassroots social movement whose participants hoped to impose what we would recognize as municipal apartheid on residential areas of U.S. cities."[10]

W. E. B. Dubois, a Harvard-trained sociologist; author of the first sociological study of urban blacks, *The Philadelphia Negro;* and a founder of one of the leading civil rights organization in the United States, the National Association for the Advancement of Colored People, abhorred permanent and complete racial segregation and the political disenfranchisement of all African Americans.[11] Dubois felt that the total and permanent disenfranchisement of African Americans was being supported by Washington. He believed that Washington was publicly asking "black people to give up at least for the present, three things . . . political power, insistence on civil rights, and the higher education for Negro youth."[12] Dubois, however, did believe that the majority of blacks were socially inferior and were in need of some type of societal discipline and control. This belief was clearly articulated in the following statement taken from his famous book *Souls of Black Folks*: "I should be the last one to deny the patent weaknesses and shortcomings of the Negro people; I should be the last to withhold sympathy from the white South in its efforts to solve its intricate social problems. I freely acknowledge that it is possible, and sometimes best that a partially undeveloped people should be ruled by the best of their stronger and better neighbors for their own good, until such time as they can start and fight the world's battles alone."[13] Historian Mia Bay concludes in her essay on Dubois and his *The Philadelphia Negro* that it is clear that Dubois believed and accepted the tenets of Social Darwinism as they pertained to the black social body. "With dispassionate detachment, Dubois refers to his subjects as a 'half-developed race' and a 'people comparatively low in the scale of civilization.'"[14] Dubois's fear of permanent social and political castigation of the entire African American social body was the reason for his advocacy of active civil disobedience. It was the "civilized" black middle class that Dubois was most concerned about, his "talented tenth," who he felt were unfairly trapped by racial segregation. Dubois stated publicly that if the reconciliation between Northern and Southern whites during this time was to "be marked by industrial slavery and civic death of . . . black men, with permanent legislation into a position of inferiority, then those black men, if they are really men, are called upon by every consideration of patriotism and loyalty to oppose such a course by all civilized methods, even though such opposition involves disagreement with Mr. Booker T. Washington. We have no right to sit silently by while the inevitable seeds are sown for a harvest of disaster to our children, black and white."[15]

The inability of African Americans to support and unify over civil rights struggles at the turn of the twentieth century and the belief in their own civic and racial inferiority contributed to the power relations that produced their historical and current state of environmental disenfranchisement. Power in this case was manifested by such legal, socioeconomic, and political policies as Jim Crow laws as well as legal racial zoning laws that segregated blacks into environmentally compromised spaces. Even the African American leadership of the time embraced the ideologies of Social Darwinism and advocated intraracial separation.[16] As a result, early black leadership was ineffectual in offering meaningful resistance to the body politic's political powers. The political fragmentation among black leadership that began with Dubois and Washington has continued in varying degrees today and is key to understanding why many African American communities have been unsuccessful in effectively dealing with environmental racism.

Nascent Struggles for Environmental Justice and Sustainability

Many environmental justice activists and scholars today believe that the modern Environmental Justice Movement in the United States is an outgrowth of the country's modern Civil Rights Movement that began to gain momentum after World War II. This is a false and ahistorical assumption. A wealth of historical evidence exists that demonstrates that concerns over environmental saliency and sustainable spaces have been present in the black community since the turn of the century.

Despite or because of their resignation to black segregation at the beginning of the twentieth century, both Booker T. Washington and W. E. B. Dubois were interested in and concerned about the environmental conditions of the African American community. Booker T. Washington advanced and promoted the idea that blacks were better off by returning to or staying in a rural and agrarian (as opposed to an urban) environment. In his visits to Washington, D.C., as a student during the Reconstruction period, Washington would lament the fate of blacks who had left their agrarian communities for the cities in search of a better life: "I saw many [black] men who but a few months previous were members of Congress, then without employment in poverty. . . . How many times I wished then, and have often wished since that by some power of magic I might remove the great bulk of these people into the country districts and plant them upon the soil, upon the solid and never deceptive nature of Mother Nature."[17] Although most of the literature about Washington emphasizes his thrust on industrial education, it is important to understand that he laid a heavy emphasis on agrarian education and black employment in an agrarian economy.

To further this emphasis, the Tuskegee Institute ran extension programs, conducted Negro conferences, and operated the Jessup Wagon (a traveling agricultural school), all of which supported rural black farmers and the development of what we now refer to as sustainable communities. Through these and similar Tuskegee Institute programs, black farmers were taught how to optimize their farming techniques to "gain and hold their own land, build and furnish their own houses and educate their children."[18] Tuskegee would become even more famous with the research work of renowned botanist and agricultural scientist Dr. George Washington Carver.[19] Louis Harlan's biography makes it clear that Washington was also concerned about the environmental health conditions of both Tuskegee Institute students and the black community in general. As a result, he founded National Negro Health Week, March 21–27, 1915, with the support of the National Negro Business League and the National Urban League.[20] According to Harlan, Washington "devoted much attention to the details of the earth closets, the night cart, and the purity of the water supply of the campus."[21] In 1908, with the support of the National Tuberculosis Association, Washington held a five-day tuberculosis conference at Tuskegee. In 1911, he asked the newly founded Russell Sage Foundation for support in a "nationwide effort to improve the sanitary and health conditions of blacks." Although the foundation did not offer its support, "Washington slated one day of the 1914 Tuskegee Negro Conference as a public health conference where demonstrations and presentations were made about sanitation, nursing, and patent medicine frauds. Additionally, George Washington Carver offered an exhibit on pure and impure water."[22]

As elucidated in chapter 1, W. E. B. Dubois was one of the first academics to systematically study blacks and their environmental conditions in the north (Philadelphia) and the south (Atlanta). Dubois's Philadelphia study clearly articulates the inadequacy of sanitary infrastructures and marginalized housing in the urban environment. In *Souls of Black Folks*, his study of southern blacks in Atlanta, Dubois characterizes rural southern blacks as poor and ignorant and compares their living conditions to those of Philadelphia blacks. Dubois observed that, like their Northern city cousins, Southern blacks were packed into substandard housing that was almost always old, bare, and unplastered, with a black and smoky fireplace in need of repair. Unlike the North, though, Dubois believed that the conditions in the rural South did offer an environmental advantage for blacks: "Of course, one small, close room in a city without a yard, is in many respects worse than a larger single country room. . . . The single great advantage of the Negro peasant is that he may spend most of his life outside his hovel, in the open fields."[23] Even though Dubois felt that city life provided greater socioeconomic opportunities for blacks, he also realized that blacks were making a trade-off in terms of their environment and health by leaving the rural agrarian workforce of the South: "The toil, like all farm toil, is monotonous, and there are little machinery and few tools to relieve its burdensome drudgery. . . . But with all this, it is work in the pure open air, and this is something in a day when fresh air is scarce."[24]

In his earlier autobiography, *Dusk of Dawn: An Essay toward an Autobiography of a Race Concept*, Dubois described in greater detail the environmental dilemmas of urban blacks (especially those he considered to be more cultured and socially accomplished) produced by voluntary and forced racial segregation. Dubois observed that "negroes" living in segregated environments found themselves living among "diseased people in a crime-ridden geography where city services of water, sewerage, garbage removal, street cleaning, lighting, noise and traffic regulation, schools, and hospitalization are usually neglected or withheld."[25] Dubois felt that any attempt by "negroes" to move away from these segregated and environmentally disenfranchised areas was beginning to be met by legislation and city ordinances that tried to legalize racial segregation. For example, one of the first efforts to legalize racial segregation occurred in Baltimore, Maryland, where blacks tried to "buy their way out of the back alleys and the slums into the better-paved, better-lighted main streets."[26] Baltimore's 1910 city ordinance that attempted to segregate blacks by law was duplicated in cities (like Atlanta, Louisville, Kentucky, and Greensboro, North Carolina) across the country for ten years. The resultant "segregation ordinance movement" was precipitated by the massive migration of rural blacks to cities in both the north and the south; in Baltimore alone, the black population had increased from 79,000 to 108,000 within the first two decades of the twentieth century. According to geographer David Delaney, "The segregation ordinance movement was a grassroots social movement whose participants hoped to impose what we would recognize as municipal apartheid on residential areas of U.S. cities. Their goal was to prevent black people from living in neighborhoods that they wanted to maintain as exclusive white spaces."[27] These efforts to legally circumscribe African Americans geographically in cities were met with legal opposition by the NAACP across the country under Dubois's leadership, terminating in the Supreme Court case of *Buchanan v. Warley*, in which white supremacists were rebuffed.[28] The NAACP would continue to wage legal battles against similar techniques of power that attempted to enforce spatial censorships of blacks (which created or exacerbated environmental inequalities) throughout the first half of the twentieth century. The final legal victory for the NAACP was the 1948 Supreme Court decision in the case of *Shelley v. Kraemer*. In *Shelly v. Kraemer* the court ruled that state actions supporting restrictive covenants were in violation of the Fourteenth Amendment.

Roots of the Modern Environmental Justice Movement

Today's Environmental Justice Movement is predicated upon the belief that disproportionate health and socioeconomic costs from pollution from industrial production and development are and have been borne by the poor, by racial minorities in the United States, and by people of color across the world.[29] The United Church of Christ's (UCC) first study on environmental racism in 1987 concluded that "race and not income was the primary determinant in siting polluting facilities and that three out of the five largest commercial waste landfills (accounting for 40 percent of the nation's garbage) were located in black and Hispanic communities."[30] Luke W. Cole and Sheila R. Foster's recent work, *From the Ground Up: Environmental Racism and the Rise of the Environmental Justice Movement*, reveals that the most recent studies by the United Church of Christ's Commission for Racial Justice (CRJ) found that "from 1980 to 1993 the concentrations of people of color in all zip codes with toxic waste sites increased from 25 percent to 31 percent." Similarly, in 1993, as in 1980, "the percentage of people of color in a community increased as commercial hazardous waste management activity increased."[31] People living in these communities are the very same people who have been historically constructed as others in their own countries and the global community. As a consequence of this construction based on ever-changing scientific and pseudoscientific notions of racial inferiority, these same groups have experienced a loss or curtailment of civil, political, and social rights for generations.

Many scholars have argued that the change from an agricultural to an industrial society led the way to a more civilized and advanced society with numerous benefits in terms of improvements in health, environment, and personal wealth for its members.[32] This change to an industrial society, however, also led to unforeseen costs for the society in the form of environmental degradation and public health problems that were directly tied to pollution produced by industrial processes. Industrial development was accompanied by an increase in what we now know can be environmental illnesses: asthma, emphysema, lead poisoning, cancer, neurotoxicity, and even miscarriages.[33] All of these illnesses can and have been tied to the presence of environmental pollutants generated by industrial processes. Since the first industrial revolution, environmental inequalities have existed among members of society. This is evidenced by the fact that everyone in the society does not and did not benefit equally from the "goods" produced by the industrial processes in the form of an improvement in the overall quality of life—better housing, better environments, and better health. Likewise, the industrial and postindustrial revolutions in society created entire populations of people who bore the inequitable costs of industrial production by disproportionately receiving an inordinate level of the "bads" in the form of environmental illness, ecological deterioration, and unsustainable communities.[34] The poor and Irish immigrant communities of Great Britain during the nineteenth century can be seen as an excellent precursive community suffering from environmental injustices. The cultural, racial, ethnic, and socioeconomic restrictions in their living spaces forced them to live in the midst of industrial production.[35] Their living spaces, like those of communities of color and poor whites today, lacked proper environmental infrastructures like sewers and privies. These communities suffered from devastating health impacts stemming from early industrial pollution in the form of respiratory illnesses and from such illnesses as typhoid fever and cholera, which can be tied to inadequate sanitation. This pattern of environmental inequity would be reflected across the Atlantic and, eventually, the globe, as industrialization spread during the nineteenth and twentieth centuries.

The current Environmental Justice Movement can be viewed as a continuing resistance to power relations that have created and continue to create an uneven distribution of environmental costs and benefits in industrialized societies across the world. Activists in the modern movement have engaged in lawsuits and protest marches that have challenged the legislative and academic techniques of those in power who have contributed to environmental disenfranchisement. The activities of environmental justice activists have caused government and environmental policy makers to critically examine how particular forms of the benefits and costs (e.g., environmental "goods" and "bads") of industrial and postindustrial society are divided among its members. In many ways, the Environmental Justice Movement provides evidence of the Foucauldian theorem on the role of modern society; that is, to provide biological protection to those considered within the social body of the state. We can now see that those lying inside the social body are those who will benefit because their communities will receive the full support of protective environmental legislation and enforcement; they will have access to uncontaminated residential spaces and to an organic food supply, or at the very least, a food supply that has not been genetically engineered or contaminated from pollutants.[36]

There is not a consistent consensus among scholars on the exact moment of birth for the modern Environmental Justice Movement. Many believe that the movement began with Dr. Martin Luther King Jr.'s 1968 move toward a "poor people" campaign and his support of protesting black sanitation workers. It is also argued that today's Environmental Justice Movement began in the 1970s with the protests of low-income families in the now infamous Love Canal in New York. Most scholars, however, agree that the 1982 grassroots protests by African Americans in Warren County, North Carolina, against toxic dumping in their communities was the pivotal and defining moment for the modern Environmental Justice Movement. By 1991, the basic objectives and strategies for addressing inequitable distribution of environmental costs in poor and racially marginalized communities had solidified.

1968––Martin Luther King Jr. and the Poor People's Campaign

There is an inextricable relationship between poverty and environmental racism and the Environmental Justice Movement. It is evidenced by the fact that it is usually poor and minority communities who are on the front line, protesting and demanding relief from environmental inequities. Activists in the environmental justice movement continually lament that it is society's poor who bear the cost of environmental pollution because they don't have the economic power to eliminate or avoid the costs of industrial production in their impoverished communities. However, their lack of economic power is due to the fact that they had been constructed as "others" and abandoned for generations. The first national leader in the second half of the twentieth century to address the systemic and total disenfranchisement (and the concomitant environmental consequences) of the poor as a result of their social construction as "others" in this country was civil rights leader and activist Reverend Dr. Martin Luther

King Jr. James H. Cone points out, in his comparative study of Martin Luther King Jr. and Malcolm X, that when Dr. King "focused on the problems of the inner city, he saw the despair . . . and the often fruitless effort of poor blacks who were trying to survive in an environment unfit for human habitation."[37] His observations led to the formal creation of the Poor People's Campaign (PPC) on March 4, 1968, which sought to ameliorate social, economic, and environmental disenfranchisement regardless of color. In 1968, under the Poor People's Campaign, Dr. King began to openly advocate plans for a multiracial march for the poor on Washington, D.C.[38] The march was planned for April 22, 1968.[39] Fifteen hundred demonstrators from fifteen regions of the country were to converge on the nation's capital to petition government agencies and Congress for an economic Bill of Rights.[40] Andrew Young, one of King's closest friends and a key leader in the Civil Rights Movement, points out in his autobiography that the leaders of the movement had reached a *gestalt* in terms of understanding the root of racism and civil disenfranchisement. People constructed to be outside the body politic were the ones suffering the most; they were usually the poor. According to Young, Martin Luther King Jr. and his fellow civil rights activists wanted to gear the movement toward a Poor People's Campaign because they recognized that "poor people in America were out of sight and out of mind. Policies that created slums and kept people in poverty were perpetuated almost unconsciously. For politicians, there was no real need to consider the impact of policy decisions on the poor since they were powerless in the political system."[41]

A critical issue in the proposed Poor People's Campaign was the need to address the problem of the poor living in unhealthy and unsanitary housing conditions. King argued that the United States could not have a democratic society if the great concentration of wealth rested in the hands of only a few members of society. Even as the plans for the Poor People's Campaign began to develop, King's commitment to environmental issues impacting the poor and racially marginalized was made even more apparent in 1968 when he traveled to Memphis, Tennessee. On April 3, 1968, he delivered his famous "I've been to the mountaintop" speech in Tennessee to a largely black group of striking sanitation workers. Following his show of support for the workers, he was assassinated on April 4, 1968. Despite his death, Dr. King's concerns about the inequitable distribution of wealth and poverty in the United States and the concomitant environmental consequences continue to be addressed by today's environmental justice activists.

The 1970s—Earth Day and Nascent Environmental Justice Ideologies

The first national Earth Day observance on April 22, 1970, which sought to address the environmental problems of the planet as a result of man's actions and mentalities, inadvertently revealed today's environmental justice concerns. Although a national movement did not emerge in the 1970s to address the environmental inequities in poor and minority communities, the philosophical and ideological underpinnings for today's Environmental Justice Movement had already emerged. Contrary to much of the published literature about the first Earth Day, African Americans and other communities of color had already begun an open dialogue about environmental justice issues. National and local articles that described the reactions by African American communities and their leaders to the emerging environmental movement began appearing in newspapers and magazines during 1970 in light of the country's newfound concerns about the environment. Their concerns mirrored those expressed by Dr. King in 1968 and revolved around the need for sanitary housing, the need for environmental infrastructures, and the illegal dumping of waste and garbage in their communities. For instance, one day before Earth Day, the prominent black Chicago newspaper, the *Chicago Defender*, ran a photographic report about the visit of Special Presidential Assistant Robert J. Brown and his task force on aid to disadvantaged communities to the impoverished community of Robbins, Illinois. The report pointed out that this poor African American community was suffering from environmental health problems because of inadequate sanitary infrastructure. The environmental problems were so severe that Robbins residents at this time were contracting hepatitis because of high levels of sewage in the standing water.[42]

The recognition of the connection between poverty and environmental disenfranchisement was also reflected in the comments by another prominent civil rights activist during this time period, Reverend Jesse Jackson. During the first Earth Week (April 1970), Reverend Jackson, at that time still a member of the Southern Christian Leadership Conference

(SCLC) and former director of Operation Breadbasket, went to Congress to discuss the country's continuing need to resolve the problems of the poor.[43] Jackson urged the government to focus its concern on the issues of hunger and sanitary housing and decried the attention that was being given to the emerging traditional environmental movement. Jackson felt that the newly emerging environmental movement was drawing attention and concerns away from the Civil Rights Movement. Jackson's sentiments and posture toward the environmental movement and its relationship to African Americans was echoed across the country by many politicians but especially by the country's first African American mayors, Carl B. Stokes of Cleveland and Richard Hatcher of Gary, Indiana. The observations of Mayors Stokes and Hatcher, elucidated in an Earth Day article, "To Blacks, Ecology Is Irrelevant," in *Business Week* on November 14, 1970, centered on the fact that blacks were more likely than whites to suffer from environmental illnesses and that their environmental problems were symptomatic of deeper societal ills such as poverty, racism, and the inequitable distribution of political power.[44] This same article also made it clear that blacks were very cognizant of their "otherness" as well as the environmental inequalities occurring in their communities and that they resented bearing only the costs of modern industrialized society without the concomitant benefits. The conclusions of *Business Week* would reflect the primary arguments of the modern Environmental Justice Movement:

- Blacks are not opposed to cleaning up pollution. Environmental woes to black leaders are symptoms of the deeper diseases infecting society: poverty, racism, and the inequitable distribution of political power.
- Blacks will not be satisfied by cleaner ghettos if they are still denied access to suburbia.
- They will not be appeased by a company that cleans up its shop if it still excludes blacks from its executive suite.
- They resent the ability of "White America" to mount a broad-based attack on pollution, like the Apollo moon program, but unable to mount a similar attack on the related problems of poverty and race.

- "Blacks are double victims. We suffer from pollution as much as anyone, but we're not beneficiaries of the affluence that produced the pollution."
- Factories that cannot be economically upgraded to meet pollution standards are being closed, often throwing blacks and low-income whites out of work.
- The environmental issue that most upsets part of the black community is population control (genocide). "Too many whites see the population problem as too many blacks."
- Many birth control clinics are in or near black ghettos—at the same time so many other vital community services are lacking.
- Black resentment is triggering a debate about priorities within the ecology movement: "The Earth and the web of life come first, man comes second" versus "The slums of Chicago must be cleaned up before the pollution in Lake Michigan."
- Environmentalists are recognizing that a movement dedicated to the survival of man and his habitat is itself ecologically unsound if it remains irrelevant to the needs of so many in squalor.

Ironically, the nationally prominent African American magazine *Ebony* featured recently slain civil rights leader Dr. Martin Luther King Jr. in its April 1970 issue. The majority of the magazine was dedicated to the accomplishments and issues of the Civil Rights Movement: unemployment, housing, and education discrimination. The issue contained only one article that focused on public health issues as environmental issues in African American communities. Despite *Ebony*'s limited coverage, the literature from African American periodicals at the time clearly shows that African Americans were cognizant of the environmental movement but that they had their own interpretation of the critical "environmental issues" for their communities.

The concerns of African Americans then and in today's Environmental Justice Movement, however, seem to be with what they perceived as a shift to an ecocentric perspective (the environment "without man") that they felt was eclipsing their basic needs for ensured survival in what they perceived as an indifferent or hostile "human" environment. An environmental justice consciousness had already emerged by the 1970s among African

Americans and on Earth Day 1970, African American Chicagoans actually had separate, communitywide environmental celebrations. At the national level, African American politicians and periodicals emphasized that the environmental issues for African Americans were grounded in basic social justice issues like hunger, adequate housing, and safe water sources.

By the end of 1970, a multiracial coalition of urban environmentalists began to focus attention on public health and working conditions and sought to reform the environmental movement to include issues of both race and class. By the late 1970s, Dr. Robert Bullard, a prominent environmental sociologist and key figure in the Environmental Justice Movement, had studied land use in Houston, Texas, and found that garbage dumps had a disproportionate impact on people of color and low-income people because of their close proximity to these dumps.

Earth Day had significance for many types of communities in the United States and served as an intellectual springboard that allowed communities to rethink human relationships with nature. The way in which people conceived of themselves with respect to this environment, however, was heavily influenced by their race during this period. African Americans, the ultimate "others" in American society, clearly felt that Earth Day observations could only be meaningful for them if they took into account that the integrity of the human environment on the most basic levels was the primary environmental concern. They also clearly understood that the environmental integrity of one's ecological space was predicated and determined by race. This long-held view and stance would prove to be the basis for the 1980s Environmental Justice Movement.

The Urban Environment Conference

Six years after the first Earth Day, the Urban Environment Conference (UEC) was developed in 1976 by a unique coalition of organizations (labor, environmental, and minority) dedicated to incorporating race and class issues into the environmental movement. This coalition initiated "City Care" conferences that were held in cities across the United States. The conferences fostered the development of the ideological and structural foundations for the modern environmental justice movement. Contrary to prevailing environmental justice myths, the UEC's activities were supported by a traditional environmental movement organization. It received its first financial contributions from the Sierra Club and labor unions.

When the UEC arrived in Michigan in 1976 for one of its first conferences it brought together representatives from labor unions, environmental groups, economic justice organizations, and churches to discuss issues of economic justice and the urban environment. As a result of the Michigan conference, the UEC received a $66,000 federal grant, which they used to fund eleven similar "City Care" conferences throughout the United States. Federal agencies that helped fund conferences included the Environmental Protection Agency (EPA) and the Departments of Housing and Urban Development (HUD); Interior; Energy; Agriculture; and Transportation. The UEC conferences and activities emanating from them led to the adoption of the first "Right to Know" legislation in Delaware. These "Right to Know" laws would become central to locally based environmental activism because future plants would be required to provide notice of potential environmental risks to the community. The knowledge of environmental risks gained by affected communities empowered urban environmental activists and laid the groundwork for research and documentation of environmental justice in the 1980s and 1990s.

In 1979, the city of Detroit, the National Urban League, the Sierra Club, and the UEC held a major national conference that would come to have a major influence on the emergence and form of today's Environmental Justice Movement. Together with approximately seventy-five national and community-based cosponsoring organizations, 750 people met for three and one-half days to listen to addresses by community leaders, share information, and set new agendas for the UEC. Nearly all of the attendees were community activists familiar with the grassroots impacts of national problems. Issues addressed included public health, neighborhood empowerment, urban parks, suburban sprawl, and public transportation.

1978––Love Canal

As discussed above, poor minority communities are not the only groups who have been constructed as environmental "others" in America. Poor and working class whites have also been constructed as environmental others and have been (and still are) toxic victims, carrying the brunt of inequitable environmental costs. Like racial minorities, their environmental problems are inseparable from their economic condition and their position as marginalized whites. Some scholars believe the modern Environmental Justice Movement began at different points in the 1960s and 1970s, but there are many scholars who believe it began in the United States on August 2, 1978. This was the day when CBS and ABC television networks first carried news of the adverse effects of toxic waste on residents of Love Canal. The New York state health commissioner had recently announced that the landfill created by the Hooker Chemical Company had created a serious and extremely dangerous public health threat to the residents of Love Canal, a predominantly white working class community in Buffalo, New York. Hooker had dumped thousands of drums of toxic waste into an abandoned navigation canal that had been filled in in 1952. The company then sold the land to the Niagara Falls Board of Education, who eventually built schools and housing. Soon after residents moved into the area, alarming health problems and birth defects began to occur. Adults, children, and animals received chemical burns from the dirt in backyards and school playgrounds. Citizens reported visual explosions. Hooker's dumping practices resulted in the resurfacing of pesticide residues and other chemicals that were seen bubbling on the ground. The community had become so poisoned that many of the residents' lawns wouldn't grow, and the few fruits and vegetables that residents were able to grow made them sick.

The grassroots environmental activism that is now so common and characteristic of the Environmental Justice Movement was critical to the successful resolution of the environmental dilemmas at Love Canal. This activism was lead and personified by Lois Gibbs, a Love Canal resident whose three-year-old son Michael developed a respiratory illness that was tied to the toxic waste in the development. Moved by her own son's illness as well as the illnesses of many of her neighbors' children, Gibbs founded the Love Canal Homeowner's Association and took their complaints to the state capital for resolution. The activism of the Homeowner's Association led to an 1978 investigation by state epidemiologists. They found abnormally high rates of birth defects, miscarriages, epilepsy, liver abnormalities, rectal bleeding, and headaches. The continued activism of Gibbs and the Homeowner's

Association convinced the federal government that they should investigate as well. By 1980, federal investigations had identified 248 chemicals in the dump site; currently, more than 400 have been found. As a result of the state and federal investigations, then-President Jimmy Carter declared Love Canal, New York, a disaster area. Residents were evacuated, the state of New York purchased more than 230 of the residents' homes and financed some of the costs of their relocation, and many homes were torn down. As well, the declaration of Love Canal as a disaster area entitled residents to federal aid that could be used for relocation. Lois Gibbs's successful environmental activism to resolve environmental inequalities in her community would eventually be imitated across the country with various levels of success by other female environmental justice leaders like Peggy Shepard, co-founder of West Harlem Environmental Action, Inc. (WE ACT); Dollie Burwell, lead member of Warren County Concerned Citizens; Hazel Johnson, founder of Chicago's People for Community Recovery (PCR); Emelda West, co-founder of St. James Citizens for Jobs and the Environment; and Margaret Williams of Citizens Against Toxic Exposure (CATE). All of these women created or participated in the development of environmental justice organizations in poor and minority communities to address or combat environmental racism in their respective communities.[45]

The 1980s—Environmental Racism and Warren County, North Carolina

Today, environmental justice has become synonymous with the concept and phenomenon of environmental racism. Another turning point, and yet another candidate for the claim to the birth of the modern Environmental Justice Movement (as well as the change in the conceptual premise from class-based to race-based) occurred in Warren County, North Carolina, in 1982. African Americans mounted one of the first national protests over the siting of a hazardous waste site in their community. "Hunt's Dump" was named for the then-governor of North Carolina, James Hunt.

After surveying ninety-three sites in thirteen counties, Governor Hunt selected 142 acres of land in Afton, a small black community in Warren County, as the disposal site for 32,000 cubic yards of dirt contaminated with toxic polychlorinated biphenyls, or PCBs. The soil had been removed from 217 miles of North Carolina state highway across fourteen counties where it had been illegally dumped by the Robert Burns and Ward Transfer Company in 1978. The Burns and Ward Company had transported the waste from Buffalo, New York, and decided to dump it illegally along the highway rather than properly storing it in accordance with federal, state, and local regulations.

The community had a high water table in porous sandy soil and most of its residents got their water from wells. This clearly was not the optimal site for the land disposal of PCBs. The water table was only five to ten feet beneath the surface; it would be only a matter of time before the well water was contaminated. Residents protested out of concern about possible PCB contamination.

Governor Hunt claimed his reasons for selecting Warren County as the disposal site were based solely on technical premises. This claim was later refuted by the chief of the EPA's hazardous waste implementation branch, William Sanjour. Sanjour, coincidently, was a supporter of Warren County residents. His assessment determined that the siting decision was political. Protests to put pressure on decision makers against locating the toxic dump in Warren County were then organized under the leadership of Afton residents Ken and Deborah Ferruccio. They organized the grassroots activist group Warren County Citizens Concerned about PCBs. Their protest actions were eventually joined by those of nationally prominent civil rights advocacy groups such as the United Church of Christ (UCC) Commission for Racial Justice and the Southern Christian Leadership Conference, as well as religious leaders, environmental activists, and political officials.

In 1982 Warren County residents peacefully protested the siting of the landfill site for over six weeks and attempted to physically block the path of over six thousand truckloads of PCB-contaminated soil. Their actions caused Warren County to become a national news story. These peaceful protests resulted in the arrest of more than five hundred people, including two civil rights activists who would prove instrumental and pivotal in the national recognition and future development of the Environmental Justice Movement: District of Columbia delegate Walter E. Fauntroy and Reverend Benjamin Chavis, then executive director of the UCC Commission for Racial Justice. The arrests of protesters, including Dr.

Joseph Lowery of the Southern Christian Leadership Conference, was the first time in American history that citizens had been sent to jail for trying to stop a toxic waste landfill. The 1982 protests by the Warren County citizens group ultimately did not prevent the siting of the landfill, but they did serve to make environmental racism a national concern. The actions of Warren County protestors had a long-term impact on influencing future national environmental policies dealing with environmental inequities in communities of color. As environmental sociologist Robert Bullard noted, "Although the demonstrations in North Carolina were not successful in halting the landfill construction, the protests brought sharper focus to the convergence of civil rights and environmental rights and mobilized a nationally broad-based group to protest these inequities."[46] Governor James Hunt eventually conceded to the Warren County residents' demands and agreed not to build additional landfills in their community; further, he agreed to have their well water monitored for PCB contamination.

The Warren County case makes it clear that the ultimate environmental others were people of color. Unlike the stereotypical images of urban and poor minorities suffering from environmental inequities, Afton was a stable minority community with a high home ownership rate—84 percent of the residents in the area surrounding the protest site were African Americans; 64 percent of these owned their own homes.

In 1983, one year after the Warren County protests, District of Columbia delegate Walter Fauntroy (who had been arrested in the Warren County protest) persuaded the U.S. General Accounting Office (GAO) to study the 1983 sitings of hazardous waste landfills in EPA Region IV. This region covered Alabama, Florida, Georgia, Kentucky, Mississippi, North Carolina, South Carolina, and Tennessee. The resultant report, *Siting of Hazardous Waste Landfills and Their Correlation with Racial and Economic Status of Surrounding Communities*, concluded that African American people and ethnic minorities were more likely than the general population to live near a commercial waste treatment facility or uncontrolled waste site. The GAO study found that three out of every four landfills were located near predominantly minority communities. The report eventually spurred the 1987 UCC Commission for Racial Justice to sponsor a study, *Toxic Wastes and Race in the United States: A National Report on the Racial and Socioeconomic Characteristics of Communities with Hazardous Waste*

Sites. The commission employed Public Data Access, a New York-based research firm, to assist in the analysis of this information. The study concluded that race was the best predictor of hazardous waste site location. Their statisticians found that there was only a one in ten thousand chance of such siting patterns occurring randomly. Environmentalists studying incinerators found the same results. In response to the findings of the report, UCC leader Reverend Benjamin Chavis coined the term "environmental racism" to reflect the fact that toxic facilities were more likely to be found in communities with high percentages of racial minorities, the poor, the elderly, and the young.

It would take more than ten years after the GAO study before a national policy response would form to deal with the phenomenon of environment racism. The changes in environmental regulation and enforcement polices under President Ronald Reagan (1980–1988) undermined the fragile coalition that had formed between minority communities, labor, and environmental groups. These groups focused most of their efforts on their own constituencies and began to fight over whatever federal funding and programmatic support remained during the two Reagan administrations and the single term of President George H. W. Bush.

The 1990s—Moving the Modern Environmental Justice Movement Forward

In 1990 a group of academics convened at the University of Michigan's School of Natural Resources and Environment to discuss their most recent findings on the relationship between race and environmental hazards. (The group would come to be known as "the Michigan Group.") This conference led to the formation of the Michigan Environmental Justice Coalition. Prompted by their findings, the group wrote letters to Louis Sullivan, then secretary of the U.S. Department of Health and Human Services, and to William Reilly, then head of the U.S. Environmental Protection Agency (EPA). A meeting with Reilly and seven of the professors resulted in the creation of the Work Group on Environmental Equity. Its primary objective was to examine the EPA's negligence or insensitivity to issues of environmental racism.

Also in 1990, environmental activists, disgusted by the policies and practices of traditional environmental groups, issued a public challenge to traditional environmentalists. Richard Moore of the Southwest Organizing Project and Pat Bryant of the Gulf Coast Tenants Organization drafted a letter that was signed by more than one hundred community leaders and sent it to the ten largest traditional environmental groups. The letter accused the traditional environmental groups of racism in their hiring and policy development processes. It created a national media frenzy when an article appeared about it in the *New York Times*. The political stir caused by this event influenced UCC Commission for Racial Justice head Benjamin Chavis (a signatory of the letter) to call for an emergency summit of environmental, civil rights, and community groups. The UCC spearheaded the planning of the summit under the direction of Charles Lee, the director for the Environmental Justice Program under the UCC Commission for Racial Justice. The summit took eighteen months of planning by Lee, Pat Bryant, Moore, Dana Alston of the Panos Institute, Indian activist Donna Chavis of North Carolina, and academic Robert Bullard. The end result was the historic First National People of Color Environmental Leadership Summit held for three days in Washington, D.C., in October 1991. It brought together three hundred environmental justice activists as delegates and four hundred observers from across the United States as well as Africa and South America who met to develop principles and issue a call for national and worldwide action.[47]

Three basic philosophies emerged from the summit: first, that environmental justice is not separate from economic and political struggles in communities of color; second, that environmental justice is intrinsically related to community empowerment; and third, that establishing a just environmental justice policy should be an exclusionary dialogue that recognizes that communities of color speak for themselves. More than 650 grassroots leaders adopted the "Principles of Environmental Justice," a platform calling for an end to the discriminatory poisoning of low-income communities and people of color worldwide. The principles (see appendix at the end of this chapter) from the summit were eventually included in President Clinton's 1994 executive order on environmental justice.

The summit concluded with a demand for a response from the EPA to address the summit's environmental justice concerns and the formation of two groups. The first group, the Indigenous Environmental Network, was formed to promote the interests of Native American activists. The second group, the Southern Organizing Committee, was formed to organize the Southern Community Labor Conference for Environmental Justice in New Orleans in 1992, a gathering of nearly two thousand activists from fourteen states. A few years later, two summit organizers, Benjamin Chavis and Robert Bullard, were appointed to President-elect Clinton's transition team to help formulate national policies addressing environmental inequalities.

On February 11, 1994, President Clinton signed Executive Order 12898 on Environmental Justice. The official title of the order was "Federal Actions to Address Environmental Justice in Minority Populations and Low-Income Populations." The order focused on the "environmental and human health conditions" of people of color and low-income populations with the goal of achieving equal environmental protection for all communities, regardless of their race, income status, ethnicity, or culture. It directed all federal agencies with an environmental and public health mission to make environmental justice an integral part of their mission. The order also made federal agencies responsible for ensuring that states and organizations receiving federal monies for environmental projects did not violate federal civil rights laws. Finally, the order established the Interagency Working Group on Environmental Justice, with membership comprised of the heads of such federal agencies as the Departments of Justice, Defense, Energy, Labor, Interior, Transportation, Agriculture, Housing and Urban Development, Commerce, and Health and Human Services, and the EPA.

In 2003, twenty-one years after the first modern environmental justice national protest in Warren County, nine years after President Clinton's executive order, and a year after the second environmental justice summit, the Warren County, North Carolina, environmental justice issue was coming to a close. In 1998, the 60,000 tons of PCB-contaminated soil was detoxified through a community-approved process known as base catalyzed decomposition (BCD). The cost for decontamination was estimated at $16.2 million. The funding came from the North Carolina General Assembly, a settlement between the U.S. Department of Justice and the Burns and Ward Company (the source of the PCBs), and from monies from environmental projects that were completed under budget.[48]

Twelve years had elapsed before the community was able to take steps to eliminate the hazards posed by the toxic wastes in the landfill. "In 1994, a working group consisting of members of the community and representatives from the state, began an in-depth assessment of the landfill and a study of the feasibility of the detoxification."[49]

The Warren County story is one of the more positive in the vast repertoire of communities who have waged battles in the modern environmental justice movement. There are now over one hundred studies on environmental justice struggles. Many document an overriding number of unhappy or disappointing endings for environmental justice struggles.[50]

The struggle for environmental justice continues. Over 1,200 environmental justice activists from around the world attended the second Environmental Justice Summit in Washington, D.C., on October 28, 2002. Summit attendees included representatives from the United States, South Africa, Colombia, Nigeria, the Philippines, and the Marshall Islands. They all came to discuss the current and future state of environmental inequalities worldwide. A major conclusion that emerged from this second Environmental Justice Summit reflects the dismal state of affairs for the current Environmental Justice Movement. Although improvements have been made in the way governments carry out environmental protection, gaps still exist. Summit attendees agreed that community groups today are still "faced with rollbacks and the steady chipping away at civil liberties, basic civil and human rights, and environmental protection."[51]

Notes

1. David Delaney, *Race, Place and the Law, 1836–1948* (Austin: University of Texas Press, 1998), 104, 132.

2. Louis R. Harlan, *Booker T. Washington: The Wizard of Tuskegee, 1901–1915* (New York: Oxford University Press, 1983), 130–35. According to Harlan's research, Washington received support from Andrew Carnegie to the tune of $600,000 in U.S. Steel bonds and $150,000 for personal use, Henry H. Rogers of Standard Oil gave Washington $500 per month, and George Eastman (camera manufacturer) gave annual contributions of $10,000 and contributed $250,000 to the memorial fund.

3. Steven Selden, *Inheriting Sham: The Story of Eugenics and Racism in America* (New York: Teachers College Press, 1999), 4–5. The Carnegie Institution financially supported the work of eugenicists, like Charles Benedict Davenport's Station for the

Experimental Study of Evolution in Cold Spring Harbor, New York, who played a key role in organized American eugenics. A primary objective of Davenport's research was to demonstrate the "value of superior blood and the menace to society of inferior blood."

4. Selden, *Inheriting Sham*, 8.

5. For a thorough description of Washington's political power in America, read Louis R. Harlan, *Booker T. Washington: The Wizard of Tuskegee, 1901–1915* (New York: Oxford University Press, 1983).

6. Harlan, *Booker T. Washington*, 429.

7. Washington, *Up from Slavery*, 107.

8. Washington, *Up from Slavery*, 107.

9. Harlan, *Booker T. Washington*, 237.

10. Delaney, *Race, Place and the Law*, 105.

11. Delaney, *Race, Place and the Law*, 106–8. The NAACP's legal efforts played a major role in arresting the segregation ordinance movement in the U.S. Supreme Court case *Buchanan v. Warley*.

12. Dubois, *Souls of Black Folks*, 40.

13. Dubois, *Souls of Black Folks*, 135.

14. Mia Bay, "The World Was Thinking Wrong about Race: The Philadelphia Negro and Nineteenth-Century Science," in *W. E. B. Dubois, Race and the City: The Philadelphia Negro and its Legacy*, ed. Michael B. Katz and Thomas J. Sugrue (Philadelphia: University of Pennsylvania Press, 1998), 52.

15. Dubois, "Of Mr. Booker T. Washington and Others," in *Souls of Black Folks*, 44–45.

16. For more information on how African Americans perceived the variation of their community and the social equality as a function of class, read Washington, *Souls of Black Folks*, and W. E. B. Dubois, *Dusk of Dawn: An Essay toward an Autobiography of a Race Concept* (New Brunswick, NJ: Transaction Publishers, 2002).

17. Washington, *Up from Slavery*, 43.

18. Harlan, *Booker T. Washington*, 205–7.

19. Harlan, *Booker T. Washington*, 205–7. While at Tuskegee, Carver developed his own method of crop rotation to conserve nutrients in the soil.

20. Harlan, *Booker T. Washington*, 235.

21. Harlan, *Booker T. Washington*, 233.

22. Harlan, *Booker T. Washington*, 233–34.

23. Dubois, *Souls of Black Folks*, 108.

24. Dubois, *Souls of Black Folks*, 111.

25. Dubois, *Dusk of Dawn*, 182–83.

26. Dubois, *Dusk of Dawn*, 238–39.

27. David Delaney, *Race, Place and the Law*, 105.

28. David Delaney, *Race, Place and the Law*, 149.

29. Robert D. Bullard, *Unequal Protection: Environmental Justice and Communities of Color* (San Francisco: Sierra Club Books, 1994).

30. Mark Dowie, *Losing Ground: American Environmentalism at the Close of the Twentieth Century* (Cambridge: MIT Press, 1995), 142.

31. Luke W. Cole and Sheila R. Foster, *From the Ground Up: Environmental Racism and the Rise of the Environmental Justice Movement* (New York: New York University Press, 2001), 55–56.

32. The relationship between public health and industrialization is discussed in Martin V. Melosi, *The Sanitary City: Urban Infrastructure in America from Colonial Times to the Present* (Baltimore: Johns Hopkins University Press, 2000), and Joel A. Tarr, *The Search for the Ultimate Sink: Urban Pollution in Historical Perspective* (Akron, OH: University of Akron Press, 1996).

33. Bullard, *Unequal Protection*.

34. Laura Westra and Bill E. Lawson, eds., *Faces of Environmental Racism: Confronting Issues of Global Injustice* (Lanham, MD: Rowman and Littlefield, 2001).

35. Mary Poovey, *Making of a Social Body: British Cultural Formation, 1830–1864* (Chicago: University of Chicago Press, 1995).

36. Westra and Lawson, *Faces of Environmental Racism*.

37. James H. Cone, *Martin and Malcolm: A Dream or a Nightmare* (Maryknoll, NY: Orbis Books, 1996), 226.

38. David J. Garrow, *Bearing the Cross: Martin Luther King and the Southern Christian Leadership Conference* (New York: Quill, Morrow, 1999), 599.

39. Beginning in 1970, April 22 was designated as the country's Earth Day, a day when the country examined its role and responsibility in creating a livable and sustainable planet for all beings (human and nonhuman).

40. Andrew Young, *An Easy Burden: The Civil Rights Movement and the Transformation of America* (New York: HarperCollins, 1996), 443.

41. Young, *An Easy Burden*, 442.

42. *Chicago Defender*, untitled photographic spread by Ted Lacey, April 21, 1970, page 15.

43. W. August Low and Virgil A. Clift, eds., *Encyclopedia of Black America* (New York: Da Capo Press, 1987), 804–805. SCLC was a civil rights organization created in 1957 as a direct outgrowth of the Montgomery Improvement Association, which had launched the Montgomery, Alabama, bus boycott (1956–1957). The mission of the SCLC led by the Revs. Martin Luther King Jr. and Ralph Abernathy was to obtain equal rights and integration for African Americans.

44. "To Blacks, Ecology Is Irrelevant," *Business Week*, November 14, 1970.

45. "EJRC-Sheroes and Heroes for Environmental Justice," www.ejrc.cau.edu/(s)heros.html, March 9, 2004.

46. Robert D. Bullard, Chapter Two in *Dumping in Dixie: Race, Class and Environmental Quality.* www.ciesin.org/docs/010-278/010-278chpt2.html, 8, March 9, 2004.

47. Cole and Foster, *From the Ground Up*, 32.

48. "PCB Detoxification at Warren County Landfill Nears Completion," Press Release, Office of Governor Michael F. Easley, State of North Carolina, August 21, 2003.

49. Warren County PCB Landfill Fact Sheet, www.wastenotnc.org/WarrenCo_Fact_Sheet.htm, December 29, 2003.

50. Westra and Lawson, *Faces of Environmental Racism.*

51. "Environmental Justice Summit Draws Over 1200 Delegates," www.ejrc.cau.edu/SummittIIdelegatenews.html, December 29, 2003.

APPENDIX 2.1

Environmental Justice Principles Adopted, Washington, D.C., October 1991 First National People of Color Environmental Leadership Summit

Preamble

We, the People of Color, gathered together at this multinational People of Color Environmental Leadership Summit, to begin to build a national and international movement of all peoples of color to fight the destruction and taking of our lands and communities, do hereby reestablish our spiritual interdependence to the sacredness of our Mother Earth; to respect and celebrate each of our cultures, languages, and beliefs about the natural world and our roles in healing ourselves; to insure environmental justice; to promote economic alternatives which would contribute to the development of environmentally safe livelihoods; and to secure our political, economic, and cultural liberation that has been denied over 500 years of colonization and oppression, resulting in the poisoning of our communities and land and the genocide of our peoples do affirm and adopt these Principles of Environmental Justice:

1. Environmental Justice affirms the sacredness of Mother Earth, ecological unity and the interdependence of all species, and the right to be free from ecological destruction.

2. Environmental Justice demands that public policy be based on mutual respect and justice for all people, free from any form of discrimination and bias.

3. Environmental Justice mandates the right to ethical, balanced and responsible uses of land and renewable resources in the interest of a sustainable planet for humans and other living things.

4. Environmental Justice calls for universal protection from nuclear testing, extraction, production and disposal of toxic/hazardous wastes and poisons and nuclear testing that threaten the fundamental right to clean air, land, water, and food.

5. Environmental Justice affirms the fundamental right to political, economic, cultural and environmental self-determination of all peoples.

6. Environmental Justice demands the cessation of production of all toxins, hazardous wastes and radioactive materials and that all past and current producers be held strictly accountable to the people for detoxification and the containment at the point of production.

7. Environmental Justice demands the right to participate as equal partners at every level of decision-making including needs assessment, planning, implementation, enforcement, and evaluation.

8. Environmental Justice affirms the right of all workers to a safe and healthy work environment, without being forced to choose between an unsafe livelihood and unemployment. It also affirms the right of those who work at home to be free from environmental hazards.

9. Environmental Justice protects the right of victims of environmental injustices to receive full compensation and reparations for damages as well as quality health care.

10. Environmental Justice considers government acts of environmental injustice a violation of international law, the Universal Declaration on Human Rights, and the UN Convention on Genocide.

11. Environmental Justice must recognize a special legal and natural relationship of Native Peoples to the U.S. government through treaties, agreements, compacts, and covenants affirming sovereignty and self-determination.

12. Environmental Justice affirms the need for urban and rural ecological policies to clean up and rebuild our cities and rural areas in balance with nature, honoring the cultural integrity of all our communities, and providing fair access for all to the full range of resources.

13. Environmental Justice calls for the strict enforcement of principles of informed consent, and a halt to the testing of experimental reproductive and medical procedures and vaccinations on people of color.

14. Environmental Justice opposes the destructive operations of multinational corporations.

15. Environmental Justice opposes military occupation, repression and exploitation of lands, peoples and cultures, and other life forms.

16. Environmental Justice calls for the education of present and future generations which emphasizes social and environmental issues, based on our experience and an appreciation of our diverse cultural perspectives.

17. Environmental Justice requires that we, as individuals, make personal and consumer choices to consume as little of Mother Earth's resources and produce as little waste as possible; and make the conscious decisions to challenge and reprioritize our lifestyles to insure the health of the natural world for present and future generations.

PART TWO

PACKING THEM IN

Justice in the Jungle: Immigrants and Environmental Racism in the Back of the Yards, 1880–1930

> Power concedes nothing without a demand. It never did and it never will.
>
> —Frederick Douglass

One of the first manifestations of environmental racism and one of the very first struggles for environmental justice in Chicago occurred at the turn of the twentieth century in the notorious Back of the Yards neighborhood of Packingtown, located on the perimeter of the South Side of Chicago. The communities that comprised Packingtown included areas now known as Bridgeport, McKinley Park, Back of the Yards, and Canaryville.[1] Of these, only one was virtually undeveloped when Chicago's Union Stockyards first opened on Christmas Day, 1865: Back of the Yards.[2] Originally part of the town of Lake, this community was sparsely settled prior to the Civil War. It eventually developed and grew along with the Union Stockyards.[3] The remaining communities, while already firmly in place in 1865, continued to grow along with the Stockyards.[4]

The Stockyards had been in operation within the city limits of Chicago for a number of years but had to be relocated primarily for environmental reasons tied to waste management practices of packinghouse industrial activities. Environmental nuisances associated with cholera and typhoid fever epidemics in the city and a desire to compete more effectively in the market, as well as the expansion of the railroad system, resulted in the creation of the Union Stockyards.[5] Citizens' complaints about the environmental nuisances and public health threats led to city ordinances that helped force the packers to the outer perimeters of the city.

When the Union Stockyards first opened on Christmas Day in 1865, five hundred pens were used to house the animals. The pens "covered sixty acres of ground. Within another three years there were 2,300 pens on a hundred acres, capable of handling 21,000 head of cattle, 75,000 hogs, 22,000 sheep, and 200 horses all at the same time."[6]

Between 1870 and 1890, Chicago had begun to earn its reputation as the "hog butcher of the world," after the meat packing industry grew by 900 percent. By 1900, meat packing was Chicago's largest industrial employer, paying 10 percent of all Chicagoan wages and producing one-third of the manufactured goods.[7] In a contemporary study, *The Social Problem at the Chicago Stock Yards*, Charles J. Bushnell asserts, "In 1900, 225,000 of Chicago's population get their living directly from the business of the square mile occupied by her Union Stock Yards, and another 225,000 get their living indirectly from the same source."[8] Historical accounts written about the stockyards emphasize its incredible growth during the thirty-five year period from 1865 to 1900. When the Stock Yard Company issued its 35th Annual Report in 1900 it reported that its 500-yard length (of which 420 yards were bricked and planked) had a livestock holding capacity of 75,000 cattle, 80,000 sheep, 300,000 hogs, and 6,000 horses. The report also described the immense infrastructures that had been built to support the "hog capital" of the world. By 1900, these infrastructures included 250 miles of railway tracks, 13,000 uncovered pens, and "8,500 double-decked or covered pens . . . connected by 25,000 gates."[9] By 1900, "more than 400 million head of live stock have been received and shipped in the past 35 years, at a total valuation of more than $5,500,000,000."[10]

The organic waste from the killing of livestock was a major problem for the meat packing industry and the public. If the meat could not be immediately consumed or preserved, the "beef and pork went through a series of mutations that rendered them first unpalatable, then inedible, and finally dangerously toxic."[11] The problem of overcoming the rapid decay of the slaughtered stock was partially ameliorated by a number of technological and scientific developments occurring in the 1870s. The packers took advantage of the development of stationary refrigeration technology as well as adopting the Appert process of "meat preservation, on a large scale, in tin cans through complete sterilization by thorough cooking; and concentration and packing in air-tight packages." Both of these developments enabled meats to be transported and held for an indefinite period in any climate, with or without cold storage.[12]

Although these technological developments were crucial in reducing the problem of rapid decay of marketable products, they did not address the problems stemming from the waste and offal generated during the packing process. The emergence of glue and fertilizer manufacturers in the latter part of the nineteenth century who could utilize some of the wastes and offal produced by the packers started the packers on the path of "byproduct utilization."[13] According to Bushnell's study of the packing houses in 1900, a 1500-pound steer generated 825 pounds of beef and its remainders would be used to produce hairpins, buttons, yellow prussiate, fertilizer glue, gelatin, isinglass, neat's foot oil, tallow, grease, stearine, fertilizer, soap works, and curled hair works. Bushnell observed that "the remaining blood and tankage and all waste of a nitrogenous or phosphatic character [were] made into fertilizers, albumen, stock and poultry food. Other products [were] phosphoric acid, phosphorous, bone black, black pigment, sulphate of ammonia, and bone oil."[14] Although the packers made attempts to minimize the negative impacts on the environment stemming from their operations by trying to utilize as much of the stock as possible for manufacture or production of byproducts, they ultimately lost the battle. As environmental historian William Cronon aptly noted in his work *Nature's Metropolis*,

> whatever was left [from the packing process] sooner or later made its way as refuse into the Chicago River. The stench that hung over the South Branch and the filthy ice harvested from it were clear signs of its pollution. Decaying organic matter, whether in the form of packing wastes, manure, or raw human sewerage, was the chief water supply problem the city faced by mid-century.[15]

The infamous polluted natural environment of the Back of the Yards was directly tied to the enormous amount of waste that came from the rapid industrial growth in the Union Stockyards. The level and nature of this waste became nationally renowned in 1906 with the publication of Upton Sinclair's novel *The Jungle*. The dismal environmental state of both the built and natural environment was also tied to the expansion of the packing house industries and the inactions of municipal government and real estate interests. The pollution of the natural environment was created by the waste disposal practices of the industries and by the failure of the city to enforce waste disposal laws or ordinances that regulated these activities for the sake of public health. The corruption of the built environment, in this case, overcrowded and dilapidated housing, was due to the city's failure to enforce housing codes that had been specifically designed to address these types of problems but were being violated by slum landlords.[16] Humans as well as animals designated for slaughter in Chicago's stockyards literally and figuratively found themselves packed into unsanitary spaces with severe consequences to public health. The water and streets of the Back of the Yards and Packingtown were littered with the minimally controlled disposal of human and animal wastes (blood and feces) generated by the rapidly expanding meat packing industry and the thousands of immigrants working in that industry. This increase in population and industrial growth caused thousands of people to literally drop dead from sewage-related diseases such as erysipelas, typhoid, and cholera.[17]

The environmental history of the Back of the Yards is a classic story of environmental racism. Both the natural and built environment were allowed to become environmentally corrupted because of who was doing the polluting—politically empowered native "white" industrialists— and who lived adjacent to the polluted area—"white" Eastern European immigrants. The area had been allowed to become industrialized by the larger body politic to protect the native "white" Chicagoan population from known public health hazards associated with this particular type of industrial waste. These conditions were not allowed to persist or even exist in "native" white communities. (This history is elucidated in greater detail in chapter 4.) Although there were no explicit legal policies or practices equivalent to race-based restrictive covenants or racial zoning laws that forced the immigrants into these spaces, the segregated geographical spaces that immigrants voluntarily created were disproportionately used as the final sink for the city of Chicago's waste as well as that of the packers.[18]

By the turn of the twentieth century, Eastern European immigrants dominated the Back of the Yards neighborhood. Harry Rosenberg's report on the 1904 packing industry and stockyards revealed that the older Irish and German immigrants and American residents of the Packingtown community had been replaced by Poles, Lithuanians, Bohemians, Slovenians, and Croatians. According to Rosenberg, the older residents had, since 1900, "gradually moved away further south and to the boulevards and prairie away from the stench and smoke of the yards."[19] This assessment of the radical change in ethnic composition is supported by Robert A. Slayton's seminal study of Packingtown, *Back of the Yards: The Making of a Local Democracy*. Slayton's study found that, by 1909, the percentage of Stockyard workers who were of Slavic descent had increased to 46.4 percent, up from 14.0 percent in 1896. The 1920 U.S. census revealed that this residential community was composed of 42.6 percent foreign-born residents. Of these, 44.6 percent were Polish, 15.9 percent were Czechoslovakian (including Slovaks and Bohemians), 12.4 percent were Russian, 7.3 percent were German, 6.7 percent were Lithuanian, and 2.5 percent were Irish.[20] The transition from a primarily Irish-German community to an Eastern European community started in the mid-1880s when Polish workers were brought in as strikebreakers. Their numbers were exponentially increased between 1890 and 1900 by an influx of immigrants coming from the old country. Poles, the most dominant of the Eastern Europeans, were poorly paid day laborers who packed themselves into the cheapest places to live. Unfortunately, these cheap places were the places proximate to the most environmentally polluted sections of the area (packinghouses, city dumps, stockyards, and railroad tracks).[21]

Like other immigrant communities across the country, Back of the Yards immigrants were accused of being and causing environmental or public health problems for the larger body politic.[22] As late as 1952, historian Bertram B. Fowler stressed that the Eastern European immigrants in the Back of the Yards created the slums themselves by bringing the "squalor and misery" from their native Europe. According to Fowler, their degraded living environment "could not be attributed to anything American. The squalor was that of poverty-stricken Europe."[23] Native Chicagoans' environmental perceptions about immigrants were in line with national beliefs. According to historian Louise Carroll Wade, Eastern European immigrants in Packingtown were constantly portrayed negatively by the larger social body and the news media, which described them as living in "indescribable filth" or as "depraved beasts and harpies."[24]

The national perception of immigrants as environmental threats is revealed by urban environmental historian Martin Melosi in *The Sanitary City*. According to Melosi, Boston's Lemeul Shattuck was an adamant nativist who firmly believed that the city of Boston's immigrants were the primary cause of its environmental woes. Melosi argues that Shattuck's *Report of the Sanitary Commission of Massachusetts, 1850,* only reinforced the view that "immigrants were primarily responsible for the degradation of the cities and the spread of disease."[25] Public health historian Charles Rosen points out that Shattuck's report included explicit recommendations for how "particular urban communities" were to be disciplined and monitored to protect the larger body politic. These recommendations included sanitary surveys, vaccinations, and the establishment of state and local health boards.[26] Immigration historian Alan Kraut's seminal work, *Silent Travelers*, demonstrated that during this period "immigrants were repelled because their very appearance suggested to their hosts' gazes a physical inferiority or vulnerability that might be contagious."[27]

Urban environmental historian Joel Tarr describes a Foucauldian separation of immigrants in the early urban environment in *The Search for the Ultimate Sink*. Tarr concludes that although the rapidly evolving city during this time period was divided into two parts—one for residential areas and the other for commercial-industrial operations—this pattern of geographical separation did not hold for the vast majority of poor and working class immigrant communities. Tarr's research has shown that immigrant communities in this era found themselves living near the core of the central business district in "highly congested living areas with problems of poor sanitation, high disease rates, and deteriorating housing."[28] This spatial pattern of separation with concomitant environmental health impacts became worse with the rise of modern transportation systems such as the rapid mass transit systems and eventually the automobile. Neither form of transportation proved affordable for most immigrants during this time frame because they were restricted to the lowest-paying jobs.

The immigrants packed themselves into the urban and industrialized core of the city and were literally and figuratively left to rot in the inner core of the polluted cities. As Tarr says, "Members of the middle and upper classes worried that . . . congested living conditions, especially among the poor and the alien, posed a danger to 'the moral integrity and unity of the community.'"[29] The stereotyping of immigrants as vectors of disease by the larger body politic played a major role in their being segregated in geographical spaces within the developing city.

Rosenberg's 1904 report concluded that the "infiltration" of recent immigrants created urban congestion and highly disparate environmental health problems in an already environmentally compromised living space that had been produced by garbage dumps, Bubbly Creek (a branch of the Chicago River), and smoke from the stockyards. According to Rosenberg's study, "the death rate . . . for [immigrant] babies [was] five times as large as the death rate on Lake Shore Drive."[30] Recent research by Chicago's noted immigration and neighborhood historian Dominic Pacyga has shown that Packingtown and the Back of the Yards was a "classic Victorian slum" with high rates of mortality among both children and adults.[31]

The Built Environment in the Back of the Yards

The environmental health problems of Back of the Yards immigrant residents were exacerbated by a marginalized built environment composed of wooden houses on dirt streets that had no connection to the city's water system, no electricity, and few gas lights.[32] Additional contemporary descriptions of the dismal built environment in Packingtown neighborhoods are found in Bushnell's contemporary monograph on the stockyards.[33] He states that there was a drastic difference between the built environment of these white immigrant communities and the native white community of Hyde Park. He asserted that there were "physical causes for the [environmental] disparity" between the two communities and observed that the Stockyard community was "badly paved where there is any paving. Most of it is wood paving, which absorbs considerable impurities from air and drainage. In Hyde Park most streets are paved with asphalt or macadam. In the Stockyard district many of the streets are for miles in rainy weather scarcely better than mud holes."[34]

Bushnell's description of the neighborhood is consistent with that of Upton Sinclair in the infamous *Jungle*, a slightly veiled, fact-based fictional account of the lives of immigrant workers who lived around and worked in the Stockyards.[35] Although *The Jungle* is known for its detailed description of the workplace environment, it also contains passages that provide descriptions of the neighborhood environment. At one point in the novel, the main character, Jurgis, learns that his child, Antanas, has been drowned in a street that had turned into a "canal" after a heavy rain because of a lack of standard infrastructures such as sewers.[36]

Polluting the Natural Environment

Like most industrial areas, the Union Stockyards used an accessible stream to dump industrial and organic wastes from slaughtered animals. In this case it was the southwest fork of the Chicago River, which became known as Bubbly Creek. Over nineteen companies poured their waste into the creek. The inability of the organic wastes dumped into the river by the packing industries to rapidly decay produced the "Bubbly Creek." As a result of the decaying material that had sunk to the bottom, bubbles of gas were constantly being released. "Local legend claims that the diameter of these bubbles had to be measured in feet. One eruption was said to have encircled a boat. In calmer moments, residents recall bubbles five to eight inches across. They remember workmen on a small barge skimming the slime off the surface and collecting it in 50-gallon drums. The water was so dense that Bubbly Creek never froze."[37] Bubbly Creek became a metaphor for the horrific corruption of the natural environment in the Back of the Yards produced primarily by the stockyard industries. The eutrophic creek became one of the most identifiable landmarks of the community. Bubbly Creek produced a sanitary nightmare that killed thousands of people for years in the Chicago metropolitan area prior to the creation of the Metropolitan Sanitary District in 1889. Bubbly Creek is described in William Cronon's *Nature's Metropolis* as "a great open sewer a hundred or two feet wide" in which grease and chemicals underwent "all sorts of transformations." It was in constant motion, "as if huge fish were feeding in it or great leviathans were disporting themselves into its depths."[38]

The environmental state of Bubbly Creek worsened after the flow of the Chicago River was reversed from north to south in an attempt to reduce and eliminate the discharge of sewage into Lake Michigan that had created numerous typhoid fever and cholera outbreaks. Thomas J. Jablonsky points out that after this reversal, "the river [Bubbly Creek] at this point still had a weak current, but it could not flush the stream clean of pollutants dumped into it by the rendering and packing companies."[39]

Contemporary technical reports describing the parameters used to determine the degree of pollution entering into the Chicago River reveal that the pollutants from the packinghouses ranged from a minimum of two and a half times (for ammonia nitrogen) to almost twenty-five times (for chlorine) that of the residential sewage from the Thirty-ninth Street Station.

Reversing the flow of the Chicago River was one means of increasing the kinetic energy of Bubbly Creek and, hence, its potential to successfully manage the sewage problem, but it didn't work. An article appearing in the *Chicago Tribune* on October 27, 1909, sarcastically declared that the river's reversal

> was successful indeed, except for Bubbly Creek! There the flow of the river, which had always been sluggish, practically stopped with the reversal of the flow in the river's main channel. Bubbly Creek became a practically stagnant pool. . . . The refuse poured into it was not carried away; it putrefied and filled in the bed of the river at the rate of almost half a foot a year from 1895 to 1908; it created a scum on the water's surface through which the putrescent gases forming below, with difficulty found their way to give the creek its name.

Bushnell's contemporary description noted that the south branch of the Chicago River just north and northwest of the stockyards had become so polluted that "small animals and fowls . . . make their way across the river upon its coating of filth and grease."[40]

The creation of the Sanitary District did, on average, ameliorate the environmental and subsequent health problems of the metropolitan region connected to the polluted waters of the area, but it also created an environmental nightmare for poor and working class immigrants who were constricted to living in the Back of the Yards. From an environmental perspective, their compromised living conditions would have to wait almost forty years from the District's implementation for a resolution.

The solid waste generated in Packingtown and the stockyards that was not dumped into the waterways made its way to dumps located in the yard. A large dump for the stables waste was connected directly to the yards and located in its most southern part.[41] Solid waste pollution occurring in Packingtown was caused not only by the packers but also by the city of Chicago. "The city's contribution to the blighted landscape was its operation of four huge holes into which Chicago dumped its garbage from a half dozen south side wards."[42] Unfortunately, the immigrants living in the Back of the Yards had an alderman living in the community who contributed to the environmental devastation of their neighborhood.[43] Thomas Carey had originally mined the land for clay and processed the material at his on-site brickyard located in the community. "Over time, four pits were excavated. One hole, west of the Leavitt street tracks [was] completely filled by 1909. The other three holes [of five, six, and ten acres] were east of the tracks from 41st to 47th streets. . . . The packinghouses used one of these dumps to burn waste; and a fire smoldered continuously, surrounded by a pool of fetid water."[44]

After the notoriety of *The Jungle* in 1906, newspaper articles that described the environmental inequities in the Back of the Yards began to appear in the mainstream native white newspapers. In late October 1909, two articles were printed in the *Chicago Tribune* that addressed the problem. The first article, "South Side Dump Menace to City, Garbage Exudes Poisonous Fumes, Is Charge of Settlement Workers," dealt with the impacts of solid waste pollution in Packingtown.[45] The objective of the article was to report the concerns and "accusations of charitable and settlement organizations of the twenty-ninth ward" who had formed an "investigating committee consisting of the workers from the University of Chicago settlement at the 47th and Robey Streets and representatives of the South Side Settlement League." The investigating committee along with "a representative of the *Tribune*, a sanitary expert and bacteriologist" had, the preceding day, "visited the garbage depository." According to the article, their goal was to "lodge complaints before the proper authorities based on facts and figures" secured. This article was accompanied by a nearly full-page spread of pictures of immigrant children playing and women scavenging in the neighborhood dumps, with captions that declared that the existence of the dumps was contributing to the death and disease in Packingtown.

The second article, which appeared two days after the first, addressed the health problems in the community that were connected to water pollution in the area.[46] This article, "Fight 'Dump' to Save Babies, Investigators Find Bubbly Creek Worse Disease Breeder, Death Rate Is Increased, City Asked to Bar All But Dry Garbage in 47th Street Ditch," reported that Bubbly Creek had now fallen under the ban of the volunteer Babies' Protective

Figure 3.1. Children Playing in an Empty Lot in the Back of the Yards at 45ᵗʰ and Laflin, n.d. Courtesy of Chicago Historical Society (negative ICHi-31535)

Agency after a committee of the organization had "visited sections of the stagnant stream lying within residence districts west of the Stockyards." This second article claimed that "127 babies under two years old had died in the 39ᵗʰ ward in the previous six months" and that "half of them had lived within three blocks of the dumps." The residents in the Back of the Yards continued their demands for environmental justice even though their "petitions . . . received by the city council and the health department . . . were quietly filed away" and "officials claimed that closing the back of the yards dumps would only transfer the nuisance somewhere else."[47] The article then went on to state that "the sewage filled, slime coated ditch was found to be in a condition more detrimental to health than ever before, according to physicians and sanitary experts, and was charged with direct responsibility for an unprecedented amount of sickness and an abnormal death rate among children." The article also quoted Dr. Caroline Hedger, a female doctor and former resident of the University of Chicago settlement, who stated, "The poor health of these children [was] directly traceable to bad sanitary conditions . . . both along Bubbly Creek and surrounding this dump at Forty-seventh and Robey Streets."

Mary McDowell, a resident and director of the neighborhood's University of Chicago Settlement House located in the Back of the Yards, also asserted that there was a direct relationship to the community's health conditions and the environmental state of the neighborhood. In her essay "Municipal Housekeeping Symposium," she observed, "The death rate for children of that district was greater than that of the city as a whole and double that of the Lake Shore Wards [who] were innocently sending garbage from their neat backyards to the dumps on Lincoln Street."[48]

In this same essay McDowell indicates that the problems in this neighborhood were so atrociously persistent that "the City Waste Committee of the Woman's City Club for five years had regularly urged upon the Health Committee and the Finance Committee of the City Council the appointment of a commission to study the whole question and report on a city wide plan for the scientific disposal of garbage." According to McDowell, these women "knew that every day 534 tons of pure garbage must be disposed of and 172 tons of rubbish must be carried from back yards and alleys." These women felt that the garbage problem was not only one of aesthetics but also a problem of sanitation and health.[49]

Although historians Louis Cain and Louise Carroll Wade have developed environmental histories of Chicago's early water pollution problems, the following observation by Mary McDowell offers the best explanation of the environmental inequities that caused Bubbly Creek and made it a dangerous nuisance to the neighborhood of Packingtown:

> This creek, once an innocent little stream with willows and wild flowers along its banks, had been turned into a cesspool. For fifty years public indifference had permitted human sewage from over a million population, as well as grease, hair and other noxious ingredients from the many Packinghouses and Stockyards within one square mile (between Ashland on the west and Halsted on the east, Forty-seventh on the south and Bubbly Creek on the north) to pour into this little stream.[50]

Environmental Justice Struggles in the Jungle

When immigrants complained about odors and public health problems they believed were tied to the environmental pollution in their community, they frequently encountered indifference and inaction from the municipal government responsible for ameliorating these problems. Recognizing the nature and extent of environmental inequities taking place in their communities, immigrants (primarily women) spoke out. With the cooperation and support of nonimmigrant settlement workers, social workers, and physicians, these women launched one of the first environmental justice struggles in Chicago's Progressive era. Their early activism was undoubtedly motivated by high infant mortalities and illnesses in the Back of the Yard, which the women believed were tied to the environmental conditions that had been observed since the mid-1880s. At that time, the infant mortality for the German parish of St. Augustine's, which had a large immigrant population, was "141.95 per 1,000, preschool deaths averaged 87.23 per 1,000; and deaths of school-age children, 13.43 per 1,000 . . . resulting in 3 out of every 20 children dying in the parish."[51] The environmental conditions in the area were lethal to children. According to one study, by 1900 the Back of the Yards child mortality rate was 40 per 1,000, compared to half that rate in the more affluent Hyde Park.[52] Even as overall infant mortality decreased in Chicago from 1928 to 1933, the infant mortality rate in the Back of the Yards actually rose.[53] These "white" immigrant women and their native "white" women political allies used the same type of strategies that are still in use today to bring attention to and ameliorate environmental inequities that have impacts on children. They organized grassroots groups in their neighborhoods to protest pollution and they conducted letter-writing campaigns aimed at local politicians to elucidate these concerns. These activist women garnered the attention and occasional support of the media, politicians, and academic and medical institutions to address the environmental problems that plagued their communities.

The primary champion for these primarily Eastern European and Catholic immigrant women who obtained some initial measure of environmental equity was a native white woman and neighbor, Mary McDowell. At its peak, the University of Chicago Settlement House located in the Back of the Yards had a parlor room, dining facilities, a library and office, meeting rooms, and quarters for seventeen residents.[54] It had been formed to provide support to the immigrant community by offering kindergarten classes, day nurseries, a mother's club, music and drama classes, and English and citizenship classes for immigrants.

The majority of the Back of the Yard immigrants were Eastern European Catholics whose religious leadership wielded a strong influence upon them. Research by historian Robert Slayton revealed that parish priests in the Back of the Yards were vehemently opposed to McDowell's settlement house and strongly discouraged parishioners' involvement with the settlement house Protestants.[55] Despite the objection of the religious patriarchy, Catholic and female immigrant parishioners still turned to McDowell, a disenfranchised native white Protestant woman, to help resolve their environmental problems.[56] These immigrants knew that they were outside the pale of native politics, which were dominated by Protestant politicians and religious institutions. They were highly unlikely to be in the right place at the right time to influence environmental politics. They consciously chose to align themselves with someone who could fight on their behalf to bring about environmental changes.

Mary McDowell was the oldest of six children, born to Malcolm McDowell and Jane Gordon McDowell in Cincinnati, Ohio, on November 30, 1854. She was born into a middle class "native" white Methodist family. Her father was a sheet iron manufacturer who worked in his own company, the McDowell Steel Company, until the mid-1880s. Her maternal grandfather was an early steamboat builder; her paternal uncle, Irvin McDowell, was a brigadier general for the Union Army in the Civil War.

McDowell's dedication to supporting others came honestly. During Mary McDowell's youth, her mother engaged in charitable works for the families of Union soldiers while her father was dedicated to the abolition of slavery. Although her mother was a graduate of Wesleyan Female College in Cincinnati, McDowell decided at age eleven not to pursue a formal education but instead to "follow her father into a modest Methodist chapel which emphasized good works."[57]

McDowell came to Chicago in 1870 with her parents. By the early 1880s, the family had permanently relocated to the Chicago suburb of Evanston. Both Mary and her father commuted into Chicago after their move to Evanston to support volunteers in socially oriented civic organizations. Mary worked closely with her father in the Methodist church doing charitable works for the poor and needy. These works included helping refugees of the Great Fire of 1871. By the time she had formed the University of Chicago Settlement House in 1894, she had met and befriended Jane Addams in 1891 and served as Addams's kindergarten teacher at Hull House.

By the time she opened the doors of the University of Chicago Settlement House, McDowell was an experienced community organizer. In the early 1880s, after hearing the corresponding secretary of the Women's Christian Temperance Union (WCTU), Frances E. Willard, at a speaking engagement, McDowell joined the organization and began "organizing women in Illinois . . . by 1887 she was the national director for this work."[58] In the same year that she opened the University of Chicago Settlement House (1894), she helped found the Chicago Federation of Settlements. From 1914 to 1915 she served as president of the National Foundation of Settlements, an organization that had patterned itself after the Chicago Federation of Settlements. McDowell served as director of the University of Chicago Settlement House until 1923, when she became Chicago's Commissioner of Public Works.

In the early spring of 1900, within six years of starting the settlement house, McDowell attended a city council finance committee meeting to morally support a confrontation between working class immigrant men and a young, aristocratic attorney representing the Chicago Reduction Company, which wanted to do business in the immigrants' ward. The immigrants lived in Packingtown and "gave up a day's wages to attend a hearing on the question of abating one of the nuisances in their district" that had been produced by a garbage reduction facility. According to McDowell, the lawyer ended up "pleading for the nuisances that these citizens were protesting against. With calm assurance he addressed th[e] committee of the alderman: 'Gentlemen of the Finance Committee, I am sure you must realize that in all great cities there must be a place segregated for unpleasant things, and of course the people living there are not very sensitive.'"[59] McDowell's papers reveal that the reduction company lost its plea for business because the people living in the district "segregated for unpleasant things" were in fact very sensitive to their living environment and were fed up with it.[60] For years, these immigrants had been assaulted by the pollution of the "open cesspool Bubbly Creek, bad odors, gases, and smoke."[61] Fed up with their environmental situation, they organized themselves with the support of McDowell to combat the polluters in their communities.

In 1905, immigrant women in the Back of the Yards were still upset about environmental problems that continued to plague their community. They convinced McDowell to go to City Hall with them to complain to the commissioner of health about the public health problems that stemmed from the pollution. According to McDowell's papers, the city proved unresponsive because the commissioner of health sent the women to the new commissioner of public works, who "told [the] outraged householders and mothers . . . that they could do nothing to change the method of garbage disposal as they [the city] had no appropriation."[62]

McDowell eventually became the environmental spokesperson for Packingtown because of the power relations that existed between immigrants and natives and between women and men. Although McDowell was a woman, she was still part of the native white community as well as an active social member and community leader of the Protestant-dominated power elite. Her settlement house received funding from the "very rich, the bankers and business leaders in faraway North Shore suburbs like Evanston and Winnetka . . . and some from the Swift and Armour clans themselves, the hated overlords of the packing plants."[63] Mary McDowell would reflect that she became spokesperson because "I was the only one of . . . mostly immigrant women who could speak to Chicago."[64]

This decision to speak out against the environmental inequalities in the Back of the Yards as well as her active political and civic involvement in the city was typical of many of her contemporaries, who were also involved in settlement work.[65] These "settlement workers together with their allies, moved in on city hall to demand massive and often coordinated efforts from the city fathers. They pleaded for better streets, regular garbage collection, more efficient sewage systems, and programs of public health and sanitation."[66] McDowell felt that "the aim of the settlement was explicitly political. . . . 'To initiate movements for city wide reforms in cooperation with city organizations to prove to the community their civic needs and then help to supply those needs.'"[67]

By all historical accounts, Mary McDowell can justifiably lay claim to being the grandmother of the environmental justice movement in Chicago. She personally and professionally championed the environmental plight of immigrants and African Americans in the city until she died on October 14, 1936. The majority of historical evidence about immigrant struggles for environmental justice in the Back of the Yards is documented in her personal papers. In her 1914 essay "Civic Experiences," McDowell recalled that one immigrant woman in the area asked her a question that struck at the heart of the Back of the Yard environmental inequities. "Why don't they dump the garbage on the bully-vards, why do they bring it near our homes?"[68] This question wasn't an isolated case. According to McDowell, another Bohemian immigrant woman together with several other "householders" came to see her at the settlement house within a few years of its formation to complain "not only of the dumps but of the uncovered wagons reeking with filth and flies."[69]

Before the end of the first decade of the twentieth century, several environmental groups formed in the Back of the Yards to combat environmental problems. The "Young Citizens Club" was composed of boys organized by the settlement house's female university volunteers; the "Neighborhood Guild" was made up of both adult men and women; "Cleaner Clubs" were made up of immigrant children from the settlement's Seward Vacation School; and the "Settlement Women's Club" was composed of immigrant or first generation women. As early as 1896, Cleaner Clubs children went through the neighborhood to record environmental complaints and log them with City Hall. The Settlement Women's Club's environmental activities focused on the physical cleanup of the community rather than on complaints. These women inspected and cleaned up the alleys and sidewalks in the Back of the Yards. "It was members of this club that routed the last 'hair field' near Ashland Avenue where one packing firm still dried the hair on animals on the vacant land nearby."[70] The Back of the Yards residents concerned about environmental issues developed cleanup "jingles" and "creeds," passed out complaint cards, and inspected alleys as a means of motivating their neighbors and themselves to stay focused on and committed to cleaning up their geographical space.[71]

The most effective and complex of these organizations was the community-based Neighborhood Guild, which served as a clearinghouse for environmental problems arising from industrial and municipal mismanagement. The guild became a bureau of environmental complaints. One of their first activities centered around closing down the glue factory located near the settlement house on Gross Avenue. Immigrant women—especially "householders"—felt the factory was a threat to the community's health because of standing water and fumes produced by the plant's operation.[72] Acting on behalf of the Back of the Yards community, the guild lodged several complaints with City Hall against the glue factory and eventually succeeded in having the operating practices modified.[73] Mary McDowell points out that "after much pressure the Glue Works was compelled to save water by using a tank on the top of the factory instead of in the holes in vacant lots and one bad odor was abated. . . . That tank is looked up to with respect today as the first monument to the first civic victory of a handful of awakened citizens."[74]

The guild also "complained of scum covered ditches, where one little child lost its life when it tried to walk on the crust of filth [a possible reference to Bubbly Creek]. They reported houses without sewer connections and the bad lighting on Gross Avenue."[75] One of the most significant impacts the guild had on the community was promoting and developing environmental awareness and activism. "One practical result of the Guild's educational work was expressed by an intelligent working man member who said 'I learned that I had a right to complain of bad conditions to the City Hall and I had my eyes opened to see what before I never noticed, scum on ditches and dirt on streets.'"[76] McDowell states that in another one of the environmental battles between Back of the Yards residents and City Hall, the residents had "found the worst tenement house in the neighborhood and reported it to the health department. 'The Boss' of the Health Department was discovered to be the owner and the city inspector laughed at us for being so fastidious for he said 'What's one more smell out here anyway?'"[77]

McDowell's efforts to help get rid of the dumps or bring them under control were also met with strong resistance from city "politicians . . . [who] sought to protect one of their own." As discussed above, Alderman Thomas Carey was initially a resident of Packingtown who also owned a business there. But when he moved from the Packingtown area to a classier neighborhood near the lakefront, his initial defense, that it wasn't a bad environmental situation because he too lived in the area, broke down.[78] This reaction was typical of those in power to the environmentally disenfranchised living in Packingtown.

Gender, Technology, and Environmental Justice

Although it was a contributing factor, McDowell's command of the English language wasn't the primary reason for her potential to be an effective spokesperson for Packingtown. Her social standing and connections were the key factors.[79] Mary McDowell was also closely connected to Jane Addams and had started her social service career in Hull House's kindergarten.[80] Immigrant women of Packingtown had not developed the requisite social and professional standing that would have allowed them to interact frequently (and effectively) to present their environmental causes to the types of audiences and social circles to whom McDowell preached her gospel of "municipal housekeeping." In a 1914 Lithuanian newspaper editorial, the writer described the status of women in their American communities and decried, "A deplorable attitude toward women has become rooted in the minds of most of our people. A girl, they believe, should be concerned only with getting married; and once she has married, her sole duty is housekeeping."[81]

Although middle class and upper middle class "native white" women did not hold or wield the same type of power as their male counterparts, they were part of the power relations in Chicago. These women had access to and influence upon male leadership through their social, political, and personal relationships. As relatives or members of the same social class they were able to influence the social and political dynamics of the city. These relationships contributed to their success in philanthropic and social work efforts. For example, Mary McDowell was able to successfully present her argument about the troubles in Packingtown to the Hyde Park Presbyterian Church. She writes, "It was here that in one of the front pews sat a just judge who came up after my speech to say, 'If you would come to my court tomorrow I will give you an injunction against the Health Department to prevent further dumping of garbage on Lincoln Street. I never knew where our refuse was taken.'"[82]

McDowell's activism resulted in her receiving the nickname of "Garbage Lady" among both her immigrant neighbors and her political and social

Figure 3.2. "Leaving the Dump," Back of the Yards area, 1905. From the Mary McDowell Settlement House Collection, Chicago Historical Society (negative ICHi-23826)

peers. The title had as much to do with her political activism as the technical expertise about sanitation she acquired by studying the available books and monographs dealing with garbage disposal. According to McDowell, she developed this expertise because:

> Wherever she went to speak she was confronted with the question and the comment, "What else is there to do with the garbage?" It evidently has to be dumped somewhere; if we abolish the Packingtown dumps that will only transfer the nuisance to another section of the city. We can't gain anything by changing garbage systems until we have a better system to substitute for what we have now.[83]

Howard Wilson's biography of McDowell points out that she became a self-taught sanitation engineer because she had become keenly aware of and aroused by the environmental inequalities that existed in her community, and the needs of her immigrant neighbors spurred her on.[84] Unlike the average immigrant resident of Packingtown, McDowell had access to manuals about garbage disposal as well as the time and the language fluency to develop the requisite expertise. Under the sponsorship of Mrs. Ethel Sturges Drummer, McDowell spent the summer of 1911 studying methods of garbage disposal in operation in the largest European cities of "England, Scotland, Holland, and Germany. She found there in the Old World . . . cities which had eliminated the evil effects apparent in the Chicago methods of disposal and which had even made the garbage a source of financial profit."[85]

Mrs. Drummer, a prominent upper class native of Chicago, was an education and health reformer and the wife of William Francis (Frank) Drummer, vice president of the Northwestern National Bank.[86] In was in Europe that McDowell saw firsthand that waste disposal practices in urban and industrialized cities could be controlled and managed for the benefit of all citizens without deadly public health consequences. She learned about European methods of incineration and early forms of waste recycling for fuel resources. She saw that special types of garbage could sometimes be "burned as fuel for the generation of electric or steam power . . . and used for the operation of street railways, laundries, baths, or lighting systems municipally owned."[87]

Immigrants in the Back of the Yards were wise in selecting her as their environmental advocate since there was very little chance that an immigrant would have received the same type of sponsorship. Cognizant of the relationship between power and knowledge, McDowell utilized her connections with the news media to educate the public at large and generate sympathy for the environmental plight of her immigrant neighbors. While still in London on her return trip from Europe, she reacquainted herself with a correspondent from the *Chicago Daily News* "whose acquaintance and friendship dated from the days of the Packingtown strike . . . and she told him how she had spent her summer."[88] McDowell then gave the reporter her consent to write and send a story about her activities to the newspaper. "The story was sent, and thus even before Mary McDowell reached her home her summer of work in Europe began its conscious task of creating public sentiment in Chicago."[89] After her return from Europe, McDowell "again appeared at clubs and societies and churches and organizations . . . armed with stories of actual living conditions in Packingtown, and with stereotypical slides and factual analysis showing practical solutions."[90]

All of McDowell's activities took place before Illinois women were given the right to vote in 1913. This is an important point, because all of the historical material on McDowell consistently asserts that her goal was to change public policy by changing public opinion. McDowell was politically astute and knew that the power of the vote was key to having direct influence on public policy:

> Another event had occurred, however, with a direct and influential bearing on the garbage situation. Woman suffrage had been accepted in the municipalities of Illinois, and with it the pressure of public force had increased tremendously.[91]

Prior to receiving their franchise, Mary McDowell and women's waste committee clubs constantly petitioned City Hall to take a more "scientific approach" to the garbage problem by examining the available technologies. They were ignored until they received the franchise. McDowell noted that

> the first visit the Women's Committee made to the City Hall, the week after receiving the vote, brought the same plea for a city-wide plan based upon a scientific study. Our breath was taken away to find that

our votes were so effective that an appropriation of ten thousand dollars was made in ten minutes and a commission with two women on it was appointed. . . . The City Waste Commission began its work the very next week. Two experienced experts (incineration, reduction systems) were hired to study and report.[92]

For decades, Mary McDowell, her contemporaries, and the immigrant women in the Back of the Yards waged battles for environmental justice in their community. They protested, petitioned government officials, and found ways to get their story into the news media. All of this historical evidence shows that they felt that there was sufficient evidence to demonstrate that these immigrants were the victim of both the "Not in My Backyard" attitude and what I have termed the "Put It in Immigrants' Backyards" syndrome. After all, the prevailing thought among the body politic was that immigrants were socially marginalized. Like many environmental justice activists today, they were unsuccessful in completely resolving all of the environmental inequalities on their own. This was no doubt due to the fact that they were women and social minorities who ultimately were not in control of the final decisions governing the environmental policies and planning for their own geographical space. Although they won some of their environmental justice battles, their efforts alone were insufficient to stand against municipal politics that wanted to use the area as the city's ultimate sink. An example of this lack of power was the citywide plan to reduce the garbage problem by purchasing the reduction plant and building two incinerator plants on the same site. This plan was conceived by the city as a result of the immigrants' environmental activism. The plan was approved but was ultimately defeated by a new Republican mayoral administration that had no relationship or history with these female environmental activists in the Back of the Yards.[93]

The primary environmental solution for immigrants living in the Back of the Yards was physical relocation into the suburbs or less polluted areas of the city. For many, this was a difficult, although not impossible, task. These immigrants were marked by language and cultural habits from Old Europe; many did not want to leave the cultural and social security of their ethnic enclave.[94]

From an environmental standpoint, the greatest contribution of settlement workers like Mary McDowell to immigrant communities was the assimilation of their latter generations to the point where they could be accepted as "white" and gain access to healthier living spaces if they so chose. Immigrants who were financially able and willing began to escape from the environmental degradation and move to other, less polluted communities or into the suburbs. As Chicago historian Thomas Philpott's history of Chicago's slums and ghettos revealed, "immigrants of all ethnicities, aliens as well as naturalized citizens, Catholics and Jews alike, had access to neighborhoods where black native Americans could not go."[95] Chicago communities that defined themselves as "white" and that enacted and enforced racially restrictive covenants or participated in sometimes violent measures to keep these geographical spaces racially "white" were composed of a large percentage of ethnic groups. Philpott observed, "In 1930, 70 percent of white Chicagoans and . . . 54 percent of white suburbanites . . . were foreign stock; thus any community that was 'only' 40 or 50 or even 60 percent ethnic could qualify as American."[96]

For immigrants who remained in the Back of the Yards area, the environmental inequalities were resolved only after businessmen and male politicians decided that the pollution in the area was a threat to Chicago's City Beautiful Plan. Their solution to the environmental pollution and environmental inequities in the Back of the Yards, discussed at length in the next chapter, was to destroy "Bubbly Creek" by filling it in and making it into a great thoroughfare, as envisioned by the City Beautiful Plan.

Notes

1. Dominic Pacyga and Ellen Skerrett, *Chicago, City of Neighborhoods* (Chicago: Loyola University Press, 1981), 475.

2. Pacyga and Skerrett, *Chicago*, 464.

3. Pacyga and Skerrett, *Chicago*, 464.

4. Pacyga and Skerrett, *Chicago*, 464.

5. Pacyga and Skerrett, *Chicago*, 464.

6. Pacyga and Skerrett, *Chicago*, 464.

7. Thomas J. Jablonsky, *Pride in the Jungle: Community and Everyday Life in Back of the Yards Chicago* (Baltimore: Johns Hopkins University Press, 1993), 10–11.

8. Charles J. Bushnell, *The Social Problems at the Chicago Stock Yards* (Chicago: University of Chicago Press, 1902), 4.

9. Bushnell, *Social Problems*, 7.

10. Bushnell, *Social Problems*, 7.

11. William Cronon, *Nature's Metropolis: Chicago and the Great West* (New York: W. W. Norton, 1991), 225.

12. Bushnell, *Social Problems*, 8–9.

13. Bushnell, *Social Problems*, 8–9.

14. Bushnell, *Social Problems*, 18–20.

15. Cronon, *Nature's Metropolis*, 225.

16. Dominic Pacyga, "Working and Living in Packingtown: Back of the Yards, 1890–1914," in *Polish Immigrants and Industrial Chicago: Workers on the South Side, 1880–1922* (Columbus: Ohio State University Press, 1991), 69.

17. According to the Illinois State Department 1927 report, "The Rise and Fall of Disease in Illinois," 105, by Dr. Issac Rawlings, "Erysipelas followed the river and bad sanitation, poverty and congestion more closely than cholera did."

18. A number of works by immigration historians, including Jania Eugenia Nowosielski's master's thesis (Northeastern Illinois University, 1971), have shown that Polish immigrants voluntarily created segregated communities for both economic and social reasons.

19. Harry Rosenberg, "Packing Industry and the Stockyards," in Mary McDowell Collection, Chicago Historical Society, Box 3, Folder 15.

20. Robert A. Slayton's seminal study of Packingtown, *Back of the Yards: The Making of a Local Democracy* (Chicago: University of Chicago Press, 1986), 25–26.

21. Jablonsky, *Pride in the Jungle*, 37.

22. Alan M. Kraut, *Silent Travelers: Germs, Genes and the Immigrant Menace* (New York: Basic Books, 1994).

23. Bertram B. Fowler, *Men, Meat and Miracles* (New York: Messner, 1952), 78.

24. Louise Carroll Wade, *Chicago's Pride: The Stockyards, Packingtown and Environs in the Nineteenth Century* (Urbana and Chicago: University of Illinois Press, 1987), 148, 297.

25. Martin Melosi, *The Sanitary City: Urban Infrastructure in America from Colonial Times to the Present* (Baltimore: Johns Hopkins University Press, 2000), 63.

26. Charles Rosen, *A History of Public Health* (Baltimore: Johns Hopkins University Press, 1958, 1993), 213.

27. Kraut, *Silent Travelers*, 78.

28. Joel A. Tarr, *The Search for the Ultimate Sink: Urban Pollution in Historical Perspective* (Akron, OH: University of Akron Press, 1996), 313–14.

29. Tarr, *Search for the Ultimate Sink*, 314.

30. Rosenberg, "Packing Industry and the Stockyards."

31. Dominic A. Pacyga, *Polish Immigrants and Industrial Chicago: Workers on the South Side, 1880–1922* (Chicago: University of Chicago Press, 1991, 2003), 71–73.

32. Pacyga, *Polish Immigrants and Industrial Chicago*, 467–68.

33. Bushnell, *Social Problems*.

34. Bushnell, *Social Problems*, 40.

35. Upton Sinclair, *The Lost First Edition of Upton Sinclair's The Jungle*, ed. Gene DeGruson (Memphis, TN, and Atlanta, GA: St. Luke Press, 1988).

36. Sinclair, *The Jungle*, 183.

37. Jablonsky, *Pride in the Jungle*, 19; Bushnell, *Social Problems*, 73.

38. Cronon, *Nature's Metropolis*, 252.

39. Jablonsky, *Pride in the Jungle*, 19.

40. Bushnell, *Social Problems*, 73.

41. Bushnell, *Social Problems*, 73.

42. Jablonsky, *Pride in the Jungle*, 20.

43. Jablonsky, *Pride in the Jungle*, and Mary McDowell, "City Waste," Municipal Housekeeping Symposium, Mary McDowell Papers, Chicago Historical Society, Chicago, Illinois.

44. Jablonsky, *Pride in the Jungle*, 20.

45. *Chicago Tribune*, October 27, 1909.

46. *Chicago Tribune*, October 29, 1909.

47. Jablonsky, *Pride in the Jungle*, 20.

48. Mary McDowell Papers, Chicago Historical Society.

49. Mary McDowell Papers, Chicago Historical Society.

50. Mary McDowell, "City Waste," Municipal Housekeeping Symposium.

51. Slayton, *Back of the Yards*, 40–42.

52. Slayton, *Back of the Yards*, 40–42.

53. Slayton, *Back of the Yards*, 40–42.

54. Louise Carroll Wade, "Mary McDowell," in *Women Building Chicago, 1790–1990: A Biographical Dictionary*, ed. Rima Lunin Schultz and Adele Hast (Bloomington: Indiana University Press, 2001), 564.

55. Slayton, *Back of the Yards*, 173–75.

56. Slayton, *Back of the Yards*, 175.

57. Wade, "Mary McDowell," 563–65.

58. Wade, "Mary McDowell," 563–65.

59. Mary McDowell, Municipal Housekeeping Symposium, 1.

60. Mary McDowell, Municipal Housekeeping Symposium, 1. The business of the Chicago Reduction Company was the transformation (reduction) of sewage waste into either a usable or less noxious form. The resultant waste would be considered usable if it could be used as fertilizer or a nontoxic filling for landscapes.

61. Mary McDowell, Municipal Housekeeping Symposium, 1.

62. Mary McDowell, Municipal Housekeeping Symposium, 1, and Lucy Eldersveld Murphy and Wendy Hamand Venet, eds., *Midwestern Women: Work, Community and Leadership at the Crossroads* (Bloomington: Indiana University Press, 1997).

63. Slayton, *Back of the Yards*, 175.

64. Mary McDowell, "Civic Experiences," Mary McDowell Papers, Chicago Historical Society.

65. Clarke A. Chambers, *Seedtime of Reform: American Social Service and Social Action, 1918–1933* (Minneapolis: University of Minnesota Press, 1963), 112. "Others, with Jane Addams, daily observed the problems of municipal housekeeping which cried for a solution if modern society were to survive. . . . They propagandized for closed sewers and for adequate garbage collection. They set in motion neighborhood self improvement crusades and clean-up crusades. Jane Addams was one of the most prominent settlement founder and leader during this time period."

66. Chambers, *Seedtime of Reform*, 17.

67. Murphy and Venet, *Midwestern Women*, 63.

68. Mary McDowell, "Civic Experiences," 14.

69. Mary McDowell, "Civic Experiences," 14.

70. Mary McDowell, "Civic Experiences," 6.

71. Mary McDowell, "Civic Experiences," 4.

72. Mary McDowell, "Civic Experiences," 2.

73. Mary McDowell, "Civic Experiences," 2.

74. Mary McDowell, "Civic Experiences," 2.

75. Mary McDowell, "Civic Experiences," 2.

76. Mary McDowell, "Civic Experiences," 3.

77. Mary McDowell, "Civic Experiences," 5. "The Boss" is the alderman of the Town of Lake.

78. Jablonsky, *Pride in the Jungle*, 20.

79. Murphy and Venet, *Midwestern Women*, 14. "Settlement workers were overwhelmingly of middle class and professional background often from families of substantial means, well educated, mostly of native-born Anglo-Saxon, Protestant inheritance."

80. Murphy and Venet, *Midwestern Women*, 114.

81. *Lietuva,* "The Question of Women's Gymnastic Clubs," December 11, 1914, 1–2, Chicago Historical Society.

82. McDowell, Municipal Housekeeping Symposium, 3.

83. Howard Wilson, *Mary McDowell, Neighbor* (Chicago: University of Chicago Press, 1928), 149.

84. Wilson, *Mary McDowell,* 149.

85. Wilson, *Mary McDowell,* 149.

86. Wade, *"Mary McDowell,"* 235.

87. Wilson, *Mary McDowell,* 150.

88. Wilson, *Mary McDowell,* 151.

89. Wilson, *Mary McDowell,* 150–51.

90. Wilson, *Mary McDowell,* 150–51.

91. Wilson, *Mary McDowell,* 153.

92. McDowell, *Municipal Housekeeping*, 5.

93. McDowell, *Municipal Housekeeping*, 7.

94. Slayton, *Back of the Yards*, 129–50.

95. Thomas Philpott, *The Slum and the Ghetto: Neighborhood Deterioration and Middle Class Reform, Chicago* (New York: Oxford University Press, 1978), 160.

96. Philpott, *The Slum and the Ghetto*, 197.

CHAPTER FOUR

Engineering and Environmental Inequality: The Rise and Fall of the Notorious "Bubbly Creek"

> All forms of power . . . draw some authority by referring to "scientific truths."
>
> —Michel Foucault

The resolution of environmental justice struggles in the Back of the Yards, as with modern struggles, occurred because of power relations that involved a legal process contingent upon the scientific, medical, and engineering validations of the "truth" of negative environmental health impacts to communities' claiming environmental inequalities and racism. Current claims of environmental racism rest upon an argument that the communities' health is damaged by virulent pollution stemming from industrial operations (through engineering design) and waste disposal practices. Likewise, any validated claims of health damage always produce a concomitant demand for changes in engineering design and operation to ameliorate environmental pollution that created the environmental inequalities.

An example of this power-knowledge dynamic occurred in July 1998 in Grand Bois, Louisiana, when Houma Indians and Cajuns lost a battle for environmental justice against the oil industry because they failed to provide "truths" that could convince the court that their health problems stemmed from the industrial operations and waste management practices of the Campbell Wells and Exxon Oil Companies. Although Campbell Wells would settle with the residents out of court, jurors did not accept the community's scientific experts' evidence that Exxon had caused them physical harm.[1]

"Bubbly Creek," the major source of environmental health problems and the ultimate sink for most environmental waste in the Back of the Yards, was originally located in the town of Lake. Its environmental state was strongly influenced by the power relations that existed among the packinghouse industry, civic, commercial, political, and engineering leadership in Chicago, the state of Illinois, and the federal government. Despite local ordinances and state and federal laws, the marginally controlled waste disposal practices of the packinghouses, slaughterhouses, and tanning industries corrupted the environmental integrity of the creek. These were the polluting industries that had been forced outside of the physical space of the city of Chicago, far from its social body, because of fears of cholera and typhoid fever from waste disposal practices. Fully cognizant of the environmental inequalities that had been produced from their own industrial operations, the packinghouse industry and its industrial allies engaged in a complex set of power relations to have a large portion of the creek destroyed. Supported by local engineers, industrial and civic leaders in Packingtown were finally able to successfully advocate for the destruction of Bubbly Creek in 1923. The federal government declared it a nonnavigable body so that the city of Chicago could complete the construction of a major road. The change of status to a nonnavigable body allowed the creek to be filled in and paved, thereby extending Pershing Road, in accordance with the Chicago Plan, an initiative by the city's Chicago Plan Commission to develop an arterial urban transportation network consisting of classes of streets: conventional residential streets, avenues for through traffic (thoroughfares), and landscaped boulevards which combined the "corridor park and the drive."[2] The planners envisioned and pushed for the closing of Bubbly Creek, which was technically and legally referred to as the west fork of the south branch of the Chicago River, so that Pershing Road, a major Chicago thoroughfare, could be extended and become one of "the great traffic arteries of the west and south sides of the city."[3]

The filling in of the creek was only one of the engineering solutions to eliminate it as an environmental nuisance. The other alternative that had been used in the past to clean the creek was to dredge the body of water and remove the waste products that were the source of its pollution. The fill-in approach was the engineering solution supported by both city planners and industrialists, who publicly claimed that this method would help them to achieve a "City Beautiful" for the benefit of workers and residents living in the Back of the Yards, as articulated by the Chicago Plan. The objectives of the industrialists and planners to eliminate the creek, however, could only be achieved with the mutual support of engineers, planners, and local, state, and federal government officials. The powers who sought to eliminate Bubbly Creek for the purpose of extending and completing Pershing Road were met by a vociferous and extended challenge from multiple powers exerted by other engineers, lawyers, statesmen, and business owners who had their own plans for the river and questioned the purported altruistic motives of Chicago engineers, businesses, and politicians in creating a "City Beautiful." As a result, the drive to destroy the environmental nightmare of Bubbly Creek was held up for almost thirty years, even after the federal government declared it to be a nonnavigable body of water. The primary delay in closing the creek was due to federal support and economic interest in the state of Illinois's plans for the development of a deep waterway connecting Lake Michigan to the Mississippi River. According to the media, however, the delay was caused by two businesswomen, Olive and Dollie Leitch.

The Leitch sisters were part of Chicago's social elite and landowners in the Back of the Yards.[4] By the time Bubbly Creek became a heated public controversy at the local, state, and federal levels, the Leitch women owned only three acres of an original forty acres of land that included riparian property situated on the south bank of the creek. All of this land had originally been owned by Dollie Leitch's grandfather, Benjamin Wilder, in 1869.[5] In 1874, the Leitch property became part of a subdivision of land that was split between the two women, the Central Manufacturing District, and the Mechanical Manufacturing District.[6] Dollie's mother, Mrs. Robert Leitch, inherited the land from Wilder in 1875 after his death and left the property to her son Robert. The land was then passed on to Dollie and Olive Leitch in 1912 after the death of Dollie's brother, Robert, a distillery owner in Packingtown. Prior to the transfer of the land to Dollie and Olive, Robert granted permission to several transportation companies supporting the packing industries to cross the land. By the time the property ended up in the hands of Dollie and Olive, it had been leased for thirty-six years to the Stockyards Company and subleased to the "Chicago Junction Railway company and others which constructed railroad tracks over it."[7] The Chicago Junction would become a strong proponent for the destruction of Bubbly Creek and would try on three occasions to unsuccessfully take possession of the land from the Leitch women by condemnation from 1916 to 1934. On April 30, 1934, the injunction the company had brought against the women dissolved and the railroad tracks were removed. The Leitch women then filed a lawsuit against the Chicago Junction, asking for $2,000,000 for the rental of their property while the tracks were on it.[8]

The media blamed the delay in closing Bubbly Creek on Olive Leitch, a graduate of the Chicago Law School. She argued that Bubbly Creek was still navigable water protected by the United States government that, despite state and local laws, was and had been under environmental assault by uncontrollable and illegal industrial practices. She decried the force of the power relations that sought to fill in Bubbly Creek. She asserted before the U.S. Congress and in several lawsuits for more than ten years that

> the city of Chicago, the sanitary district, municipal corporations (through the City Council of Chicago) and officers of the State of Illinois did collude and conspire with the private corporations, the Union Stock Yards and Transit Company and the First Trust and Savings Bank by fraud and misrepresentations did unlawfully and illegally close the South Branch of the South Fork of the Chicago River and . . . the Secretary of War and the chief engineers of the United States Government cooperated with these private and public corporations to jointly, illegally, and unlawfully, by fraudulent misrepresentation, cause the above described part of the Chicago River to be filled and the right of navigation thereon to be destroyed.[9]

The existence of environmental inequities in the Back of the Yards, although visible to anyone living or visiting the area, had to be publicly validated by the environmental "truths" of engineers, scientists, and medical professionals before any legal action could be taken to ameliorate the environmental nuisances. This scientific and technological validation of water pollution and its environmental consequences by engineers was a classic example of Foucault's thesis that the execution of power works in tandem with knowledge. Leitch's assessment supported Foucault's belief that there was "no power relation without the correlative constitution of a field of knowledge, nor any knowledge that does not presuppose and constitute at the same time power relations" manifested in the battle to have Bubbly Creek declared nonnavigable water.[10] In this case it was the engineering power-knowledge that facilitated the power relations needed to destroy the creek and eliminate an environmental nuisance that disproportionately impacted Eastern European immigrants living in the Back of the Yards. Despite the legal-power and science-power that the Leitchs brought into the power relationship, no doubt their gender impacted the saliency and acceptability of their argument. No other opponents of the fill-in for Bubbly Creek would be demonized in the public eye the way the Leitch sisters were. Contemporary articles appearing in Chicago newspapers portrayed the Leitch women as being the thorns in the city's plan for ameliorating the environmental problem and its desire to develop the area.[11] "The Irish Lick Bubbly Creek; Now They Can Go to the Zoo" ran in the *Chicago Daily News*; "Close 'Bubbly Creek' Urges Commerce Body" ran in the *Central Manufacturing District Magazine*. None of these articles ever mentioned the Illinois Deep Waterway and the role of the state in initially halting the project.

Rising Bubbles: Polluting the Creek in the Back of the Yards

Bubbly Creek, also known as the west fork of the south branch of the Chicago River, represented the horrific environmental conditions in the Back of the Yards produced by the packinghouse industries. As discussed in chapter 3, the creek was one of the worst polluted water sources and one of the most identifiable landmarks in the region. The environmental and public health consequences of that pollution were not limited to one place; they impacted an entire region. The goal of this section of the chapter is to elucidate an environmental history of Bubbly Creek, which explains how it came to be an environmental problem for Chicago. A number of environmental histories have already been written that examine or include the history of the Chicago River. These include Louis Cain's *Sanitation Strategy for a Lakefront Metropolis: The Case of Chicago*, William Cronon's *Nature's Metropolis*, Thomas Jablonsky's *Pride in the Jungle: Community and Everyday Life in Back of the Yards Chicago*, Donald L. Miller's *City of the Century*, and Louise Carroll Wade's *Chicago's*

Pride: The Stockyards, Packingtown and Environs in the Nineteenth Century.
None of these provides a complete history of Bubbly Creek, nor do they
examine the critical role of engineers and planners in the power relations that
both created and ameliorated Bubbly Creek as one of the primary sources of
environmental inequalities for immigrants in the Back of the Yards.[12]

Bubbly Creek originally flowed north into Lake Michigan, the source of
the city's drinking water. Organic wastes poured into the creek by the packers
produced a sanitary nightmare that resulted in thousands of deaths from
typhoid fever, cholera, and other sewage-related illnesses in the metropolitan
Chicago area. In his 1869 report to the Illinois State Board of Health, Dr. John
H. Rauch, sanitary superintendent of the city of Chicago, would state that
the amount of sewage generated by the slaughterhouses by 1863 had grown
so large that it had become equal to or exceeded the amount produced by the
human population. As a result, the city's sewage system could not keep up with
this production and "in 1863 a remarkable epidemic of erysipelas occurred
which prevailed exclusively in close proximity to the south branch and to the
main river. The great amount of animal refuse thrown into the south branch
was supposed to have been the cause of this epidemic."[13] Dr. Willis O. Nance,
trustee of the sanitary district, reported in his study, "The Sanitary District of
Chicago: Its Influence on Chicago's Health," that in 1891, Chicago "lost over
1,900 citizens by death from typhoid, and had at least 15,000 more cases, and
that the death rate from typhoid in that year was 174 per 100,000."[14]

The Back of the Yards, home of Bubbly Creek, was originally part of
the town of Lake. This city was sparsely settled prior to the Civil War but
eventually developed and grew with the industrial developments in Chicago's
Union Stockyards.[15] Louise Carroll Wade's seminal history of Packingtown
points out that the nuisances created by the packing and related industries
in Chicago (i.e., slaughtering and rendering) resulted in the issuance of city
ordinances in 1849, 1851, and 1865.[16] According to Wade, when the 1849 and
1851 ordinances failed, the city turned to the state legislature and, in February
1865, secured an "Act to Provide Sanitary Measures and Regulations for the
city of Chicago." Wade's work fails to mention another and extremely lengthy
ordinance (eighteen sections), "An Ordinance Concerning Nuisances," that
was passed by the city in December 1862, before it turned to the state for help.
Section five of the 1862 ordinance established a financial penalty between $25
and $100 for "any distiller, tanner, butcher, pork or beef packer . . . or other

person whatsoever who shall cause or suffer any offal, manure or rubbish . . . to be discharged out of or flow from their premises . . . into the Chicago River or either of its branches or any of its slips or canals connected therewith or into Lake Michigan within the jurisdiction of the city."[17]

On November 27, 1865, the city of Chicago filed the ordinance "Order to Remove All Rendering Establishments from the City Limits" after the state act was created. This was followed by the passing by the city of "An Ordinance Concerning Slaughtering within the Limits of the City of Chicago." Together these acts prohibited slaughterers, packers, and renderers from putting offensive matter into the Chicago River or any of its branches, canals, or slips. These ordinances arose because city officials felt that the disposal practices of these industries were "destructive of the health of our citizens and are [a] good source of arrogance to the people generally."[18] Numerous complaints from citizens and city workers about the environmental pollution produced by these industries (which were referred to as "nuisances") were filed with the city of Chicago. These complaints gave rise and support to the creation of the ordinances that attempted to regulate these environmental nuisances. The ordinances were inspired and driven by the concerns of the medical community in the newly emerging field of public health who believed that there was a definite link between cholera, typhoid fever, and the improper management of human and animal waste.

The power relations involving the public health officials (who were primarily medical doctors) were not the classic displinarian powers articulated by Foucault but were the beginning of a new form of power that Foucault referred to as *biopolitics.* Biopolitics emerged as a means of controlling "a multiplicity of men . . . not as individual bodies . . . but a global mass affected by overall processes characteristic of birth, death, production and illnesses." According to Foucault, biopolitical power is a power that seeks "control over human beings . . . and their environment . . . the milieu in which they live."[19] Furthermore, the actions of physicians as public health officials in this situation were typical of the actions Foucault ascribed to biopolitical power. In this case, biopolitical power sought to reduce the mortality rates of Chicago citizens stemming from the environmental degradation of its drinking water source that had been caused by the sewage contamination. Thousands of people had to be protected. The only way to achieve this goal was to regulate and eventually eliminate the source of the environmental contamination, which came from the disposal practices of the packers.

On July 12, 1865, twenty-two citizens filed a "Resolution Ordering the Board of Police to Send a Health Officer to 188 Wells Street to Abate the Nuisance of the Stench Coming from the Packing House." The resolution pointed out that the citizens' complaints stemmed from the fact that the packinghouse was also being "used for rendering, which caused a stench that is intolerable."[20] Prior to and in support of the 1862 ordinance, the city's Committee on Health filed its own report based on a five-week study of the packinghouse industry. The "Report of Committee on Health on the Nuisances Produced by Distilleries and Slaughterhouses on the South Branch" concluded that although there were many businesses that operated hygienically there were also many who were found "pouring their blood and offal, most if not all, into the River." This report also contained statements from over a dozen of its inspectors. Many of these statements were similar to that of inspectors Culberton and Jones, who observed, "These parties are running their filth and blood into the water, their house is located on a creek, and the water at this place is red with blood." Similarly, inspector Troughman remarked that at "the gut cleaning place, he is running all his filth into a creek, the condition of his place is awful."[21]

The environmental conditions of both Lake Michigan and the Chicago River prior to the reversal of the river in 1900 (as discussed in chapter 3) were in the same as those of Bubbly Creek. According to testimony given by civil engineer George M. Wisner on behalf of the Sanitary District of Chicago against the United States, the waters were "filthy, dirty sewage polluted water, in a septic condition, with gas bubbles rising, having large cakes of floating sewage mud. This mud was held at the surface by the gas being generated by it. . . . It was a disgrace to a civilized community."[22] The waste generated by industries, especially by the packing industries, combined with a rapidly increasing metropolitan area, resulted in the city of Chicago being granted permission by the state to "deepen the Illinois and Michigan (I & M) Canal in order to divert more of the sewage from the Chicago River, and this was completed in 1871" with the initial reversal of the Chicago River.[23] By the late 1880s the original sewage system and the deepening of the I & M Canal was recognized as being insufficient to handle or keep pace with the waste generated by the packers and the growing population. "In 1889 the Sanitary District of

Chicago was created to provide complete diversion for Chicago sewage."[24] The district was never limited to the city of Chicago, and at its inception "included territory outside the borders of the city proper . . . and since 1889 more and more territory has been added, until it embraces a considerable portion of Cook County, including parts or all of 61 communities."[25] The formation and implementation of the sanitary district resulted in the development of the Sanitary Ship Canal, whose primary engineering objective was to permanently reverse the flow of the Chicago River so that water would have sufficient volume and kinetic energy to treat sewage.

By the end of the second decade of the twentieth century, the Chicago Sanitary District, the metropolitan institution responsible for water management, would find itself embroiled in several federal lawsuits based upon the pollution produced by the packers. The legal fight involving multiple states (Missouri, Wisconsin, Michigan, and Louisiana) and the international community was rooted in the amount of water being taken to treat the sewage problem generated by the human population and the packers in the Chicago metropolitan region. The following letter written by the chief engineer to the Sanitary Board of Trustees in the "Report on Industrial Wastes from the Stockyards and Packingtown in Chicago, 1921: The Sanitary District of Chicago" illuminates the gravity of the situation:

> In view of the injunction suit now pending in the Federal Court to determine our right to take diluting water from Lake Michigan over and above 4167 cu.ft.sec . . . and the diversion controversies, both national and international, and the condition of the IL river, which is steadily growing worse, in large part because of the spurt in the packing industry, I urge that your honorable Board of Trustees make every effort to arrive at a formal agreement with the Packers and Stockyards interests, so that actual work can be started upon a constructive plan. . . . For many years tons of material has been thrown away as useless by Packers. I hope soon with the cooperation of all concerned that a notable step toward utilization can be made and a commercial fertilizer produced from the material now polluting our Main Channel and the IL river.
>
> Respectfully submitted, Albert W. Dilling, Chief Engineer[26]

Dilling's report goes on to state that the packers' efforts to reuse and recycle enough of the animal waste continued to be insufficient to reduce the environmental load in the form of sewage for the Ship Canal. This situation exacerbated the condition of Bubbly Creek. Dilling lamented that "there is still much material which passes away, in the aggregate several thousand tons a year, to which the practical manufacturer attaches little importance. To the sanitary engineer these wastes, containing large amounts of suspended matter with a liquid highly putrescible, are of great importance."[27] The sewage generated by the stockyards grew along with the expansion of the yards, but the receiving waters––the Chicago River and its branches––remained constant.

The wastes generated by the packing industry in the Union Stockyards contributed substantially to the treatment load handled by the sanitary district and the death of the Bubbly Creek. "In 1920 the total load on the main channel was approximately 4.5 million. One million from Packingtown; approximately 2.8 million from total population of the Sanitary district; 370,000 from Corn Products refining company at Argo, and other miscellaneous industries (400,000)."[28]

The water pollution problems of the stockyards arose not only because of the amount of solid waste produced from handling human waste but also because of the enormous amount of wastes generated from storing, killing, and processing the livestock relative to the mass of the receiving waters. This is why "many sanitary engineers of standing (at that time) felt the legal actions that had been brought against them."[29]

The sanitary engineers recognized that the reversal of the Chicago River had not completely solved the environmental problems of the area in its entirety. Their testimonies in all of the court depositions made it quite clear that the reversal of the river had in fact worsened the environmental conditions in the Back of the Yards in ways that they had not anticipated. In effect, the reversal of the river had decreased the kinetic energy of the Bubbly Creek so much that it became an almost inert, foul pool of water. Since the waste pouring into the stream continued to flow from the stockyards without a substantial increase in volume in the receiving waters (i.e., Bubbly Creek), it began to accumulate and become fetid as the aerobic content of the water rapidly declined. This decaying and immobile animal waste posed health hazards for the region, which sanitary engineers felt could only be reduced (at that time) by increasing the volume of water drawn from Lake Michigan. The creek became so static from the decaying waste that local animals were frequently seen walking across water.[30] The Chicago River's reversal had an immediate and positive impact on improving the environmental health of

Figure 4.1. Union Stockyards from Ashland Avenue, Cabbages in Vacant Lot, Packingtown Skyline, 1910, Courtesy of Chicago Historical Society (negative ICHi-01869)

the most affluent residents or more fortunate citizens of Chicago. The reversal, however, led to the least fortunate residents in the Back of the Yards bearing the inequitable cost of this improvement from both environmental and public health perspectives.

Burying Bubbles: The Power Relations of Nonnavigable Waters

The final fate of Bubbly Creek would be determined by the Chicago River congressional hearings conducted before the Subcommittee of the Committee on Interstate and Foreign Commerce in the House of Representatives, Sixty-seventh Congress, on December 15, 1921; May 19, 1922; and October 6 and 7, 1922. The subcommittee was formed to decide whether the creek was a nonnavigable water as articulated by House bills H.R. 9049 and H.R. 8648 and Senate bill S. 3177. The bulk of the testimonies heard by the subcommittee that would influence its decision would occur at the October meeting, which was held in Chicago, Illinois, at the Federal Building. Of the

Figure 4.2. Skimming Bubbly Branch, 1905, Courtesy of Chicago Historical Society (negative ICHi-23820)

thirty-two witnesses who testified at the Chicago River hearings in October 1922, twelve represented the business and industrial sector, claiming they were representing civic interests; thirteen witnesses were engineers employed by various levels of the government; and seven were attorneys representing business interests. Given these statistics it is clear that the fate of Bubbly Creek was heavily determined by the power relations that revolved around business power-knowledge and engineering power-knowledge. Although the *Chicago Daily News* in 1937 would proclaim that "The Irish Lick Bubbly Creek, Now They Can Go to the Zoo," the historical record is clear that the death of the creek had very little to do with the environmental protest of immigrants in the Back of the Yards. Rather, it was due in large part to the power maneuverings of predominantly native white Anglo Saxon Protestant (WASP) men, especially engineers. This group would act first in the economic interests of the state and federal government for the Illinois deep waterway project and finally in the economic interests of the city of Chicago to complete Pershing Road as the optimal thoroughfare to facilitate and complement economic growth occurring on the city's South Side under the guidance of the City Beautiful Plan.[31]

Civic Power and Knowledge

As alluded to by the Leitch women, the drive to fill in Bubbly Creek as a critical path to extend Pershing Road was supported and promoted by many individuals, politicians, and business interests who claimed they were representing civic interests. A consortium of those active in the demise of the creek included the Central Manufacturing District Association (CMD), the Chicago Plan Commission, the Pershing Street Association, the 39th Street Association, the City of Chicago (mayor and council), United States congressmen, Illinois state representatives, Chicago Metropolitan Sanitary District engineers, city engineers, and Packingtown aldermen. All of these entities would provide crucial testimony in the U.S. Congress Subcommittee Hearings on October 6 and 7, 1922, that would lead to Bubbly Creek being declared nonnavigable water.

Although immigrants had complained for years about the environmental state posed by Bubbly Creek, less than 10 percent of the thirty-two witnesses who gave testimony at the Chicago River Hearings were born outside of the United States and only one of the witnesses was a woman, Olive Leitch. One newspaper account that announced construction on Pershing Road had finally begun claimed that "back in the days when Archer Avenue was Archy road, the Irish, who were among the noisiest, and the rest of the people of the 11th ward better known as Bridgeport were raising a fuss and fume about that odoriferous little appendage of the Chicago River called Bubbly Creek."[32] Illinois State Representative David E. Shanahan, an Irishman, was one of only three ethnic witnesses who testified at the Chicago River Hearings on behalf of the community. Shanahan had been a resident of the Packingtown area for thirty years at the time of the hearing and was a proponent of the efforts to bury Bubbly Creek once it was declared nonnavigable water. He testified that he was in favor of the creek being closed for economic reasons, not environmental ones. "Our particular interest is to have this street (Pershing Road) opened in order that the people over here will have an opportunity to go over to their employment in the east end of the city, and that people living in the east end will have an opportunity to go over here to this great industrial district for employment."[33] Illinois congressional representative John W. Rainey's terse testimony in support of closing the creek concurred with that of Shanahan. Rainey, however, pointed out that the creek had been an environmental problem for the community. At the hearing, he declared, "It is insanitary, it is unhealthful, and all the people out there are very anxious to have it filled in." Although Rainey testified that the creek had been considered an eyesore in the community for years, it had now, more importantly, become an obstacle that stood in the way of a much-needed transportation route for "100,000 to 150,000 people." Rainey asserted that opening Pershing Road to the other side of the city limits would establish "an avenue of transportation for all the laboring people there and for all of the employees of the stockyards."[34] Both of these political representatives offered "truths" that justified the closing of the creek based on the economy. They put very little emphasis on the environmental degradation that had taken place in Bubbly Creek and the concomitant health issues of the community at large. Their goals were to engage in power relations that would support and sustain economic development for the Packingtown community and the city at large.

Another important member of this civic consortium was Mary McDowell. Although not a physical witness at the October Chicago River Hearing, she heavily influenced the power relations that sought the demise of Bubbly Creek. McDowell was the first woman garbage commissioner for the city of Chicago and she became known as the "Duchess of Bubbly Creek." Her engagement in these power relations was motivated because she felt strongly that at least three-quarters of a mile of Bubbly Creek posed "a menace to the health of the surrounding district."[35] Her biography makes it clear that she began her fight to have Bubbly Creek eliminated beginning with the stockyards strike of 1904 and used her "friendship with Admiral Dewey . . . to reach the War Department in an effort to get the national government to fill in Bubbly Creek."[36]

On January 15, 1907, one year before the Chicago Plan Commission was approved by Chicago voters, McDowell wrote to Secretary of War Bixby, asking for guidance on how to have the creek declared a nonnavigable body and filled in to eliminate it as an environmental nuisance. Her letter was offered in the hearings by Olive Leitch to help show the court the long-term formation and existence of a consortium of power groups who actively sought out physical destruction of the creek for economic purposes, not for environmental reasons. Leitch accused McDowell of "being a representative of the stockyards interest, who purported to be working in the interest of public health."[37] McDowell saw her efforts in influencing individuals and institutions whom she believed held power over the fate of Bubbly Creek as being in the environmental interest of the community, not of the packinghouses. In her biography, she described the packinghouses as commercial enterprises "not as interested in municipal sanitation as a humanitarian would desire."[38] When McDowell's efforts with the War Department failed to get the creek filled in, she concentrated her efforts on getting rid of the creek through the city's health department and the Sanitary District. Her commitment to having the creek eliminated resulted in her taking part in the agitation for the 1927 "Bubbly Creek" state bill, S.B. 74, introduced in the state legislature by Senator Frank McDermott. The bill was strongly supported and endorsed by the South Side Chamber of Commerce, who "through its representatives, spent much time at Springfield (Illinois) working for the passage of the 'Bubbly Creek' bill."[39] This bill met with opposition from the Leitch sisters but was passed in June 1927. The bill gave the city of Chicago eminent domain powers, allowing it to fill in Bubbly Creek after it had been declared nonnavigable water.[40] The city's ability to implement the passed state bill and fill in Bubbly Creek would be thwarted and delayed by an injunction filed by Olive Leitch and Dora Leitch with federal judge James H. Wilkerson, who still contended that Bubbly Creek was a navigable water as defined under the Northwest Ordinance of 1787, "subject only to control by the federal government."[41] This resistance of the Leitchs to the efforts to fill in the creek persisted even though the federal government had abandoned the creek as a nonnavigable waterway.

The Central Manufacturing District Association (CMD) was another one of the primary self-described civic forces in the power relations that sought out the physical termination of the creek. The Central Manufacturing District, approximately three hundred acres formerly known as the "Cabbage Patch" property (which was a geographical location within the stockyards), was acquired by the Chicago Junction Railway company. This was the very same company that would try to use legal power to eliminate the Leitch women from the debate over Bubbly Creek. Situated on the South Side of Chicago, the CMD was primarily located between Thirty-fifth and Thirty-ninth streets, extending from Morgan Street on the east to Ashland Avenue on the west and portions of Robey Road near Forty-third Street. Bubbly Creek became a critical issue for the association because "through the center of the District ran the south and west forks of the south branch of the Chicago river."[42] The CMD Club opened in 1912 and was created to "fill a very important place in the daily routine life of the business men in the Central Manufacturing District."[43] Since Bubbly Creek was in the middle of the district, its business members became actively engaged in the power relations that sought to bury the creek and promote continued economic development in the area, which they felt was contingent on the completion of Pershing Road (formerly Thirty-ninth Street) as a major transportation route. The continued development of transportation infrastructures was consistent with the objectives of the CMD's owners. From the very beginning, they would claim that "splendid roads lead from the District in all directions, making it possible to team freight to all portions of the city at a minimum expense."[44]

The CMD was highly aggressive in its political efforts to get rid of Bubbly Creek. It hosted a luncheon for the U.S. congressmen who conducted the Chicago River Hearing on the very same day of the hearing, for the express purposes of influencing the decision to declare the creek a nonnavigable waterway. In its own magazine, CMD stated that it hosted the luncheon for several federal congressmen and local and regional politicians at the Central Manufacturing District Club to discuss the matter of *The People vs. the Open Sewer*. According to the article, "Every speaker voiced grievances against the obscene rivulet (Bubbly Creek) and the meeting . . . went on record as urging Congress to close Bubbly Creek."[45] The sentiments of the CMD members can be summarized by the comments of County Treasurer P. J. Carr, who said that the river "hadn't been worth anything to anybody for ten years and that it should be closed to make way for a needed improvement, Pershing Road" and that he "knew the creek when it was crystal pure and estimated that now 100,000 workers talk about the odor every day to the disgrace of Chicago."[46] The article further pointed out that "the filling in of the stream is not only advocated by CMD, the Pershing Road Association and the Council Committee, but by the Chicago Association of Commerce and other civic bodies as well."[47]

Immediately following the CMD luncheon, a large percentage of the guests, especially from the Pershing Road Association, walked to the Federal Building in Chicago to give testimony in the Chicago River Hearings.

Of the more than twenty witnesses who testified at the Chicago River Hearings in support of the closing of Bubbly Creek, one-fifth were members or affiliates of the Pershing Road Association. In his testimony on behalf of the Pershing Road Association, its secretary, Mr. B. H. Heide, asserted that the organization was associated "with the Greater Thirty-ninth Street Improvement

Figure 4.3. Rooster Walking on the Sludge of Bubbly Creek at Morgan Street, 1911, Photo Credit: Chicago Daily News, Courtesy of Chicago Historical Society (negative DN-0056899)

Association, the Oakland Business Association, the Southside Businessman's Association, the West Side Businessman's Association . . . and several other civic organizations . . . which banded together and formed as its chief mission the building of a road from the lake––Lake Michigan––to the proposed or planned zoological gardens just outside of the western limits of the city of Chicago."[48] The testimony of the president of the Pershing Road Association, Mr. Edward E. Maxwell, was consistent with that of the association's secretary and emphasized economic growth and expansion as the primary reason for filling in the creek. Maxwell pointed out that the matter of physically eliminating large portions of the creek was a "question of the greatest good for the greatest number and this is absolutely essential because that district west of Ashland Avenue is growing very rapidly. It is becoming a very large industrial district all the way west there and not only industrial but there are many homes there."[49]

The president of the Greater Thirty-ninth Street Association, Mr. E. A. Munger, testified that his organization was the "parent organization" of all those that had organized around the closing of Bubbly Creek and the development of Pershing Road, including the Pershing Road Association. The organization had formed between 1904 and 1907 and represented "61 affiliated downtown and south-side clubs with a membership of about 225,000 who . . . unanimously endorsed this proposition." Munger testified that the association had had a long and difficult battle to close the creek and "get this street opened" and had "met with every imaginable difficulty that could be devised . . . beginning with the stockyards and the owners of the property along Bubbly Creek."[50] Munger's testimony also demonstrated his desire to utilize the power of the civic and business community in deciding the fate of the river as well as elucidating the historical force of this particular issue in power relations in Chicago. His statements during his testimony made it very clear that his organization's position was held and supported by a large number of citizens who also exercised a considerable amount of political power and influence in Chicago. His objective is clearly evidenced by the following statement he made at the hearing:

> I want to say further, Mr. Chairman, that there is not now any man in office on the south side of Chicago who was not elected on a platform resolving to close Bubbly Creek and open Thirty-ninth Street. I do not know what the official sanitary board say through the engineers here, but I know when we go down there they all stand up on their hind legs and say that they are for it and for it hard.[51]

Munger's concern over the weight of engineering power and knowledge in determining this hearing was well-founded.

Engineering Power-Knowledge

The final decision to declare Bubbly Creek as nonnavigable water was primarily driven by the engineering power-knowledge provided by local, state, and federal engineers during the 1922 congressional hearings.

The engineers constituted at least 33 percent of the thirty-two witnesses who testified before the subcommittee. The most influential engineering testimony in the hearing was that of Major Rufus W. Putnam, district engineer of the United States Army Corps of Engineers, and to lesser extent, that of Mr. A. T. Grohmann, civil engineer with the U.S. Engineering Office (U.S. Army Corps) in Chicago, Illinois. Major Putnam was from a very prominent and old American military family. His father, William Rice Putnam, was the son of Edwin Putnam, one of the sons of the famous General Rufus Putnam, thus making Major Rufus W. Putnam the great-grandson of General Putnam.[52] Putnam testified that this particular portion of the Chicago River had not been under improvement by the federal government since 1919. Putnam pointed out that "the river and harbor act of March 2, 1919, definitely abandoned as a project for improvement all of the South Branch of the Chicago River, which included the south fork up to the Chicago Junction Railway bridge."[53]

Illinois Deep Waterway Project

Although the local Chicago media scapegoated the Leitch women as being the thorns in the City Beautiful Plan, the real conflict was between state and federal engineers and local planners and engineers in Chicago. This fact was supported by the subcommittee's final decision, which stated that it was a "local controversy over closing a river that is strenuously urged by the city of Chicago and the various civic and industrial organizations that appeared in the interest of the city and just as seriously opposed by representatives of the state."[54] The heart of the problem was whether the entire creek, both the southwest and southeast forks of the south branch of the Chicago River, should be classified as nonnavigable and filled in for local highway improvements (e.g., Pershing Road) to support economic development in the city of Chicago, or whether parts of the creek could still be classified as navigable waters. If parts of the creek remained navigable, it would benefit the federally sponsored and endorsed Illinois Deep Waterway Project, which sought to develop a waterway course from Lake Michigan to the Mississippi River. This deep waterway project was planned and designed to support interstate commerce using these waterway routes.

Major Putnam testified that the federal government was very interested in the deep waterway project because it had a stake "not only in returns on its $2,000,000 investment in the Illinois River but in its use as a highway for this possible increased traffic."[55] Putnam's statements supported those of the state's superintendent and chief engineer of the division of waterways, C. R. Miller, who was also director of public works and buildings. On behalf of the state, Miller protested against the declaration of all portions of the south branch as a nonnavigable waterway because the "State of Illinois is now engaged in improving the Des Plaines River so as to connect the Mississippi River with the drainage canal and Lake Michigan by a 9-foot channel and $20,000,000 and bonds have been issued by the State for that purpose."[56] The state engineers made it very clear during the hearings that it was very probable that "all available navigable portions of the Chicago River will be required to handle the commerce which we are advised . . . will navigate through these waters."[57] The real fight was between Illinois waterways and Chicago highways. Although both interests (city and state) would be served in the long term, the city planners successfully predicted during the hearing that the age of automobile transportation and railway transportation would soon eclipse that of waterway transportation.

The power relations in Chicago at this time demanded the interest and involvement of prominent business, political, and governmental leaders and institutions in addition to the civic protest of Packingtown residents to bring some type of satisfactory closure to the environmental nightmare posed by Bubbly Creek. Industrial activities (especially by the packers) produced Bubbly Creek, and it was long recognized by everyone in Chicago that industrial leadership, together with governmental leadership, was critical in resolving this particular environmental nuisance in the Back of the Yards. The decision of the congressional subcommittee echoed that belief when they rejected the proponents' first of two arguments for declaring the creek a nonnavigable body. The first argument was based on Bubbly Creek being "foul, insanitary, and a nuisance to the health of the people in that part of the city." The committee agreed that, although the creek had become extremely polluted, the level of pollution had occurred because "authorities of the City of Chicago could have prevented it and could still prevent it if they chose to do so."[58] Congress decided to declare Bubbly Creek a nonnavigable body only because of the transportation infrastructures needed to support the economic development that the industrial and civic interests had convincingly testified was occurring in the area and specifically in the Central Manufacturing District.

Congress also made it very clear in its decision that it was "impressed with the great importance of the deep waterway project promoted by the State of Illinois" and "would not recommend the enactment of any legislation that would hinder or embarrass the State of Illinois" in the completion of the project.[59] In the end, the congressional subcommittee decided that the federal government would relinquish its control over Bubbly Creek to the state of Illinois as a navigable waterway based on the testimony of engineers from the federal and state governments. Its decision was also based on its legal power provided by a precedent that established that it was within the power of "Congress to abandon a navigable waterway, if it does not think it wise to expend public funds to improve it."[60] Congress did not merely abandon its rights to the state but urged in the passing of Senate Bill S.B. 3177 that the power relations in the state settle the fate of the creek. Congress would declare that it had abandoned control "to the end that the city of Chicago and the State of Illinois may themselves freely settle all questions involved."[61]

State and Municipal Political Power-Knowledge

The city of Chicago, the state of Illinois, and the federal government eventually resolved the conflict between Bubbly Creek and the deep waterway project once the federal government had abandoned its authority over the creek as navigable water in 1923. It would take another fourteen years of power relations between primarily the municipal and state governments to have Bubbly Creek filled in and Pershing Road completed by 1937. During the 1920s and 1930s, the state of Illinois experienced a decline in waterway traffic. "Traffic on the Illinois River in the 1920s totaled only 100,000 to 200,000 annually. In 1933, until the first tow came up from New Orleans, there was no traffic at all between Lockport and Starved Rock."[62] Furthermore, the Army Corps of Engineers decided that the optimal deep waterway route to Lake Michigan would be the Sag Channel, completed between 1911 and 1922. The corps made this decision because this route would avoid the "increasingly congested central Chicago area" that had been slowed down with too many lift bridges.[63] A federal act of July 3, 1930, extended the federal project on Illinois waterways to the heads of federal projects in Chicago and Calumet. This same act also transferred control of all of the Illinois water projects and the canals of the sanitary district to the federal government. The move to the Sag Channel as opposed to the Sanitary Ship Canal helped clear the path for building Pershing Road by removing the south branch of the Chicago River as a viable route to Lake Michigan in the deep waterway project. The delays in building Pershing Road then became driven by legal actions of property owners along Bubbly Creek. Some of these owners engaged in legal fights with both the city of Chicago and the state to either halt the destruction of the creek or be properly compensated for the loss of economic opportunities that would occur once the creek was eliminated.

Despite these obstacles, the city of Chicago and the Chicago Plan Commission continued to move forward and have Bubbly Creek filled in and Pershing Road completed in 1937. The improvement of Pershing Road had been advocated by the Chicago Plan Commission before the 1923 navigability decision. The street was mentioned in the *11th Annual Report* of the Chicago Plan Commission, 1920, as a street that was critical to improving traffic conditions in the stockyards and to providing residents with access to Lake Michigan and the zoo.[64] In 1921, officers of the Plan Commission "appeared before the City Council committees in connection with the ordinance for the filling in of Bubbly Creek between Halsted Street and Racine Ave. (necessary for the continuation of Pershing Road)."[65] In 1921, Ward Five Alderman Eaton had presented a resolution that urged "the necessity of filling in the west fork of the south branch of the Chicago River."[66] In 1925 the Chicago Plan Commission identified Pershing Road as one of the streets in their through-traffic street plan that they recommended for the city of Chicago to adopt and implement. According to the Plan of Chicago, 1925, the city's adoption and execution of the through-street plan would play a major role in "relieving the present condition of congested traffic and in bringing us nearer to a solution of the traffic problem."[67] The 1925 plan specifically recommended that Pershing Road be opened and widened "from lake front to western city limits, a distance of about eight miles."[68] According to Chicago Plan Commission reports, the plans for Pershing Road remained stagnant and in "status quo" from 1922 through 1927. This was probably due to the fact that it was not until 1927 that the state of Illinois, through the passage of the Bubbly Creek bill, would grant the city of Chicago the right of eminent domain to fill in the creek and develop the road. In 1928, the Chicago Plan Commission's executive committee appointed a Pershing Road Committee that was tasked with overseeing the implementation of the road. In that same year, during the "election of April 10, 1928 a bond issue of $2 million dollars for Pershing Road was defeated by a vote of 381,529 to 184,751."[69]

Strongly influenced by the recommendations provided by the Chicago Plan Commission, the city of Chicago (and eventually the state of Illinois) passed a number of ordinances and engaged in legal proceedings beginning in 1929 that were directed at getting Bubbly Creek filled in. On February 4, 1929, the city government ordered that the "the Commissioner of Public Works be authorized and directed to . . . proceed with the filling in of Pershing Road and . . . the filling in of Bubbly Creek between Ashland Road Avenue and Thirty-ninth Street."[70] On June 3, 1929, the Chicago City Council "passed an ordinance for the opening and improvement of Pershing Road 108 feet wide between Lowe and Damen Avenues."[71] The Chicago Plan Commission reported that in 1930 on "November 5, a paving ordinance covering the portion of Pershing Road, as when opened and widened was submitted to City Council" and that the ordinance was favorably approved by the city's Committee on the Judiciary on December 11, 1930. Less than six months from the issuance of this ordinance, the city of Chicago made a condemnation agreement with one of the major property owners in the areas near Bubbly Creek, the Chicago City Railway Company.

The final boost to filling in Bubbly Creek and completing Pershing Road was accomplished during the Depression, in the watershed period from 1931 to 1935. On January 21, 1931, the city council passed the "Chicago City Railway Company Agreement in Connection with Condemnation Proceedings for the Opening and Widening of W. Pershing Road from S. Damen Avenue to Lomen Avenue."[72] This agreement was based upon a petition that the city had filed in the Superior Court of Cook County, Illinois, and sought to "condemn certain property for the opening of widening of Pershing Road . . . and for a levy to pay for the costs."[73] The agreement resolved the dispute between the two parties and resulted in the Chicago Railway withdrawing its petition against the condemnation action of the city. On March 25, 1931, the condemnation suit ended and special assessments began to be collected. Prior to the end of the lawsuit, the city had passed a paving ordinance for a widened Pershing Road on January 10, 1931.[74] In 1934, the Chicago City Council passed an arterial ordinance recommending that the state include Pershing Road as one of many arterial thoroughfares that could be improved with motor fuel tax funds. This recommendation was approved by the state of Illinois's Department of Public Works and Business Division Highway on August 31, 1934.[75] On November 21, 1934, the city of Chicago was informed by the commissioner of public works that an ordinance had been passed "granting permission to the State of Illinois to improve W. Pershing Road from S. Ashland Avenue to S. Halsted Street as a State Highway."[76]

One of the final obstacles to the filling in of Bubbly Creek was removed on May 22, 1935, when Ward Eleven Alderman Hugh B. Connelly introduced an easement ordinance. Connelly's proposed ordinance was consistent with his motto: "Maintenance of all necessary services at the lowest possible cost."[77] The ordinance was unanimously accepted by the City Council on June 6, 1935, and provided "for the acceptance of easements from certain property owners for the use of property for street purposes in advancement of awards . . . to permit the early improvement of W. Pershing Road."[78] By July 21, 1935, five critically important property owners accepted the easement agreement; their decision would virtually erode the conflict to get rid of Bubbly Creek for the sake of Pershing Road. These owners included Albert and Massie Lettermann, the Anglo-American Provision Company, the Union Stock Yard and Transit Company of Chicago, and the Central Manufacturing District. Another of the final hindrances was removed with the November 5, 1936, city ordinance for granting "Authority for an Agreement with the Barrett Company in Connection with the Filling in of Part of the West Fork of the South Branch of the Chicago River, the Construction of Certain Sewers and the Opening and Extending of W. 31st Street."[79]

When Pershing Road finally opened on October 24, 1937, Alderman Connelly (an Irishman) received public recognition for his "getting the project through the maze of legal technicalities involving federal, state and city authorities." Connelly not only had a bridge named after him for his deeds in closing Bubbly Creek, he received an old shovel that had been carved from a tree that had grown on the banks of Bubbly Creek in 1860. Connelly received the shovel because "legend . . . had it that this shovel was saved because it had been used to throw the first spadeful of dirt in the creek."[80]

Notes

1. J. Timmons Roberts and Melissa M. Toffolon-Weiss, *Chronicles from the Environmental Justice Frontline* (New York: Cambridge University Press, 2001), 154–58.

2. Commercial Club of Chicago, *Plan of Chicago* (Chicago: The Commerical Club, 1909), 64, 72.

3. "Association of Commerce Backs 'Bubbly Creek' Bill," *Central Manufacturing District Magazine,* April 1927.

4. "Women Delay Bubbly Creek," *Chicago Tribune,* March 9, 1946.

5. "Bubbly Creek Bubbling Its Last," *Chicago Post,* September 9, 1920. In 1869, Benjamin Wilder "purchased the land with scrip and buffalo robes he received in payment for the building of Jefferson Barracks in Missouri near St. Louis."

6. *Chicago River, Hearings before Subcommittee of the Committee on Interstate and Foreign Commerce of the House of Representatives,* October 1922, 87.

7. "Jail Confronts Two in Old War on Bubbly Creek," *Chicago Tribune,* January 23, 1935.

8. "Jail Confronts Two."

9. Olive Leitch's "Testimony" in *Chicago River, Hearings before Subcommittee of the Committee on Interstate and Foreign Commerce of the House of Representatives,* October 1922.

10. Michel Foucault, *Discipline and Punish: The* Birth *of the Prison,* trans. Alan Sheridan (New York: Vintage Books, 1979), 27, and Alec McHoul and Wendy Grace, *A Foucault Primer: Discourse, Power, and the Subject* (New York: New York University Press, 1997), 59.

11. "The Irish Lick Bubbly Creek; Now They Can Go to the Zoo," *Chicago Daily News,* October 23, 1937; The Greater Southside, "Close 'Bubbly Creek' Urges Commerce Body," *Central Manufacturing District Magazine,* December 1927, 24–25.

12. Louis Cain, *Sanitation Strategy for a Lakefront Metropolis: The Case of Chicago* (DeKalb: Northern Illinois University Press, 1978); William Cronon, *Nature's Metropolis: Chicago and the Great West* (New York: W. W. Norton, 1991); Thomas Jablonsky, *Pride in the Jungle: Community and Everyday Life in Back of the Yards Chicago* (Baltimore: Johns Hopkins University Press, 1993); Donald L. Miller, *City of the Century: The Epic of Chicago and the Making of America* (New York: Simon and Schuster, 1996); and Louise Carroll Wade, *Chicago's Pride: The Stockyards,*

Packingtown and Environs in the Nineteenth Century (Urbana: University of Illinois Press, 1987).

13. Illinois State Board of Health, *Report of the Sanitary Investigations of the Illinois River and its Tributaries* (Springfield, IL: State of Illinois, 1901), XI.

14. Dr. Willis O. Nance, "The Sanitary District of Chicago: Its Influence on Chicago's Health," in *Sanitary District Report* (Chicago, 1891), 3.

15. Dominic Pacyga and Ellen Skerrett, *Chicago, City of Neighborhoods* (Chicago: Loyola University Press, 1981), 475.

16. Wade, *Chicago's Pride*, 40.

17. Chicago, *An Ordinance Concerning Nuisances,* December 1862.

18. Chicago, *Order to Remove All Rendering Establishments from the City Limits,* November 27, 1865.

19. Michel Foucault, *Society Must Be Defended: Lectures at the College de France,* ed. Mauro Bertani and Alessandro Fontana, trans. David Macey (New York: Picador, 1997), 242–44.

20. Citizens of Chicago, *Resolution Ordering the Board of Police to Send a Health Officer to 188 Wells Street to Abate the Nuisance of the Stench Coming from the Packing House* (Chicago), July 12, 1865.

21. Chicago Committee on Health, *Report of Committee on Health on the Nuisances Produced by Distilleries and Slaughterhouses on the South Branch*, December 1862.

22. George M. Wisner, "Deposition Testimony," in *United States v. Sanitary District.*

23. Max R. White, *Water Supply Organization in the Chicago Region* (Chicago: University of Chicago Press, 1934), 58.

24. Wisner, *U.S. v. Sanitary District.*

25. White, *Water Supply Organization,* 58.

26. The Sanitary District of Chicago, *Report on Industrial Wastes from the Stockyards and Packingtown in Chicago* (1921), vol. II.

27. Sanitary District of Chicago, *Report on Industrial Wastes,* vol. II, 6.

28. Sanitary District of Chicago, *Report on Industrial Wastes,* vol. II, 6.

29. Sanitary District of Chicago, *Report on Industrial Wastes,* vol. II, 7.

30. Charles J. Bushnell, *The Social Problem at the Chicago Stock Yards* (Chicago: University of Chicago Press, 1902), 73.

31. "Irish Lick Bubbly Creek."

32. "Irish Lick Bubbly Creek."

33. Statement of Mr. David E. Shanahan, *Chicago River Hearings* (Chicago), 1922.

34. Statement of Hon. John W. Rainey, *Chicago River Hearings* (Chicago), 1922.

35. Statement of Hon. John W. Rainey, *Chicago River Hearings.*

36. Howard Wilson, *Mary McDowell, Neighbor* (Chicago: University of Chicago Press, 1928), 160–61.

37. Leitch's "Testimony" in *Chicago River Hearings,* 74.

38. Wilson, *Mary McDowell,* 164.

39. *Central Manufacturing District Magazine,* December 1927.

40. Fifty-fifth General Assembly, State of Illinois, *No. 21, Final Legislative Synopsis and Digest,* June 30, 1927.

41. Wilson, *Mary McDowell,* 164, and Central *Manufacturing District Magazine,* December 1927.

42. "The Center of Chicago, 'The Great Central Market,'" *Central Manufacturing District Magazine,* 1911.

43. "Resume of Its First Year's Activities," *Central Manufacturing District Magazine,* 1913.

44. "Resume of Its First Year's Activities," 9.

45. *Central Manufacturing District Magazine,* 1922.

46. *Central Manufacturing District Magazine,* 1922.

47. *Central Manufacturing District Magazine,* 1922.

48. "Statement of Mr. Heide, Pershing Road Association," *Chicago River Hearings* (Chicago), 1922.

49. "Statement of Mr. Edward E. Maxwell, Pershing Road Association," *Chicago River Hearings* (Chicago), 1922.

50. "Statement of Mr. Munger, Greater Thirty-ninth Street Association," *Chicago River Hearings* (Chicago), 1922.

51. "Statement of Mr. Munger," 30.

52. Rowena Buell, ed., *The Memoirs of Rufus Putnam and Certain Official Papers and Correspondence* (Boston: Houghton Mifflin, 1903).

53. Major Rufus W. Putnam Testimony, *Chicago River Hearings* (Chicago), 1922.

54. Report No. 1352, 67th Congress, 6.

55. Putnam Testimony, 6.

56. Report No. 1352, 67th Congress, 4th Session, 5.

57. C. R. Miller Statement at Chicago River Meeting, December 15, 1921.

58. Report No. 1352, 67th Congress, 4th Session, 4.

59. Report No. 1352, 67th Congress, 4th Session, 5.

60. Report No. 1352, 67th Congress, 4th Session, 11.

61. Report No. 1352, 67th Congress, 4th Session, 11.

62. Army Corps of Engineers, *History of Transport on Upper Mississippi and Illinois Rivers,* 1970.

63. Army Corps of Engineers, *History of Transport,* 68.

64. Chicago Plan Commission, *11th Annual Report* (1920), 117.

65. Chicago Plan Commission, *12th Annual Report* (1921).

66. City of Chicago, *Journal of City Council*, 1921–1922.

67. Chicago Plan Commission, *The Chicago Plan Annual Report, 1925*, 26.

68. Chicago Plan Commission, *The Chicago Plan Annual Report, 1925*, 32.

69. Chicago Plan Commission, *The Chicago Plan Annual Report*, 1928.

70. City of Chicago, *Chicago City Council Proceedings*, 1928–1929.

71. Chicago Plan Commission, *20th Annual Report of the Chicago Plan Commission*, 1929.

72. City of Chicago, *Chicago City Council Proceedings*, 1931.

73. City of Chicago, *Chicago City Council Proceedings*, 1930–31.

74. Chicago Plan Commission, *Twenty-third Annual Report of the Chicago Plan Commission*, 1931.

75. City of Chicago, *Chicago City Council Proceedings*, 1934–35.

76. City of Chicago, *Chicago City Council Proceedings*, 1934–35.

77. Citizens Association of Chicago, *Chicago Citizens Handbook for the Aldermanic Election*, City of Chicago Municipal Archives, Chicago Public Library, 10.

78. City of Chicago, *Chicago City Council Proceedings, 1934–35*.

79. City of Chicago, *Chicago City Council Proceedings, 1936–37*.

80. "Irish Lick Bubbly Creek."

PART THREE

BROKEN PROMISES

CHAPTER FIVE

Planning and Environmental Inequalities: Race, Place, and Environmental Health in Chicago

To try to achieve a decent environment without social justice is comparable to efforts to build the city beautiful by concentrating on the boulevards and ignoring the indecencies of life that exist in the densely packed slums behind the façade.
––Robert C. Weaver, Colloquium, U.S. Congress, 1968

The colored man is asked to live decently and keep clean when all the conditions are against him.
––Benjamin Rosenthal, Reconstructing *America Sociologically and Economically*

African Americans who migrated to northern cities in the late nineteenth and early twentieth centuries were not welcomed with open arms by the larger body politic and social body. They were regarded and treated by the larger white social body as undesired and unwanted environmental and public health "nuisances" and forced to live and work in unhealthy and (physically and socially) degraded urban environments. Their continual movement north into racially constricted and congested areas created a self-perpetuating cycle, since these environmental conditions subjected African

Americans to various contagious diseases, such as tuberculosis, which they contracted at disproportionately high rates. This high rate of contagious disease among African Americans then fueled fear and prejudice among whites, who redoubled their efforts to keep them contained in the same degraded environments that had contributed to their health problems in the first place. Nowhere were the mechanics of this vicious cycle more clearly evident or the implications more bluntly expressed than in Chicago.

Chicago became the city of choice for migrating African Americans during the first half of the twentieth century. It also became one of the most racially segregated cities in the United States starting in the Progressive era and was the site of contemporary charges of environmental racism. The massive migration of African Americans to northern cities gave rise to the "Negro problem," considered at that time to be the country's "most grave and perplexing domestic problem."[1]

The scientific and medical communities viewed African Americans as health and moral hazards unfit to occupy the same geographical space as the white social body and body politic unless they were restricted, disciplined, and confined. In his landmark 1915 study, *America's Greatest Problem: The Negro*, Robert W. Schufeldt asserted that "the gravest problem to be faced in dealing with the . . . negro . . . is the danger to the public of his or her contagiousness and infections from the standpoint of physical and moral disease."[2] African Americans who contracted environmentally related contagious diseases like tuberculosis (also known as the "white plague" or "white death" in the postbellum period) were articulated by medical doctors and scientists across the country as being a "menace to the white population." Dr. Fred J. Mayer, a southern physician from Opelousas, Louisiana, declared at the 1913 Southern Medical Association meeting that "in so far as the negro is concerned in his relation to public health, it is but one phase of that sinister problem that looms large and low on the horizon . . . as a carrier and transmitter of disease he is a standing menace to the white race."[3] The prevailing thought of African Americans as "diseased bodies" contributed to planning policies that restricted their geographical space. As a result of these race-based geographical restrictions legally imposed by the white body politic, the environmental conditions that scientists and the medical community knew contributed to the proliferation of tuberculosis worsened and played a major factor in the abysmal mortality rates for African Americans for the first half of the twentieth century. In 1905, Kentucky physician John E. Hunter pointed out that the environmental conditions that exacerbated the tuberculosis epidemic in "colored settlements" were "illy ventilated dwelling places, too many in one room, many tenement houses in alleys and other places cut off from sunshine and pure air."[4]

Nowhere was the policy of racial restriction more harshly developed and enforced in northern cities than in Chicago, Illinois, which had become a leader in racial planning policies in the first decades of the twentieth century. Chicago's history is an exemplary history of how planning and planners created and formed separate geographical spaces for African American communities that would for generations be subjected to environmental disenfranchisement. Although many scholars traditionally point to the rigid patterns of forced racial separation from the emergence of Jim Crow laws in the southern United States in the post-Reconstruction era, northern cities and states developed and executed austere and rigid race-based segregation planning policies for ethnic and racial groups, especially African Americans. Planning as a profession began during this time period and it was not untouched by nativist and racist philosophies. Although initiated as a response to "improving the blighted physical environment in which people worked and lived," the planning profession became "a mechanism for protecting property values and excluding undesirables." As planning scholar Yale Rabin points out, the "two interest groups that were regarded as the undesirables were immigrants and African Americans."[5] As a leader in race-based planning policies, Chicago literally forced black migrants––environmental undesirables––into racially isolated spaces.

Chicago's residential planning policies were conceived and highly influenced by the extremely prominent Chicago real estate board and middle class neighborhood associations like the Woodlawn and Hyde Park–Kenwood associations. These organizations would initiate or encourage policies and practices like restrictive covenants and, ultimately, violence in order to keep African Americans outside of optimal environmental living spaces that were being preserved for "white" citizens.

A number of Chicago historians and scholars have written about the racially segregated settlement patterns of African American migrants that formed in Chicago from the turn of the twentieth century until midcentury.[6] Some of these scholars have alluded to both voluntary and involuntary racial segregation of African Americans in Chicago; however, the bulk of historical evidence clearly points to the fact that African Americans entering the city of Chicago from the slavery period until the middle of the twentieth century had very little choice in determining where they lived. The majority of African Americans during this period became severely racially segregated because of legal and extralegal racial policies and planning practices that were repeatedly enforced by life-threatening violence from citizens and citizen groups. The violently enforced racial segregation policies contributed to African American communities' environmental marginalization.

Whether legal or extralegal, racial planning created Chicago's notorious "Black Belt." The Black Belt, which eventually grew to encompass a geographic area seven miles long and a mile and a half wide from 22nd to 63rd streets between Wentworth and Cottage Grove, actually started in Chicago's downtown area.[7] The Black Belt was initially contained in an area whose northern border was the Chicago River; southern border, 16th street; western border, the south branch of the Chicago River; and eastern border, Lake Michigan.[8] Although African Americans voluntarily came to the area, many of them were forcibly moved into the Belt as a form of social control. The Belt was described in contemporary local newspapers as a geographical space that "the entire city believes . . . to be a bad place. The neglect of it is a standing disgrace to the city . . . and the only means of cleaning it up to the standard of the whole community as a whole . . . is by keeping white persons out of it."[9] Chicago residents interviewed after the infamous 1919 race riot stated that their interest in racial separatism was spurred by the demonstrated "depreciation of property by Negroes."[10] An article in the February 1920 issue of the *Property Owners Journal*, a monthly periodical of the Chicago real estate board, asserted that "you keep the Negro in his place, amongst his people and he is healthy and loyal. Remove him, or allow his newly discovered importance to remove him from his proper environment and the Negro becomes a nuisance."[11]

African Americans claimed that their racial isolation and separation was the basis for their victimization from what is commonly referred to as environmental racism and the concomitant development of environmental illnesses. A number of medical and public historians have shown that racial segregation was a significant factor contributing to the development of a disproportionate and higher level of mortality and morbidity among African Americans from widespread epidemics and plagues like pneumonia and tuberculosis, which were driven by environmental factors. Historians have pointed out that the frequency and deadliness of these epidemics were directly tied to marginalized environmental conditions in segregated spaces.[12]

In his highly esteemed and exhaustive study, *An American Dilemma: The Negro Problem and Modern Democracy*, Gunnar Myrdal makes it clear that whenever African Americans entered the northern states after the Civil War, "they met considerable social segregation and discrimination."[13] Myrdal points out that the restriction of African Americans into particular segments of the city was achieved through legal and extralegal planning tools like "local zoning ordinances, restrictive covenants, and terrorism."[14] The first part of this chapter provides a history of the planning techniques used in Chicago that created separate and unequal environmental living spaces for African Americans from the antebellum period until 1948, the year in which the United States Supreme Court decided in *Shelly v. Kraemer* that the use of restrictive covenants as race-based private zoning was unconstitutional. The second part of this chapter discusses the environment and environmental health consequences that stemmed from this racial segregation.

Medical historian Vanessa Northington Gamble makes clear in her book, *Germs Have No Color Line: Blacks and American Medicine 1900–1940*, that the failure of southern African Americans to become racially extinct after slavery and instead develop a higher susceptibility to diseases like tuberculosis, pneumonia, syphilis, and pellagra also created a "negro health problem." Their migration northward made their problem "a national, not just regional, dilemma."[15] The Negro health problem became identified in 1914 as the "white man's burden" by Georgia physician L. C. Allen at the meeting of the American Public Health Association.[16] In Chicago and other northern cities like Detroit and East St. Louis, the large-scale African American migration led to violent contests over access to the physical environment between African Americans and whites. This violence was driven by attitudes regarding the racial inferiority of African Americans and was also heavily influenced by the fact that African Americans were seen as serious environmental health threats to the large white social body. African Americans were medically documented as having a propensity for developing the most deadly contagious diseases that lingered in the environment, especially tuberculosis. Katherine Ott's social history of tuberculosis, *Fevered Lives: Tuberculosis in American Culture since 1870*, reveals that physicians across the country during the early migration era frequently identified African Americans, European immigrants, and poor whites as conduits of disease. According to Ott's history, a Chicago physician of the time "warned that the rapid increase in tuberculosis among African Americans was a 'menace to the white population.'"[17] With regard to tuberculosis infection from African Americans, white physicians and statesmen alike lamented that they were "ever subject to the death-dealing micro-organism at their hands."[18]

In 1908, former Georgia governor W. J. Northern stated before the Southern Medical Association in Atlanta that "tuberculosis among the negroes covers only one aspect of the danger from the diseased negro. If to this disease should be added the loathsome diseases, directly traceable to the negro's excessive immorality, the evidence of menace would be so strikingly cumulative as to alarm the most indifferent citizen in the most obscure community."[19] Likewise, Dr. Edward Mayfield Boyd of Washington, D.C., overwhelmed the medical and public health literature of that time with the notion that African Americans, like other vermin, were vectors of contagion and "an arch-carrier of disease germs to white people."[20] This articulation of African Americans as threats to the larger white social body and their subsequent (and occasionally violent) segregation was an excellent example of the exercise of Foucault's biopolitical power throughout white American society. Whites at all levels in America tried to exercise power that sought "control over human beings . . . and their environment [and] the milieu in which they lived."[21]

This contest for the environment and the fight to protect the large white social body from what was generally perceived as the environmentally leprous and contagious black social body may have influenced the infamous four-day race riot in July 1919. Considered one of America's bloodiest race riots, it resulted in 38 deaths, 537 injuries, and 1,000 homeless people. Historians who have studied the riot have concluded that the most important underlying factor for its occurrence was geographical space, especially housing.[22] The riot began when a young African American teenager, Eugene Williams, violated the extralegal rule and planned policy governing the use of a white-only beach on Lake Michigan. Williams drowned after being stoned to death by white youths while still in the waters of Lake Michigan.[23]

Organized African American struggles for healthy environmental living spaces and access to the commons in Chicago persisted during the first half of the twentieth century when they were literally and figuratively packed into a rapidly deteriorating Black Belt and then into Chicago's South Side. In the late 1970s, Chicago witnessed the appearance of nationally and internationally recognized African American "environmental justice" groups like People for Community Recovery, led by Hazel and Cheryl Johnson, residents of the city's public housing community Altgeld Gardens. People for Community Recovery has claimed for almost twenty-five years that residents in their racially isolated community have been dying or suffer from environmental illnesses like cancer, miscarriages, and developmental disorders as a direct result of inequitable environmental planning practices and policies sanctioned or supported by their landlord, the Chicago Housing Authority, surrounding industries, and the government (federal, state, local, and county).[24] The struggle for sustainable living spaces has continued into the new millennium.

Most African Americans in Chicago (and in other northern industrialized cities like Cleveland, Detroit, and Pittsburgh) are (or were) either Southern migrants themselves or the descendants of Southern migrants who came to Chicago during the Great Migration periods. Urban historian James R. Grossman asserts in *Land of Hope* that these migrations "drew upon black southerners who looked to urban life and the industrial economy for the social and economic foundation of full citizenship, and its perquisites." A number of excellent studies about the formation of Chicago's black communities have demonstrated in varying degrees that Chicago's African Americans were packed into these ghettos because of implicit and explicit racist formal and informal planning policies and practices.[25] Their literature is critical in illuminating that environmental inequalities and racism in Chicago emerged from this long-term or historical geographical separation from the larger "white" social body.[26] Many of the existing histories about Chicago's black migration, however, have failed to clearly articulate the environmental health consequences of this migration population being forcibly and densely packed into segregated spaces in the Black Belt and eventually Bronzeville. Although environmental scholars have historically focused a considerable amount of attention on the emergence of environmental racism in Southern and rural African American communities, they have now begun to research and discuss the northern problem of race-based environmental inequities.[27] A 1949 report by Dr. Arthur W. Levitt in the U.S. Public Health Service's *Chicago—Cook County Health Survey* concluded that the high tuberculosis mortality rate among African Americans (which comprised 35.8 percent of the total deaths in the city) in 1945 was directly related to the notorious overcrowding conditions of African American communities, noting that "the largest and most congested district, with an area of 4. 72 square miles contains the living quarters of 300,000 people."[28] Current charges of environmental racism are rooted in and supported by the historical legacy of blacks being forced to live in unsustainable geographical spaces in the northern cities. Even today, there remains a high number of racially segregated communities formed during the Great Migration periods whose geographical landscapes have become environmentally marginalized and whose residents are suffering from environment-related illnesses.[29] These communities have been documented as having a disproportionate allocation of unwanted environmental uses (like landfills, incinerators, and toxic disposal sites), which have been linked to these illnesses.

This geographical pattern of racial segregation, isolation, and concomitant environmental inequalities has been particularly insidious for African American communities who, aside from Native Americans, have had the longest history of racial isolation and separation of any ethnic group in the United States. Gunnar Myrdal's 1944 study of the "Negro problem" concluded that "residential segregation . . . even though it was voluntary at the beginning or caused by 'economic necessity' has been forced upon the group from the outside: the Negro individual is not allowed to move out of the 'Negro' neighborhood."[30] Regardless of topography (north or south) or locality (urban, rural, or suburban), African Americans in the United States were subjected to disciplinary actions that enforced their physical separation by law, social custom, or physical force. George M. Fredrickson's monograph, *The Black Image in the White Mind*, is filled with the historical racial philosophies that developed and impacted American policies and practices toward African Americans. Popular ideologies of polygenesis set forth or advanced by influential intellectuals like Dr. John H. Van Evrie or emigration and colonization by President Abraham Lincoln all belied a philosophy that African Americans were not American citizens but were permanent outsiders who should be removed and isolated. This ideology would be reflected in the Supreme Court's 1857 *Dred Scott* decision, which "affirmed that the Declaration of Independence applied to whites only . . . 'in accord with the natural relations of the races.'"[31]

As discussed in chapter 1 of this book, African Americans would continue to be articulated and consequently treated as the ultimate outsiders in America's postbellum, modern, and postmodern eras because of Social Darwinist and eugenic ideologies, as well as legal decisions by the country's courts, including the Supreme Court's decision in *Plessy* v. *Ferguson,* which supported a "separate but equal" philosophy.[32] Various solutions to the "negro problem" emerged during this time frame; all were predicated on the environmental isolation or eradication of African Americans from the physical environs of the "white" social body. These solutions included "the deportation of 12,000,000 Negroes to Africa, the establishment of a separate Negro state in the United States, complete separation and segregation from the whites, and the establishment of a caste system or peasant class and hope for a solution through the dying out of the Negro race."[33]

Between 1818 and 1865 in the state of Illinois, the Illinois Black Laws reflected the widely held national belief that African Americans could not and should not be included in the larger "white" social body. These laws constricted and limited the physical spatial environment and movement of African Americans through that space. The Black Laws forbade African Americans from voting and initially demanded that they could only live in the state if they had a Certificate of Freedom; without the certificate, they could be sold back into slavery to the highest bidder. Under these laws any African Americans coming into the state had to post a $1,000 bond. The physical restriction of their movement extended to their living spaces and immediate environs. Black slaves or indentured servants who were found traveling without a pass more than ten miles from their master's home could be whipped with up to thirty-five lashes by the order of a local justice of the peace, who could find them in violation of the Illinois Black Laws. One hundred years later, African Americans found moving outside of Chicago's extralegally defined Black Belt were severely beaten, bombed, or killed by white gangs and white residents who wanted to restrict them to their "rightful" place. The undesirability of African Americans occupying the environmental or physical spaces reserved for whites during Illinois's antebellum period is also reflected by the fact that African Americans from other states were not allowed to stay in the state for more than ten days. Any African American violating this rule could be arrested, jailed, fined, or removed from the state. The Illinois Black Laws hardened when Congress passed the Fugitive Slave Law of 1850.

The historical irony of the creation of the Illinois Black Laws in Chicago was that the founder of Chicago was a black man, Jean Baptiste Point DuSable; the city itself eventually became a hotbed for abolitionists and the Underground Railroad.[34] According to the famous African American and Chicago businessman and real estate savant Dempsey Travis, DuSable was the first nonnative to own land in Chicago. According to Travis, DuSable's claim of owning the land was based on "alloidal tenure . . . that is by right of law."[35] Despite the Illinois Black Laws, the city of Chicago had seventy-seven African American residents upon its incorporation in 1837, at least one of whom owned real estate property. The African American population in the city decreased from seventy-seven residents to fifty-three residents from 1837 to 1840, but the acquisition of real estate by African Americans increased.[36] In 1844 there was a net gain in the African American population and in propertied African Americans. By 1844, there were 155 free African Americans living in Chicago; 5 of them owned real estate in the city. This level of land ownership doubled by 1847. All of the real estate owned by African Americans was "located in the original 1st and 2nd Wards of the city in downtown Chicago on the following streets: Lake, Madison, Fifth Avenue (Wells), and two parcels on the corner of Clark and Harrison Streets and at Buffalo (Federal) and Harrison Streets." The initial implementation of the Fugitive Slave Law had a direct environmental impact on the first African American residents and property owners of Chicago because it drove many of them into Canada and caused them to "dispose of their property at great sacrifice. The result was a net reduction in black property owners from ten in 1847 to seven in 1850."[37] Allan Spear's study of the formation of the "Black Ghetto" points out that African Americans were physically separated from the environmental spaces of whites from the beginning of Chicago's history. The majority of African Americans lived on the South Side and "as early as 1850, 82 percent of the Negro population lived in an area bounded by the Chicago River on the north, Sixteenth Street on the South, the south branch of the river on the west and Lake Michigan on the east."[38]

The 1860 census revealed that during the ten-year period after the promulgation and implementation of the Fugitive Slave Law, African Americans would continue to enter and acquire (albeit segregated) residential space in the predominantly white environs of Chicago. By 1860, the city had thirty-five African American property owners, whose properties ranged in value from $100 to $17,000. At the time, African Americans were led by a small group headed by a well-to-do tailor, John Jones, who had participated in antislavery activities and was active in voicing "the grievances of a people who already found themselves the victims of segregation and discrimination."[39] By the beginning of the Civil War, Chicago had one thousand African American residents, the majority of whom were fugitive slaves, but the number did include "free-born persons of color."[40] The greatest factors in ushering in a large mass movement of African Americans into the predominantly "white" environment in Chicago were the emancipation that came with the cessation of the Civil War and the repeal of the Black Laws on February 7, 1865.

Even with these turns of events, African Americans were still unwelcome in the physical environment of "white" Chicago. This repulsion by some whites formerly supportive of early African American Chicagoans after the end of slavery is discussed in the 1945 groundbreaking study of African Americans in Chicago, *Black Metropolis: A Study of Negro Life in a Northern City*, by St. Claire Drake and Horace R. Cayton. They point out that after the Civil War many whites who were active in the antislavery movement became concerned about how the city was going to deal with the sudden influx of African American freedmen and were hoping that they would voluntarily leave and colonize outside of the country. This particular group of whites became angry when only forty-seven African Americans in the city of Chicago accepted an invitation to emigrate to the island of Haiti in 1865. When the majority of African Americans made it apparent that they were not going to emigrate, "the editor of the *Northwestern Christian Advocate* was so incensed at what he called their 'impolitic and ungrateful behavior' that he threatened to withdraw his support from a financial campaign of the impecunious African Methodist Episcopal Church."[41]

African Americans were tightly segregated in Chicago between 1865 and 1885 and their children were forced to attend the "Black School" until parents rose up in civil protest. Together with other African Americans in Illinois, blacks in Chicago convened a Colored Convention within five years of the Civil War to demand "equal school privileges throughout the state."[42] In 1870, African Americans were guaranteed the right to vote, and in 1874 segregation in the school system was abolished.[43] In 1885, a state civil rights bill designed to protect the liberties of African Americans, especially in southern Illinois, was passed, and it was amended in 1903 and 1911. This bill essentially prohibited racial discrimination in public places.[44] No legislation, however, was developed in the state of Illinois during the immediate postbellum period to protect or encourage the ownership of private property by African Americans.

Although the environmental space occupied by Chicago's African Americans suffered minimal infrastructural damage during the Great Fire of 1871, it became severely impacted by the city's decision to permanently shift the physical location of the vice district (gambling, prostitution) to their communities. The Great Chicago Fire of 1871 caused approximately $200,000,000 in property damages, including the destruction of 17,000 buildings and the city's renowned red-light district. Drake and Cayton's seminal work on the evolution of the Black Metropolis reveals that a direct result of the Great Chicago Fire was the permanent relocation of the bulk of the city's gamblers and prostitutes into a geographical space that was only three blocks long and fifteen blocks wide, with 2,500 residents. Even after the "city was rebuilt . . . the gay underworld remained among the Negroes."[45] This was the beginning of the community's eventual long-term problem with what planning scholar Yale Rabin has termed "expulsion zoning," the practice of planners' putting locally unwanted land uses in the geographical spaces of minority communities.[46]

The policy of locating vice in African American communities would continue for generations in Chicago because "Black people were helpless to prevent the authorities from locating the red-light district where they lived, just as they were unable to stop whites from segregating them."[47] The persistent location of vice was the first precursive locally unwanted land use (LULU) in Chicago's African American community.[48]

The physical environment of late-nineteenth-century African American Chicagoans would be most severely impacted by the fire of 1874, which began on July 14 at 449 S. Clark Street. This fire burned continuously for twenty-four hours, moving in a northeasterly direction, and consumed 47 acres and 812 buildings. The fire of 1874 is believed to have consumed 85 percent of the African American–owned property in the city, which was concentrated in the South Loop area known as Dearborn.[49] Although half of the African American families that survived the fire dispersed among white residents, the other half relocated in a permanent black enclave that developed in "a long thin sliver of land sandwiched between a well-to-do white neighborhood and that of the so-called 'shanty Irish' . . . [where] most of Chicago's colored residents and their major institutions . . . concentrated during the next forty years."[50] This physical terrain became known as Chicago's Black Belt. Historian Thomas Lee Philpott concluded in his seminal work, *The Slum and the Ghetto: Immigrants, Blacks and Reformers in Chicago, 1880–1930*, that "the Black Belt and its satellites . . . were great physical entities, sharply outlined, and the border all around them was the color line."[51] For a little more than twenty years, between the Great Fire and Chicago's first World's Fair, the African American population would continue to increase and expand the Black Belt because of white movement to the more environmentally "desirable lake-front or . . . suburbs."[52]

The continued migration and movement of African Americans into Chicago's Black Belt (composed of the 2nd, 3rd, and 4th wards) is reflected in the distribution of African Americans by wards in 1880, 1890, and 1900. Data from the 1890 census reveal that African American housing showed an increase of 208 colored owners of area real estate, from 39 in 1870 to 247 in 1890. By 1893 there were 15,000 Negroes living in the city of Chicago.[53]

The U.S. Supreme Court's 1896 *Plessy v. Ferguson* decision ushered in an era of legally sanctioned racial segregation policies nationwide and the emergence of Jim Crow policies in the South. Jim Crow policies severely curtailed the physical, political, and social freedom of blacks in the South and proved to be a major impetus for their migration northward to the "lands of hope." This mass migration of blacks to Chicago resulted in their representing 1.9 percent or 30,150 out of a city population of 1,698,575 in 1900. According to urban historian Thomas Lee Philpott, "the residential confinement of the blacks [in Chicago] was nearly complete at the turn of the century."[54]

Extralegal Measures for Racial Segregation: Neighborhood Associations

The restriction and concentration of African Americans into segregated spaces during this time period was heavily influenced by white neighborhood clubs and associations that served as "extralegal agencies to keep Negro and white residences separated."[55] Chicago's Hyde Park Improvement and Protective Club was formed in 1906 to clean up the vice districts in the adjoining African American community and to "make sure that no blacks resided outside of those districts."[56] Likewise, the Washington Park Court Improvement Association changed its function in the same period "from planting shrubbery and cleaning streets to preventing Negroes from getting into the neighborhood."[57] These associations would resort to violence when persuasion could not be used to drive African Americans from their geographical space.[58] Their actions were key in consolidating African Americans into their own extremely racially homogenous ghetto. Between 1900 and 1910, African American residency in areas that were more than 20 percent "black" had doubled, from one-fourth to one-half.[59] In 1910, 40,000 African Americans lived among the two million heterogeneous inhabitants of Chicago. Of these 40,000, 30 percent lived in the predominantly African American ghetto and 60 percent lived in areas that were more than 20 percent African American.[60] By 1915, the physical ghetto housing Chicago's African American population had been formed. The vast majority of African Americans in Chicago were now living in "a large almost all-Negro enclave on the South Side with a similar offshoot on the West Side."[61] The rapid population increase of African American migrants in Chicago created a violent competition for urban space and jobs with whites, especially recent European immigrants.[62]

This growth in Chicago's African American population continued as blacks literally ran from harsh and violent social conditions in the South. Their continued migration into Chicago because of perceived economic opportunities and social freedom necessitated an expansion in the geographical space of the Black Belt. The expansion of the Black Belt between 1917 and 1921 "could be measured by the bombings: between July 1, 1917 and March 1, 1921 bombings occurred on an average of once every twenty days."[63] A total of fifty-eight bombs were used against African Americans in Chicago to prevent their incursion into white communities during this time. This violence erupted with a new force and frequency in Chicago after cities were legally barred from using racial zoning to separate African Americans from the larger white social body in 1917. The Chicago Commission Race Riot Report found that the six-month period that ended on October 1, 1920, "witnessed as many bombings as the entire thirty-five months preceding."[64] Not only were African American residents bombed, but the properties of real estate agents (both black and white) and African American bankers were also bombed as a "general scheme to close the channels through which the invasion proceeded rather than a protest of neighbors."[65] The bankers were bombed because they made the loans that enabled African Americans to buy the property and support their mortgages; the real estate agents were bombed because they sold or rented the contested property. The office of prominent African American real estate agent and banker Jesse Binga, along with an apartment building owned by the Appomattox Club, was bombed in January 1919.[66] The bombings resulted in the deaths of two African Americans, injuries to both white and African American residents, and over $100,000 in property damages.[67]

A societal philosophy of racial segregation for African Americans boosted by the 1896 *Plessy v. Ferguson* Supreme Court decision became the foundation for both legal and extralegal planning policies and practices throughout the country until the 1917 Supreme Court decision in *Buchanan v. Warley*. When the U.S. Supreme Court struck down blatantly racial zoning in *Buchanan v. Warley*, communities turned to less obvious but legal ways to create segregated living environments. Planning scholar Marsha Ritzdorf's historical research on race, class, gender, and land use planning has revealed that "prior to the 1920s, municipalities used both zoning and residential district laws to segregate residential areas by race and ethnicity."[68] Christopher Silver, another highly regarded planning scholar, asserts in his essay "The Racial Origins of Zoning in American Cities" that although explicit racial zoning was undermined by the 1917 decision, the decision did not deter cities from trying to achieve their objectives of explicit racial apartheid. In direct response to this decision, "cities [legally] engaged professional planners to prepare racial zoning plans and to marshal the entire planning process to create the completely separate black community."[69] Planning scholar Yale Rabin has pointed out that "the nation's planning movement, not just its Southern branch, regarded land use controls as an effective social control mechanism for African Americans and other undesirables . . . [and] Chicago became a bastion of racial zoning enthusiasts."[70]

One of the primary methods used to support racial separation planning efforts in Chicago after the 1917 decision was the creation of property owners' associations. These associations had formed across the country, and they "served as organized extralegal agencies to keep Negro and white residences separated."[71] The associations were organized on the idea of keeping "undesirables" out of their communities; they considered all African Americans to be undesirables.[72] "Niggers are different from whites and always will be, and that is why white people don't want them around."[73] As historian William M. Tuttle points out in his monograph *Race Riot: Chicago in the Red Summer of 1919,* these associations (with the support of realtors) "focused their efforts on forcing out the blacks already residing in their neighborhoods and on insuring that no others entered."[74] Immediately after the Supreme Court's *Buchanan* decision, however, these associations turned to violence. The property owners' associations literally and figuratively waged war against African Americans. With the formation of these associations it "became commonplace for mobs of fifty to two hundred chanting people with bricks, bats, and lengths of pipe to surround the home of a 'black invader,' deface the interiors, and smash all of the windows."[75] In 1918 the most notorious of these associations in Chicago would form: the Hyde Park-Kenwood Property Owners' Association. Claiming over a thousand paying members, this association sought to establish an "exclusively white neighborhood" along Grand Boulevard from 29th to 39th Streets and then along Michigan Boulevard from 39th

Street south to 63rd Street.[76] Although two other race-based property associations existed in 1919, only the Hyde Park–Kenwood association became associated with the bombing of black residents to keep them out of their geographical space. Tuttle's study of the 1919 race riot revealed that "waves of bombings ensued straightaway" after the association denounced "blacks in vitriolic language."[77]

Not only were African Americans unwanted in existing environmental spaces, their presence was also considered an anathema to new public and private housing developments at the time. Beginning in 1921, fifty thousand new homes and thirty thousand apartment buildings were constructed in a seven-year period; all of the subdevelopments prohibited black occupancy. The beginning of this housing boom in 1921 coincided with the Chicago Real Estate Board's unanimous vote to expel any member who either rented or sold properties in white blocks to African Americans and with the entry of the Ku Klux Klan into the city.[78] However, the board did not object to its members selling or renting properties to African Americans in transitioning communities as long as new housing was being developed. Ninety-five thousand African American families packed themselves into the seventy-six thousand homes left behind by whites who fled the city during the building boom. As the new housing supply dwindled for whites toward the end of the 1920s, violence as a segregationist planning mechanism reemerged.

The Legal Construction of Separate Black Geographical Space: Restrictive Covenants and the Chicago Real Estate Board

The end of the housing boom for whites in Chicago coincided with the emergence of restrictive covenants in the city. These covenants were developed by the Chicago Real Estate Board. Urban geographer David Delaney argues in *Race, Place and the Law* that restrictive covenants essentially negated the impact or effect of the *Buchanan* racial zoning decision and effectively blocked for more than twenty years the entrance of African Americans into white geopolitical space. Eighty percent of Chicago would become covered by covenants until the 1948 Supreme Court decision of *Shelly* v. *Kraemer,* which struck down the use of restrictive covenants.[79] Covering large tracts of area, these covenants were, in effect, simple and legally supported private zoning measures that made "the housing stock available to black families . . . less than it would have been under a formal segregation regime."[80] The use of restrictive covenants in racial planning efforts in Chicago was supported in 1926 by two Supreme Court decisions.

In 1926 the Supreme Court decided that it had no jurisdiction in the Washington, D.C., restrictive covenant case, *Corrigan v. Buckley,* brought before it by the NAACP. The court dismissed the case on the basis that there was no constitutional question involved. As a result, it "was construed by subsequent state courts as having effectively said it all. In restrictive covenant cases for the next twenty-two years, state and inferior federal courts consistently asserted that the Court had established the constitutional validity of restrictive covenants."[81] Racial planning across the country as well as in Chicago also gained support that same year from the Supreme Court's decision in *Village of Euclid v. Ambler Realty Corporation.* This case, considered to be a "bellwether event in planning history," led to the Court's embrace of zoning, which became "the most widely used weapons in the planning profession's arsenal to regulate private land use."[82] The court's six to three decision "legitimized zoning as a way of controlling land use" and as a viable means of upholding the "character of a community" from industrial development; it was also heavily influenced by nativist and racist ideologies held by the justices themselves.[83] Planners like Marc Weiss have shown that when the Court supported zoning in the 1926 *Euclid* v. *Ambler* case it was "clearly concerned with issues of social segregation."[84] According to planning historians, "an examination of the papers of the justices and lawyers involved in this case have since revealed how strongly a desire for neighborhood racial and ethnic purity fueled the approval of this tool."[85]

Prior to the 1920s, restrictive covenants were rarely used in Chicago, although they had been used with force across the country. Deed restrictions blocking the sale of individual properties had been used. Historian Thomas Lee Philpott demonstrated in his study of Chicago's slums and ghettos that the restrictive covenant "vested a large group with an interest in maintaining racial boundaries vigilantly, and it gave them the means to do it."[86] After the 1926 *Corrigan v. Buckley* Supreme Court decision, the Chicago Real Estate Board enlisted the support of Nathan William Machesney, one of the city's most prominent lawyers and a member of the Chicago Planning Commission, to draw up the format for a restrictive covenant. Machesney was also a former resident of the Hyde Park and Kenwood community who held many appointive posts in the government and was an officer of both the national and state bar.[87] In his role as general counsel to the National Association of Real Estate Boards, Machesney authored Article 34, an amendment that forbade realtors (upon penalty of license revocation) from allowing members of any other race entry into white neighborhoods because they could cause property damage. This amendment was then added to the board's Code of Ethics. Machesney then drafted a real estate licensing act to give it force. The article eventually became enforceable by the state commissions and was adopted by thirty-two states.[88] The final form of the restrictive covenant was completed by Machesney in 1927 and its restrictions only applied to African Americans, who were defined as persons who were one-eighth "negro" or persons commonly known as "colored." The Machesney covenant "barred 'negroes' from renting, buying or otherwise acquiring covenanted property." The only way African Americans could occupy the same geographical space under the Chicago restrictive covenant would be for them to be employees of the whites residing in that space, as janitors, chauffeurs, or house servants.[89]

The enforcement of restrictive covenants prepared for the Chicago Real Estate Board was limited to twenty-one years, and they were only enforceable for an area if all or a certain percentage of the property was signed for by the owners. Although the board's goal was 100 percent participation for property owners, it decided to have "the agreements go into effect once 75 percent of the property was signed for; and then drive for total coverage throughout the entire district."[90] The Chicago Real Estate Board recommended that areas implement covenants that would cover six to seven "blocks" at a time for effective enforcement. The Chicago Real Estate Board then aggressively marketed the use of the restrictive covenants by making "rounds to YMCAs, churches, women's clubs, PTAs, Kiwanis Clubs to advocate keeping their communities 'Pure White—99 44/100s.'"[91] The board advertised the restrictive covenants as constitutionally supported mechanisms that could be used to halt the Negro invasion. "By the spring of 1928, the *Hyde Park Herald* was pleased to announce that a 'fine network of contracts' extended 'like a marvelous delicately woven chain of armor' from the northern gates of Hyde Park at 35th and Drexel Boulevard to Woodlawn, Park Manor, South Shore, Windsor Park, and all the far flung white communities of the South Side."[92] The notion of African Americans as undesirables in white geographic space was not peculiar to the Chicago real estate community. In his seminal work *Crabgrass Frontier: The Suburbanization of the United States*, urban historian Kenneth Jackson revealed that "so commonplace was the notion that race and ethnicity were important that prominent appraising texts, such as Frederick Babcock's *The Valuation of Real Estate* (1932) and *McMichael's Appraising Manual* (1931) advised appraisers to pay particular attention to 'undesirable' or 'least desirable' elements and suggested that the influx of certain ethnic groups was likely to precipitate price declines."[93]

Regardless of the widely held view that African Americans—especially migrants—were undesirables, blacks continued to encroach into and take over white geographical spaces. The restrictive covenant could only go so far in halting the African American presence and essentially became a "coarse sieve, unable to stop the flow of black population when put to the test."[94] African Americans managed to enter into white communities that lay at the borderline of the Black Belt with the help and assistance of both white and black real estate speculators who engaged in "block busting."[95] These agents made enormous profits by scaring vulnerable white homeowners out of covenanted areas by convincing them that the "undesirable" African Americans had already gained entry into their community. According to sociologist Thomas Sugrue, the block busters "bought houses from panicked white sellers at below market prices" and then "sold the houses at substantial markups to blacks willing to pay a premium for good-quality housing in an ostensibly racially mixed neighborhood."[96]

This continuous encroachment upon white geographical space for more than two decades sprang from the housing demands arising from the unrelenting influx of black migration into Chicago. This in-migration of African Americans reached its peak from 1940 to 1950. The migration of African Americans during this period greatly exceeded that of the first migration period. In the earlier migration period (between 1910 and 1920), the African American population increased by 65,355; between 1940 and 1950 the population increased by 214,534.[97] The African American presence was even more threatening to Chicago during the second migration period. They had grown from representing only "4.1% of the city's total population in 1920, 8.2% in 1940 . . . to 13.6% of the city's total in 1950."[98] The nonwhite population in Chicago "increased by 80.5% between 1940 and 1950, but the number of dwelling units they occupied increased by only 72.3%."[99] This rapid and large increase of African Americans generated renewed violence from white covenanted communities who tried to keep them out of their geographical spaces.[100] Historian Arnold Hirsch explains that, although the violence over contested geographical space was not reported by the local media, it was as menacing as that of the earlier period. According to Hirsch's history of the formation of Chicago's second ghetto, "Beginning in January 1945, there was at least one attack every month and twenty-nine of the onslaughts were arson bombings. At least three persons were killed in the incidents."[101] The violent opposition to African Americans in white geographical spaces in Chicago would continue into the last decades of the twentieth century even after the Supreme Court's 1948 decision in *Shelly* v. *Kraemer* declared the judicial enforcement of the restrictive covenant unconstitutional and in violation of the Fourteenth Amendment.[102]

The White Plague and Black Migrants: Environmental Consequences of Racial Planning in Chicago

The built and natural environment that Chicago's African Americans found themselves occupying, as a result of austere and violent segregation efforts, contributed to their mortality and morbidity from environmentally influenced diseases. Tuberculosis became an insidious and national epidemic among African Americans, especially those living in urban settings and in the north after the Civil War. By 1912, physicians like Dr. E. Mayfield Boyle were already articulating what they believed to be the "whys and wherefores" of the tuberculosis epidemic among African Americans. For Dr. Boyle, "among the numerous . . . causes of tuberculosis in the American Negro" were to be included "unsanitary and unmodern houses . . . poverty and its allied disadvantages, promiscuous kissing, crowded apartments; sleeping with consumptives and in unfumigated apartments; moving from house to house."[103] Likewise, Dr. H. M. R. Landis asserted in his essay "Tuberculosis and the Negro" that "it is well known and generally conceded that the association of tuberculosis and poverty is a strong one. In any community tuberculosis is always most prevalent where poverty and poor living conditions are greatest."[104] The most influential report on "Negro" health and its relationship to the environment was written by Dr. Louis I. Dublin, statistician for the Metropolitan Life Insurance Company. Dublin's report, "The Health of the Negro," written in 1924, stated that it was his opinion that the large disparity in mortality rates between "Negroes" and whites

> is largely one of environment. The very diseases and conditions from which the Negro suffers point out clearly that we are not concerned to any serious degree with weakness of stock or of stamina. Other races when subjected to similar conditions of housing, hard work, limitations on food . . . show mortality rates no better than those of Negroes. . . . I therefore consider the outlook for the future of the Negro as entirely hopeful, provided the race can improve its environment.[105]

In 1933, more than twenty years later, tuberculosis was described by nationally prominent African American leader W. E. B. Dubois as being "the most serious disease among Negroes."[106] Dubois asserted in his 1933 *Crisis* article, "The Health of Black Folks," that the African American's susceptibility to tuberculosis was environmental and not simply due to genetic predisposition. In his opinion, tuberculosis had developed "among poor people who are poor and live in poor surroundings, with bad air and bad habits, dirt, lack of proper food, [and] who sleep in crowded unventilated rooms."[107] At the time of Dubois's article, over 50 percent of the African American population was expected to have contracted tuberculosis upon maturity and their mortality rate from the disease (although declining) far exceeded that of whites. Although the mortality rate had declined from "463 per hundred thousand in 1910 to 239 in 1921," the death rate for whites was 85.7 per hundred thousand in 1920.[108] The 1925 health statistics from Chicago's Public Health Department revealed an African American mortality rate due to tuberculosis of 382.5 compared to 83.2 for whites.[109] The 1925 study "Negro Mortality Rates in

Chicago" by Dr. H. L. Harris found that, although white mortality due to tuberculosis declined substantially between 1918 and 1925, the mortality of African Americans "increased rapidly." Dr. Harris concluded that the increase in tuberculosis mortality was due to the environmental conditions the large influx of African Americans faced when they entered into the city. "The high death-rate in the Negro wards, comparable, however, to the rate of the most congested area inhabited by white persons, suggests that environmental conditions may affect decidedly the health of the Negro citizens."[110] The tuberculosis mortality and morbidity of Chicago's African Americans was always greater than that of whites and consistent with the national pattern. From 1900 to 1950 the death rate of mature blacks from the "white death" in Chicago varied from four to six times the rate for whites despite the fact that blacks only represented 4 percent to 13 percent of the total population of Chicago in the same time frame.[111] In 1939, with the use of X-ray machinery, the medical community found that the death rate among adult African Americans on the South Side of Chicago was "275 (per 100,000) as compared to 36 among white residents."[112]

The legal, extralegal, and violent efforts by Chicago's white social body and body politic to keep African Americans (especially migrants) in their own restricted geographical space resulted in the vast majority of them being crowded into unsanitary and deadly living spaces. Public health specialists and the medical community in both Europe and the United States had known for years that cramped environmental spaces (especially those like Chicago's infamous kitchenette apartments) were a major contributing factor in urban populations' vulnerability to tuberculosis. Although tuberculosis had been around for centuries, it did not become a "mass killer" until the first industrial revolution in England (and other European countries) in the first half of the nineteenth century, when agrarian and small-town populations (both native and foreign like the Irish) flocked into the urban centers and lived in crowded and poorly ventilated spaces.[113] Thomas Dormandy's *The White Death: A History of Tuberculosis* and Rene and Jean Dubos's *The White Plague: Tuberculosis, Man and Society* both demonstrate Great Britain's public knowledge of the connection between poverty, overcrowded living and working conditions, and the ravishment of tuberculosis. These histories elucidate how large crowds of small children taken from the workhouses in London and

Westminster to work in crowded factories and mills developed symptoms of and perished from tuberculosis and scrofula. The 1843 report of the Children's Employment Commission on Trades and Manufactures described the victims as "stunted in growth, their aspect being pale and sickly . . . and the diseases most prevalent among them are . . . deformity of the limbs, and disease of the lungs, ending in atrophy and consumption."[114]

Like typhoid fever and cholera, tuberculosis was directly related to the environmental conditions of urban populations and is transmitted by the airborne aerobic tubercle bacillus *Mycobacterium tuberculosis* (human form) or *Mycobacterium bovis* (cow form). The transmission of tuberculosis via the rod-shaped bacterium tubercle bacillus was discovered in 1882 by German scientist Robert Koch, who had earlier established the "germ theory" of disease by isolating the bacterium that causes anthrax.[115] "Tuberculosis can only be spread from human to human and primarily through the absorption of either form of the bacteria directly into the lungs. The transmission of tubercle bacilli would occur if someone sneezed, coughed, talked or sang or laughed in the same space as their victims."[116] The airborne transmission of tubercle bacilli is heavily determined by environmental conditions. Tubercle bacilli cannot survive in external environmental conditions that expose them to open air and the ultraviolet rays of sunlight for more than an hour.[117] These same germ-transmitting bacteria can, however, survive for days or years if released in a closed and unventilated area.[118] Overcrowded tenements and housing, therefore, became the breeding ground for tuberculosis among the poor and especially African Americans who were forced into these living spaces for generations.

To meet the housing demands of the racially restricted African American migrating population in Chicago, white and African American real estate speculators bought apartment buildings and homes and physically rebuilt them so that they would have more than twice the number of occupants as the original structure. As a result, many of these dwelling units were overcrowded and poorly ventilated and lacked windows and private bathrooms. Several studies were conducted in the first half of the twentieth century on the physical housing conditions of African Americans; all found the same results. African Americans were being forced to live in overcrowded, poorly ventilated, and unsanitary housing. A 1912 housing study by Alzada P. Comstock of the two largest African

American communities in the city (the South Side and west side of Chicago) found overwhelming dilapidation in the African American housing stock and that "inside, the houses were gloomy, dark and damp."[119] On the South Side of Chicago, where the African American community was more racially "homogenous," Comstock found residents who "ascribed cases of severe and prolonged illness to the unhealthful condition of the houses in which they were living."[120] Her study found both original and converted two-story, two-flat homes in these African American communities that were frequently overcrowded and had "rooms . . . poorly lighted and ventilated . . . sanitary provisions . . . inadequate and the alley and ground around the house usually disfigured with rubbish and refuse."[121]

The 1920 "cursory survey" of physical conditions of African American housing by the Chicago Commission on the Negro Problem and 1919 Race Riot found that over 84 percent of the population lived in the worst type of housing: "C" or "D" housing. These types of housing were characterized as being dilapidated, overcrowded, and in such degraded physical states that it was difficult and almost impossible to enforce health regulations. The commission reported that "most of these dwellings were frail, flimsy, tottering, unkempt and . . . some literally falling apart."[122] A later study in 1924, led by Sophonisba Breckenridge and Edith Abbot from the University of Chicago at the request of Mary McDowell, by this time commissioner of public welfare for the city of Chicago, found that the housing conditions had grown worse since they were first studied in 1912. According to the 1924 study, "sleeping rooms were darker and more crowded."[123] A 1938 study of African American housing conditions in Chicago by the Chicago Housing Association found the stereotypical housing for this population to be the "kitchenette apartment" and that 67 percent of the housing for African Americans "lacked the complete facilities of central heating, gas electricity, unshared kitchen and private bath."[124] The 1940 Chicago census revealed that overcrowding existed in 55,157 residential units occupied by African Americans and 206,103 units had either no private baths or were in need of major repairs.[125] Between 1940 and 1950 the number of these carved-up units lacking private baths increased by 52.3 percent.[126] The residences of African Americans living in these areas were plagued with rats and massive amounts of garbage both inside and out––city services and the enforcement of nuisance ordinances and building codes were minimal or nonexistent in these neighborhoods.[127]

Chicago's public health community was well aware of the connection between environment, contagious diseases, and housing. One of the primary duties of Chicago's first Board of Health, created on June 19, 1835, was the examination of housing, which led to owners being legally responsible for getting rid of all nuisances and "predisposing causes of disease."[128] As tenement housing became overcrowded in the latter half of the nineteenth century, concern arose in the medical community. A survey of tenement housing by thirty-three physicians led to the 1880 passage of the Tenement and Workshop Act in the city and the 1881 Tenement House law in the state legislature.[129] The passage of the Tenement House law in 1881 resulted in the city of Chicago making routine inspections of dwellings for sanitary purposes. Six years later, in 1887, inspections of 31,171 structures made by the city's health authorities found "85 percent to be seriously defective in ventilation, drainage and plumbing."[130] The City Homes Association, a nongovernment organization dedicated to improving tenement housing conditions, conducted and published its own study of tenement housing conditions in 1901 under the title *Tenement Conditions in Chicago*. Their research revealed extensive overcrowding and "inadequate light and ventilation" in tenement structures. Their research led to the passage in 1901 of Chicago's Tenement House law which, unfortunately, had very little impact on sanitary quality of tenement housing over the years.

The U.S. Public Health Service's Chicago–Cook County Survey of 1949 lamented the fact that very little had been done since the creation of the Board of Health and subsequent departments (like the Division of Housing and Sanitation, created in 1912) to deal with the tuberculosis epidemic among "negroes," which they knew was tied to housing conditions. The report asserted that "tuberculosis and the respiratory diseases are more readily transmitted under crowded conditions" and that their "study of the deaths from tuberculosis . . . which occurred in each community area from 1940 to 1944, inclusive, showed that rates were highest in areas where overcrowding was the greatest and that these conditions are filled notoriously in the Negro residential districts of Chicago."[131] The death rate of 1946 had increased from an earlier period between 1939 and 1941, when the African American death rate from tuberculosis constituted 33.3 percent of the total deaths in Chicago even though blacks represented only 8.3 percent of the total population.[132] Calling for some type of external and internal reforms to optimize the environs of Chicago's African American community, Dr. Newitt, a public health researcher who had studied tuberculosis mortality rates in Chicago, made it very clear in his report to the U.S. Public Health Service that the public health and medical community had known for years that the "greatest prevalence of tuberculosis is found under conditions of poverty, overcrowding and lack of proper facilities for cleanliness." Tuberculosis thus can be seen as one of the early environmental illnesses that stemmed from environmental racism. In this case the racism was the physical segregation of blacks into densely packed and unsustainable living spaces that were denied environmental protection due to the lack of enforcement of existing laws and ordinances that were specifically designed to address these problems.

The abysmal death rates of African Americans living in Chicago during this time were also clearly tied to the awful and inequitable environmental conditions that were a direct result of legal and extralegal racial segregation policies. This environmentally based mortality and morbidity of African Americans as a function of planning forces foreshadowed the current phenomenon of environmental justice, which occurs concomitantly with death and environmental illnesses in racially segregated and isolated communities.

Notes

1. The Chicago Commission on Race Relations, *The Negro in Chicago: A Study of Race Relations and a Race Riot in 1919* (Chicago: University of Chicago Press, 1922), xxiii. Gunnar Myrdal, *An American Dilemma: The Negro Problem and Modern Democracy* (New York: McGraw Hill, 1964).

2. David McBride, *From TB to AIDS: Epidemics among Urban Blacks since 1900* (Albany: State University of New York Press, 1991), 17.

3. C. E. Terry, M.D., "The Negro, A Public Health Menace," in *Germs Have No Color Line: Blacks and American Medicine 1900–1940,* ed. Vanessa Northington Gamble (New York: Garland Press, 1989), 463.

4. John E. Hunter, M.D., "Tuberculosis in the Negro, Causes and Treatment," in *Germs Have No Color Line,* 252.

5. Christopher Silver, "The Racial Origins of Zoning," in *Urban Planning and the African American Community: In the Shadows,* ed. June Manning Thomas and Marsha Ritzdorf (Thousand Oaks, CA: Sage, 1997), 24–25.

6. The classic histories dealing with black migration to Chicago and neighborhood development are St. Claire Drake and Horace R. Cayton's *Black Metropolis: A Study of Negro Life in a Northern City* (New York: Harcourt Brace, 1945), Allan Spear's *Black Chicago: The Making of a Negro Ghetto* (Chicago: University of Chicago Press, 1967), James Grossman's *Land of Hope: Chicago, Black Southerners and the Great Migration* (Chicago: University of Chicago Press, 1989), Thomas L. Philpott's *The Slum and the Ghetto: Neighborhood Deterioration and Middle-Class Reform, Chicago 1880–1930* (New York: Oxford University Press, 1978), and William Tuttle Jr.'s *Race Riot: Chicago in the Red Summer of 1919* (Chicago: University of Illinois Press, 1970).

7. Maren Stange, *Bronzeville* (New York: The New Press, 2003), 7.

8. Spear, *Black Chicago*, 11–12.

9. Chicago Commission, *The Negro in Chicago*, 567.

10. Chicago Commission, *The Negro in Chicago*, 118.

11. Chicago Commission, *The Negro in Chicago*, 122.

12. Gamble, *Germs Have No Color Line*; McBride, *From TB to AIDS*.

13. Myrdal, *An American Dilemma*, 599.

14. Myrdal, *An American Dilemma*, 623.

15. Gamble, *Germs Have No Color Line*, ii.

16. Gamble, *Germs Have No Color Line*, ii.

17. Katherine Ott, *Fevered Lives: Tuberculosis in American Culture since 1870* (Cambridge: Harvard University Press, 1996), 122–23.

18. Gamble, *Germs Have No Color Line*, 20.

19. Gamble, *Germs Have No Color Line*, 29.

20. Gamble, *Germs Have No Color Line*, iii.

21. Michel Foucault, *Society Must Be Defended: Lectures at the College de France, 1975–1976*, ed. Mauro Bertani and Alessandro Fontana, trans. David Macey (New York: Picador, 1997), 245.

22. Tuttle, *Race Riot*, 159.

23. Travis, *An Autobiography*, 20, 26.

24. Illegal PCB disposal practices by CHA in collusion with Commonwealth Edison. The plight of the Altgeld Gardens residents represents a continuing pattern of pathologies and morbidity tied to an environmentally degraded environment that has grown steadily worse with zoning and planning decisions and policies external and internal to the public housing community.

25. Thomas Lee Philpott's *The Slum and the Ghetto: Immigrants, African Americans and Reformers in Chicago, 1880–1930*, Allan H. Spear's *Black Chicago: The Making of a Negro Ghetto*, Arnold R. Hirsch's *Making the Second Ghetto: Race and Housing in Chicago, 1940–1960*, William M. Tuttle's *Race Riot: Chicago and the Red Summer of 1919*, and Chicago Commission's *The Negro in Chicago: A Study of Race Relations and a Race Riot in 1919*.

26. Grossman, *Land of Hope*, 19.

27. For the most complete discussion of this phenomenon, read Robert D. Bullard, ed., *Unequal Protection: Environmental Justice and Communities of Color* (San Francisco: Sierra Books, 1994).

28. U.S. Public Health Service, *Chicago–Cook County Health Survey* (1949), 502.

29. African Americans in Chicago are twelve times more likely to have asthma than whites. African American children are five times more likely to be poisoned by lead than whites. Rates for environmental illnesses among Hispanics in Chicago are much lower than for African Americans but still substantially higher than for whites.

30. Myrdal, *An American Dilemma,* 620.

31. George M. Frederickson, *The Black Image in the White Mind* (Hanover, NH: Wesleyan University Press, 1971), 92.

32. W. August Low and Virgil A. Clift, *Encyclopedia of Black America* (New York: Da Capo, 1987), 251. In *Plessy v. Ferguson* the United States Supreme Court was asked to decide the legality of Jim Crow laws. The plaintiff, Plessy (a Creole who was not white and did not consider himself black), was arrested for refusing to ride in the Jim Crow "colored" cabins as prescribed by the Louisiana state law, which advocated separate but equal facilities for whites and blacks. The Supreme Court ruled in 1896 in favor of the state, sanctioning the segregationist public policy of separate but equal accommodations for races in public facilities.

33. Chicago Commission, *The Negro in Chicago,* xxiii.

34. Drake and Cayton, *Black Metropolis,* Spear, *Black Chicago,* and Travis, *Autobiography.*

35. Travis, *Autobiography,* 2.

36. Travis, *Autobiography,* 9. "The total population of the city in 1840 was 4,417 of which 53 were Blacks, a decrease of 24 from the 77 Blacks included in the 1837 census" (9).

37. Travis, *Autobiography,* 9.

38. Spear, *Black Chicago,* 12.

39. Spear, *Black Chicago,* 5.

40. Travis, *Autobiography,* 10, and Drake and Cayton, *Black Metropolis,* 39.

41. Drake and Cayton, *Black Metropolis,* 41–42.

42. Drake and Cayton, *Black Metropolis,* 44.

43. Drake and Cayton, *Black Metropolis,* 50.

44. Drake and Cayton, *Black Metropolis,* 50, and Chicago Commission, *The Negro in Chicago,* 232.

45. Drake and Cayton, *Black Metropolis,* 46–47.

46. Yale Rabin, "The Persistence of Racial Isolation: The Role of Government Action and Inaction," in *Urban Planning and the African American Community: In the Shadows,* ed. Judith Manning Thomas and Marsha Ritzdorf (Thousand Oaks, CA: Sage Publications, 1997).

47. Philpott, *The Slum and the Ghetto,* 159.

48. LULUs would include incineration, landfills, etc.

49. Travis, *Autobiography,* 10–11.

50. Drake and Cayton, *Black Metropolis,* 47.

51. Philpott, *The Slum and the Ghetto,* 146.

52. Drake and Cayton, *Black Metropolis,* 47.

53. Drake and Cayton, *Black Metropolis,* 51.

54. Philpott, *The Slum and the Ghetto,* 121.

55. Myrdal, *An American Dilemma,* 624.

56. Philpott, *The Slum and the Ghetto,* 156.

57. Myrdal, *An American Dilemma,* 624.

58. Myrdal, *An American Dilemma,* 624.

59. Philpott, *The Slum and the Ghetto,* 131.

60. Spear, *Black Chicago,* 17.

61. Spear, *Black Chicago,* 11.

62. Travis, *Autobiography,* 13, and Drake and Cayton, *Black Metropolis,* 53.

63. Travis, *Autobiography,* 20.

64. Chicago Commission, *The Negro in Chicago,* 122.

65. Chicago Commission, *The Negro in Chicago,* 123.

66. Chicago Commission, *The Negro in Chicago,* 123, and Allan Spear, *Black Chicago,* 220. Binga's private bank became a state bank in 1920.

67. Chicago Commission, *The Negro in Chicago,* 122.

68. Marsha Ritzdorf, "Locked Out of Paradise: Contemporary Exclusionary Zoning, the Supreme Court, and African Americans," in *Urban Planning and the African American Community: In the Shadows,* ed. Judith Manning Thomas and Marsha Ritzdorf (Thousand Oaks, CA: Sage Publications, 1997), 43–44.

69. Christopher Silver, "The Racial Origins of Zoning in America," in *Urban Planning and the African American Community: In the Shadows,* ed. Judith Manning Thomas and Marsha Ritzdorf (Thousand Oaks: Sage Publications, 1997), 32.

70. Silver, "Racial Origins of Zoning," 24–25.

71. Myrdal, *An American Dilemma,* 624.

72. Philpott, *The Slum and the Ghetto,* 165.

73. Chicago Commission, *The Negro in Chicago,* 453.

74. Tuttle, *Race Riot,* 171.

75. Philpott, *The Slum and the Ghetto,* 169.

76. Philpott, *The Slum and the Ghetto,* 165.

77. Tuttle, *Race Riot,* 178.

78. Philpott, *The Slum and the Ghetto,* 185.

79. Myrdal, *An American Dilemma,* and David Delaney, *Race, Place and the Law, 1836–1948* (Austin: University of Texas Press, 1998).

80. Delaney, *Race, Place and the Law,* 151.

81. Delaney, *Race, Place and the Law,* 154.

82. Mary Corbin Sies and Christopher Silver, eds., *Planning and the Twentieth-Century American City* (Baltimore: Johns Hopkins University Press, 1996), 213.

83. In the forty years between *Euclid* and the Supreme Court's reentry into the zoning arena, a variety of tools were used to maintain the "color line" in American suburbs: restrictive covenants, manipulation of the real estate market, refusal to accept federal dollars to build publicly funded housing, or the acceptance of money only for senior citizen housing.

84. Sies and Silver, eds., *Planning and the Twentieth-Century American City*, 9.

85. Sies and Silver, eds., *Planning and the Twentieth-Century American City*, 44.

86. Philpott, *The Slum and the Ghetto*, 191.

87. Philpott, *The Slum and the Ghetto*, 192.

88. Philpott, *The Slum and the Ghetto*, 192.

89. Philpott, *The Slum and the Ghetto*, 193.

90. Philpott, *The Slum and the Ghetto*, 193. The board allowed for the abrogation of the agreement if property values declined and selling to blacks became profitable.

91. Philpott, *The Slum and the Ghetto*, 193.

92. Philpott, *The Slum and the Ghetto*, 195.

93. Kenneth Jackson, *Crabgrass Frontier: The Suburbanization of the United States* (New York: Oxford University Press, 1985), 197–98.

94. Arnold R. Hirsch, *Making the Second Ghetto: Race and Housing in Chicago* (Chicago: University of Chicago Press, 1983), 30.

95. Hirsch, *Making the Second Ghetto*, 31–34.

96. Thomas Sugrue, *The Origins of the Urban Crisis: Race and Inequality in Postwar Detroit* (Princeton, NJ: Princeton University Press, 1996), 196.

97. Hirsch, *Making the Second Ghetto*, 16.

98. Hirsch, *Making the Second Ghetto*, 17.

99. Hirsch, *Making the Second Ghetto*, 24.

100. B. J. Bolden, "Lorraine Hansberry," in *Encyclopedia of Chicago Women: A Biographical Dictionary* (Bloomington: Indiana University Press, 2001). The plight of blacks in being forcibly packed into Chicago's Black Belt after the second migration was immortalized in the African American play *A Raisin in the Sun*, written by Hansberry.

101. Hirsch, *Making the Second Ghetto*, 53.

102. Delaney, *Race, Place and the Law*, 150; Douglass S. Massey and Nancy A. Denton, American *Apartheid: Segregation and the Making of the Underclass* (Cambridge: Harvard University Press, 1993), 188; Sugrue, *The Origins of the Urban Crisis*, 182.

103. E. Mayfield Boyle, M.D., "The Negro and Tuberculosis," *Journal of the National Medical Association*, vol. 4, no. 4, 347–48.

104. H. M. R. Landis, M.D., "Tuberculosis and the Negro," in *Germs Have No Color Line*, 86.

105. Louis I. Dublin, "The Health of the Negro," in *Germs Have No Color Line*, 82.

106. W. E. B. Dubois, "The Health of Black Folks," *Crisis,* February 1933, 31.

107. Dubois, "Health," 31.

108. Dubois, "Health," 31.

109. Harrison Llewellyn Harris, M.D., "Negro Mortality Rates in Chicago," *Germs Have No Color Line,* 64.

110. Harris, "Negro Mortality Rates," 68–69.

111. Michael M. Davis, "Problem of Health Service for Negroes," in *Germs Have No Color Line,* 446.

112. Lewis Hunt, *The People versus Tuberculosis: Being the 60 Year Record of Organized Action* (Chicago: The Tuberculosis Institute of Chicago and Cook County, 1966), 81–82.

113. Rene and Jean Dubos, *The White Plague: Tuberculosis, Man and Society* (Boston: Little, Brown, 1952), 63.

114. Dubos and Dubos, *The White Plague,* 201, and Thomas Dormandy, *The White Death: A History of Tuberculosis* (London: Hambledon Press, 1999), 74.

115. Diane Yancy, *Tuberculosis* (Hillside, NJ: Enslow Publishers, 1994), 22, and Robert Alvin and Virginia Silverstein, *Tuberculosis* (Brookfield, CT: Twenty First Century Press, 2001), 15.

116. Alvin and Silverstein, *Tuberculosis,* 38.

117. Alvin and Silverstein, *Tuberculosis,* 50.

118. Alvin and Silverstein, *Tuberculosis,* 49.

119. Philpott, *The Slum and the Ghetto,* 114. Comstock was a student of Miss Sophonisba Breckenridge at the University of Chicago's School of Social Service Administration.

120. Philpott, *The Slum and the Ghetto,* 157–58.

121. Philpott, *The Slum and the Ghetto,* 157–58.

122. Chicago Commission, *The Negro in Chicago,* 192.

123. Philpott, *The Slum and the Ghetto,* 250.

124. Devereux Bowly Jr., *The Poorhouse: Subsidized Housing in Chicago, 1895–1976* (Carbondale: Southern Illinois University Press, 1978), 30.

125. Bowly, *The Poorhouse,* 34.

126. Hirsch, *Making the Second Ghetto,* 25.

127. Hirsch, *Making the Second Ghetto,* 23–25.

128. U.S. Public Health Service, *Chicago–Cook County Survey* (1949), 390.

129. U.S. Public Health Service, *Chicago-Cook County Survey* (1949), 391.

130. U.S. Public Health Service, *Chicago–Cook* County Survey (1949), 391.

131. U.S. Public Health Service, *Chicago–Cook* County Survey (1949), 397.

132. U.S. Public Health Service, *Chicago–Cook County Survey* (1949), 501.

CHAPTER SIX

"We Fight Blight": Block Beautiful and the Urban Conservation Movement in Chicago's Black Belt, 1915–1954

Find out just what any people will quietly submit to and you have found the exact measure of injustice and wrong which will be imposed upon them and these will continue till they are resisted.

—Frederick Douglass

No other fight is more important at this time as the right to live where one is able.

"Your Civil Rights in Chicago," Chicago NAACP brochure

The primary and most critical civil rights issue for African Americans in Chicago between 1915 and 1954 was undeniably an environmental one as stated in the 1936 Chicago NAACP brochure, "Your Civil Rights in Chicago." African Americans, especially those who could be identified as such because of their skin color, physiognomy, or reputation, were legally and extralegally barred during this period from stable, sustainable housing, as well as from stable and sustainable communities that were

175

not plagued with dilapidated housing stock, poor city services, and inadequate infrastructures, through the use of restrictive covenants.[1] The only communities that were environmentally stable and sustainable during this period were all-white communities. Upper echelon and middle class African Americans in Chicago and their interracial supporters during this time frame, however, did not quietly or simply capitulate to the degraded and deadly living conditions that had been forced upon them and the larger black masses. They launched the first "conservation" movement specifically targeted to deal with the unsustainable living spaces created by the restrictive covenants and by the violence of whites virulently opposed to their presence in white communities.

The long-term fight for sustainable communities for African Americans in Chicago was spearheaded by the Chicago Urban League from the moment that Southern African American migrants began pouring into the city in 1915. The league's effort would eventually be supported by the *Chicago Defender* and the Chicago NAACP to address the legal barriers that constricted and restricted this population to environmentally degraded living spaces. More than twenty-five years after the establishment of the Chicago Real Estate Board's 1927 restrictive covenant, Chicago's African American organized communities in the Black Belt would cry out: "We Fight Blight."[2] This battle cry spoke to their involvement in the Urban Conservation Movement. The seeds for the movement were planted with the creation of the league in 1915 and 1916, would be regenerated in 1940, and would grow exponentially to the benefit of the larger African American community until 1954. The year 1954 was critical for African Americans in Chicago and across the country––the U.S. Supreme Court decided that legal racial segregation was unconstitutional in the landmark case of *Brown v. Board of Education,* which overturned the 1896 *Plessy v. Ferguson* decision.

The period of 1953 to 1954 was also a watershed time for the city of Chicago––during this time period the city enacted legislation (with funding) to enforce its newly created Urban Community Conservation Act, which was designed to fight blight through slum clearance and redevelopment. The success of the league's Urban Conservation Movement was due in large measure to the influence and leadership of its president, attorney Earl B. Dickerson. Dickerson, known as the "Dean of Chicago's

Black Lawyers," was first elected president of the Chicago Urban League in 1939 and held this position until 1954 with few interruptions.[3] As president, Dickerson exerted an incredible influence on the league. In the same year that he was first elected Urban League president, he also defeated William L. Dawson to become alderman of Chicago's 2nd Ward; 1939 was also the year that Dickerson organized the NAACP Legal Defense and Educational Fund.[4] Further, in 1939, Dickerson acted as the leading Chicago NAACP attorney in the Supreme Court case *Lee v. Hansberry*, which initially struck down the use of restrictive covenants in Chicago's Washington Park neighborhood.[5] Earl B. Dickerson was one of the few African American attorneys in the country during this era who held dual leadership positions in both the local Urban League and the NAACP organizations; this undoubtedly influenced the depth of activism around housing issues in Chicago's Urban League.[6] Articles throughout this period about the housing issues for African Americans tied to restrictive covenants frequently quoted Dickerson, himself a Mississippi migrant who had come north to Chicago when he was fifteen years old, after "his mother bribed railroad porters to hide her son aboard a train to escape racial oppression in the South."[7]

In 1940, the year after Dickerson became president of the Urban League, the "Block Club Movement" was again revived by Mrs. Maude Lawrence on the South Side and Mrs. Rachel Ridley on the west side under the executive secretaryship of Mr. A. L. Foster.[8] The Block Club Movement was the core movement for the eventual Urban Conservation Movement. The goal of the Block Club Movement was to organize neighbors and engage them in activities in their neighborhoods that promoted what we now refer to as sustainable communities (clean, crime-free, economically viable living spaces). By 1953, 175 organized blocks participated in the league's eighth annual "Block Beautiful" contest, and over 450 block meetings were held in 1954. The league pointed out in 1954 that "53,000 residents in the contesting blocks were influenced constructively."[9] "We Fight Blight" was the formal title for the league's annual community leaflet, Score, that reported its community's activities in 1954. *Score* also asserted to its readership in 1954 that the league "was the first to organize and to use block groups as a medium to prevent physical decay of neighborhoods." Pointing out the successful grassroots nature of the Urban

Conservation Movement, which had developed numerous civic leaders within the community, the league leaflet emphasized that "the league's neighborhood program is the largest adult movement in the city outside the areas of labor, politics and religion."[10]

Attempts to physically quarantine "visibly black" African Americans from white communities through the use of restrictive covenants, bombings, and brick-throwing tactics hardened with the mass migrations of rural and Southern African Americans between 1915 and 1954.[11] This persistent effort by the league and its affiliates to secure sustainable housing and communities for African Americans, especially between 1945 and 1954, is even more remarkable when one takes into consideration that this movement began before and lasted through the first half of America's Cold War period and the notorious "Red Scare." As social historian Manning Marable notes in *Race, Reform and Rebellion: The Second Reconstruction in Black America, 1945–1990,* the Cold War was a period when leading national civil rights organizations like the NAACP and lesser ones like the Congress on Racial Equality (CORE), "instead of confronting the racists politically . . . accepted the prevailing xenophobia of the times, and in the end undercut their own efforts to segregate society."[12] The overall reluctance of national organizations to launch massive civil protest movements was influenced and affected by the political and legal persecutions of some of its most prominent and vocal civil rights leaders during the "Red Scare." These included W. E. B. Dubois and Paul Robeson, who were blacklisted and professionally disenfranchised in the United States at this time.[13]

The Urban Conservation Movement did not focus solely on educating urban African Americans about how to create sustainable communities at the grassroots level in the face of hardened racial segregation. The movement also actively and openly supported and encouraged African Americans and their collective communities to exercise their civil rights in achieving this objective by writing letters and holding meetings with responsible government officials to address violations in zoning laws, building codes, and gross deficiencies in city services. This grassroots movement was created and perpetuated by the existence of block clubs and neighborhood councils that had been formed with the help and guidance of the league in its earlier "Block Club Movement."

Foundations of the Urban Conservation Movement, 1915–1940

The Block Club Movement was the first national organized attempt to deal with unsustainable African American communities in urban settings that emerged from the first Great Migration. The Block Club Movement was initiated by the National Urban League's affiliate in Pittsburgh, Pennsylvania's, Hill District between 1915 and 1920. The formation of the Block Club Movement was consistent with the three-pronged objective of the Urban League: to help migrating African Americans with employment, housing, and assimilation or adjustment.[14] The movement was based upon the formation of block clubs that were "designed to be a bulwark of strength for communities to urbanize people in a better way of life."[15] The first block club in Chicago, formed by Chicago Urban League staff member Frayser T. Lane, was the South Side Block Club.[16] The league's first secretaries were responsible for organizing and supporting the early neighborhood improvement clubs.[17]

Within the first year of its formation, the Chicago Urban League recognized that poor housing was a critical problem for migrating blacks and the rapidly expanding black population. As early as 1917, the league began utilizing African American women to do their "block work," which entailed going into the homes of newly arriving migrants and giving them advice "about health, cleanliness, deportment in public places, care of children, overcrowding and efficiency."[18] The league's first annual report in 1917 emphasized that the housing problem in 1916 was bad for African Americans and that the organization was going to work several angles to resolve the problem. These included getting corporations and capitalists interested in housing construction; having the "city see the necessity of preventing occupancy of physically unfit houses"; and asking city departments to enforce city ordinances in African American communities. By engaging in these activities, the league sought to create livable spaces for the rapidly expanding African American population by reducing the "number of insanitary houses and immoral resorts" and preventing "overcrowding and extortionate rentals."[19] By the fall of 1917, Chicago Urban League secretary T. Arnold Hill formally requested white "civic-minded capitalist" families to construct new dwellings for Negroes in Chicago's Negro districts.[20] Although the league emphasized in its second annual report that its civic activities in 1917 included using one of its female staff members "to go into the homes of the unenlightened and to visit the small insanitary and unsightly churches . . . to call a spade a spade and touch the heart of the careless, indifferent and troublesome man and woman," one of its foremost plans for 1918–1919 was still to "draw attention to insanitary and unfit houses and to high rents until relief is furnished."[21] In 1919, the same year as the Chicago race riot, sustainable housing and access to sustainable housing were the highest priorities for the league. This is not surprising, since many studies about the riot have since concluded that the fight over housing was one of the triggers for the bloodbath.[22] In its 1919 annual report, the league averred that they stood

> ready to cooperate with responsible, fair minded organizations or bodies of men in the North or South whenever they publicly announce for districts in which they have known influence, policies which we feel justified in accepting as guarantees: 1. That working and living conditions of Negroes will be fair and decent. . . . 4. That the Negro will be given fair treatment and be protected in buying and selling. . . . 5. That the life and property of every Negro will be protected against all lawless assaults.[23]

The same level of emphasis and specificity on demands for adequate housing for African Americans did not appear in the league's 1920 annual report. This deemphasis on housing may have been due to many factors, including a decrease in the rate of migration after World War I, which the Urban League asserted was "not as large as when the war was on . . . but remains steady and constant."[24] This assessment of the steady influx of African Americans into Chicago is consistent with that of E. Franklin Frazier in his study *Black Bourgeoisie*. Frazier asserted that "by 1920 the proportion of Negroes in the North had increased to over 14.1 percent, and five-sixths of those in the North were in cities, principally large cities."[25] The period immediately following the race riot was a period of decline at the Urban League. According to historian Arvarh Strickland, the decline was exacerbated by racial apathy and a reduced demand for Negro labor. Although the league continued to ask for financial support for "its work to adjust migrants to urban living . . . migration became increasingly unpopular."[26] Instead of using its female staff workers to assimilate the Southern migrants, the league gave out little cards that instructed the migrants about their services and admonished them to "be careful of their conduct and habits at home and in public places."[27] This philosophy and methodology of the league in assimilating recent Southern migrants and poorer African Americans in public or social etiquette was extended and employed in their efforts to create and maintain respectable and sustainable African American communities and public places in Chicago. As James R. Grossman points out in his monograph on African American migration to Chicago, *Land of Hope: Chicago, Black Southerners and the Great* Migration, a primary concern during this time period for the Urban League, the *Chicago Defender,* churches, Chicago's old-timers, and its middle class African American community was that their constituency not give fuel to the flaming fires of racial stereotyping that justified the use of racial planning and quarantining in the city. Grossman's work reveals that "'respectable' Black Chicagoans recognized that even if they could avoid living among migrants they would still be associated with them."[28] In cooperation with the *Chicago Defender,* the leading national African American newspaper of this period, the league frequently published "do's and don'ts" for African Americans that influenced their social construction as environmental undesirables. These included:

Don't live in unsanitary houses or sleep in rooms without proper ventilation.
Don't violate city ordinances, relative to health conditions.
Don't make yourself a public nuisance.
Don't allow yourself to be drawn into street brawls.[29]

According to historian Thomas Philpott, the efforts of the league and other "negro uplift" organizations to make the Southern migrants more socially acceptable were in vain during this time, since "to most residents of white neighborhoods, all blacks still looked like 'low grade plantation-niggers.'"[30] Between 1920 and 1924 the Urban League's Civic Department was dissolved. It was reformed in 1925–1926 as the Department of Civic Betterment to continue to address the perpetual issue of unsanitary housing and the concomitant environmental and health troubles associated with this problem.[31] Considered by the league to be its "outstanding achievement during the period," the department was formed as a standing committee of the league. Its first director and chairperson were women: Maude A. Lawrence and Mrs. Frank Brown.[32] This revised Civic Department was advised by an interracial civic committee containing eighteen members. All but two were women and all were drawn from representatives of the most prominent and politically influential social agencies and organizations in Chicago: the West Side Women's Club; the North Side Community Center; the Neighborhood Improvement and Protective Association; the Chicago Federation of Colored Women's Clubs; United Charities; the Social Hygiene Council; the Lower North Community Council; the Association of Commerce; the Community Center Council; the Elizabeth McCormick Memorial Fund; the Chicago Woman's Club; the Chicago Commons; the Northwestern University Settlement; and the Chicago Council of Social Agencies.[33]

The first-year efforts of the newly revised department concentrated on civic activities in the areas of thrift, health, recreation, neighborhood clubs, speakers bureau, and participation in a housing conference that had been called by Mary McDowell.[34]

In its second year of renewed operation, demands for the league's Department of Civic Betterment increased, as a larger than anticipated number of Southern migrants came into the city as a direct result of flooding in the South as well as the typical problems of high rent and "lack of proper housing."[35] The great Mississippi flood of 1927 was considered to be one of the most threatening natural cataclysms in local history and proved devastating to those living in the Delta, destroying homes, possessions, and crops.[36] The 1926–1927 period was a watershed year for the Civic Department. In addition to the unexpected influx of migrants from the South, they began to form new neighborhood clubs and supported the older and existing clubs with speakers. They also began to push clubs' involvement with the city's Neighborhood Improvement and Protective Association.[37] In addition to supporting the development of neighborhood clubs, the department created and implemented three active health committees in the Black Belt that were located on the city's west side, the lower north side, and the mid-south side. These committees held a Tuberculosis Institute on the city's west side at the Hayes School; conducted a series of health lectures in conjunction with a health exhibit on the city's north side; and developed a Social Hygiene Institute on the mid-south side.[38] The activities of these committees were also supported by the city's health department, which lent out health films to neighborhood clubs, schools, and churches, and by the Elizabeth McCormick Memorial Fund. The department also joined with the YMCA, YWCA, the Medical Society, and other health agencies in the city to celebrate the national "Negro Health Week" in 1927.[39] In addition to all of the above activities, in 1926–1927, the department conducted "several important surveys and studies . . . of day nurseries, of summer camps and of several neighborhoods."[40] The 1927 annual report for the league declared that "the most important neighborhood study embraced the two blocks bounded by 33rd and 35th Streets on Calumet Ave." and that evidence gathered from this study on twenty-three homes was presented by the league's executive secretary at the Housing Conference conducted by the Women's City Club. According to the 1927 annual report, the survey provided "important pictures showing the bad housing conditions . . . secured by the Civic Department and used for exhibition purposes."[41]

The following year, the Civic Department participated in an All Day Housing Conference and Exhibit at the Women's City Club and held its own conference on housing on March 30, 1928, at the Wabash Avenue YMCA. This was an all-day conference that included a morning session titled "Problems of Rehabilitation"; an afternoon session, "The Relation of Housing and Health," that was led by Dr. Arnold H. Kegel, the city's commissioner of public health; and an evening session, "The World's Fair and What It Will Mean to Chicago," that had a "special emphasis on the housing situation."[42] The department also went around the city with the Chicago Urban League's own DeVry motion picture machine conducting health talks "with significant films such as 'Sun Babies' for . . . rickets and 'Big Gains for Little Babies' for talks on tuberculosis."[43] In 1929, the same year that the league completed its two-year "Study of the Negro Family in Chicago" under the direction of E. Franklin Frazier, the department held a "Morning Conference on Health and Housing" that featured Dr. Arnold Kegel as the principal speaker.[44] The conference addressed the health department's plans to demolish housing stock that was "a menace to health and good citizenship."[45]

Although the 1929 stock market crash on Black Tuesday and the ensuing Depression circumvented many organized attempts by African American leaders to effectively deal with environmental inequalities and unsustainable living conditions, their commitment to addressing these issues stayed alive. An article, "Hovels or Homes," which appeared earlier that year in the league's *Opportunity Magazine* and was written by Chicago League member Mary McDowell, emphasized that Southern African American migrants in Chicago were being pushed into crowded living conditions that were causing diseases (like tuberculosis) and crime. McDowell ended her article with a strong recommendation that the city of Chicago's three commissions, the City Plan Commission, the Zoning Commission, and the Housing Commission, all have one slogan: "'Slums Must Go!' 'Together we will demolish slum areas and slum houses before 1933.'"[46]

The Chicago Urban League's Civic Department eventually dissolved in 1930 due to a lack of funds and did not function again as a separate department in the league until 1934, after the worst part of the Depression had passed.[47] Like earlier efforts, the league's Civic Department during the Great Depression dealt with the environmental marginalization of a large majority of African Americans in Chicago, who were constricted to living in poor housing stock as a direct result of societal perception that they were agents of blight and undesirables. In its twentieth annual report, published in 1935, the league stated that despite the fact that there were no segregation laws in Illinois at that time, the "active work in neighborhood improvement associations in the vicinity of Woodlawn, Hyde Park, Englewood, Oakwood, Kenwood" had created "a veritable barrier . . . prescribing Negroes within the limits of 22nd to 68th Streets, Cottage Grove to Wentworth Avenues."[48] In the league's 1936 report to the Welfare Council, this racialized geographical reality was cited as the purpose for the recreation of the Civic Department. The league's 1936 report, slightly more specific than its annual report, explicitly stated that the Civic Department had been reinitiated because of the environmental consequences produced by the racially restrictive activities of the neighborhood improvement associations in Woodlawn, Hyde Park, Englewood, Oakwood, and Kenwood, which had prevented "Negroes . . . from moving into these districts," resulting in the "mid-south side area becoming very crowded."[49]

The reestablishment in 1934 of the Civic Department, now known as the Department for Social and Civic Improvement, was made possible in part by support from Works Progress Administration (WPA) workers and National Youth Administration workers. The new department was headed by the nationally renowned community organizer Frayser T. Lane, who had started the league's first block club in Chicago in 1917.[50] Lane came to the Civic Department after having served six years as the executive director for the Kansas City Urban League, four years as the manager of the People's Finance Corporation, and another four years as the activities secretary for Chicago's Wabash Avenue YMCA.[51] A former caseworker for the Cook County Bureau of Public Welfare, Lane began his career in community services with the Chicago League, where he served for two years as their activities director.[52] When Lane took over the Civic Department in 1934 with his two assistants, Miss Juliette Boykin (former club secretary) and Mrs. Florence J. Scott, the league was dedicated to serving more than 200,000 African Americans who were primarily concentrated on the city's South Side.[53] Lane continued the focus of the department on neighborhood improvement, but now this goal was to be achieved by setting up "block systems as a unit of activity" and then coordinating these systems into a "community council" that would work to improve their neighborhoods. The new department concentrated most of its efforts on a test area that lay between 47th and 51st Streets and from Cottage Grove to Wentworth Avenues.[54] Prior to initiating its theories on the test area, the league held a two-day conference at which the "outstanding problems of the area were discussed by 355 registered delegates from women's clubs, social welfare agencies, public schools, churches and auxiliary groups."[55]

This organizational approach of developing community strength through block clubs was a critical move in the development of the future and successful Urban Conservation Movement. This was also the era that marked the beginnings of beautification campaigns by the league in the African American communities. The beautification campaigns successfully increased community-led efforts in planting grass in the neighborhoods and removing eyesores like abandoned cars and trucks for aesthetic purposes. In 1935 the Civic Department declared that "out of the 620 front yards in the area, 116 had not been beautified as of August 31st. This shows five times as much grass planted as was true in the past five years."[56] These activities were consistent with the league's goals for African American communities, which were to have them "develop a common mind on the fact that for many years people are going to be living within this area, and it is up to them to decide on the future value of their property and present moral conditions of their neighborhood."[57] Pamphlets passed out to these communities in this period asked residents to "1. Request landlords to make necessary repairs and to beautify the lawns; 2. Train the children to protect the grass and shrubbery and to refrain from destroying parts of the buildings, and . . . 7. Insist upon the rigid enforcement of zoning laws."[58] The pamphlets also provided a specific list of conditions that led to blight and slums, including "dilapidated houses, dirty streets and alleys, unclean yards and porches and piles of junk and rubbish."[59] By the end of the first year of the reestablished Civic Department in 1935, the Urban League reported that they had conducted 159 talks on "neighborhood improvement" for 3,180 people; had interviewed 1,350 residents and 150 businessmen and public officials "in regard to community betterment"; and held 16 block meetings whose average attendance was 14 people per meeting.[60] The end of 1935 also marked the formation of two of the most powerful community clubs in the Urban Conservation Movement—the West Side Community Council and the Washington Park Federation of Neighborhood Improvement Clubs.[61]

In addition to working on the test area project in 1936, the Civic Department also conducted two other neighborhood improvement projects, "the Community Improvement Project (WPA Project 2526)" and the "model block experiment."[62] The Community Improvement Project, whose motto was "A Club in Every Block in the Area," used 145 WPA workers to achieve its objective of "improvement, mental, moral and physical" for the targeted geographical area in cooperation and in conjunction with the Wabash Avenue YMCA.[63] In this case, the targeted area was from 26th Street to 43rd Street and Cottage Grove to Wentworth Avenues. Classes for adults and youths conducted in club settings by the league and the YMCA to foster solidarity and cooperation among residents included "sewing, knitting, cooking, health classes, beauty talks, citizenship classes, Negro history, clean blocks, lawn planting, interior decoration, religious education and dancing."[64]

The "model block experiment" program objectives were similar to that of the league's main "test areas," whose emphasis was on the development of "civic pride" among residents and "absentee landlords" by "keeping the property in good repair, beautifying property by painting buildings, planting grass and flowers, and keeping the neighborhood in such good condition that the value will improve rather than be lessened."[65] This particular project was conducted with interracial cooperation and financial support from the Celia Parker Woolley Committee of the Chicago's Women's Club and focused on buildings on Evans Avenue from 46th to 49th Streets.[66] In 1936 the league also opened up a west side office branch to deal with similar issues of housing and neighborhood pride.

The grim fact of little and extremely poor housing stock for black Chicagoans was espoused before the Chicago Urban League on February 26, 1936, by Harold L. Ickes, U.S. secretary of the interior and administrator of public works, who had formerly been the president of the Chicago NAACP.[67] In his address to the league, Ickes announced plans for the development of forty-seven federal housing projects in the country's larger cities, which would be open to "negroes." According to Ickes, public housing was being built because the Democratic-driven Public Works Program had recognized the "wretched living conditions of thousands of Negro families" and was undertaking "a slum clearance program on the theory that one of the primary needs of a sound Democracy is good housing, and in the belief that if our economic system makes it impossible for a large portion of the population to have good housing, there is something wrong with that system."[68] He criticized a legal system that had an ecocentric view toward land use and planning as opposed to a homocentric view when it came to urban redevelopment. Lamenting before the Chicago Urban League that more sustainable housing in the form of public housing for African Americans could have been created, Ickes stated:

> There would be many more if the courts had not questioned the right of the Federal Government to condemn property for housing projects. It seems that under our system it is permissible to condemn land for wildlife refuges, for parks, for roads, for post offices, and even for court houses, but some judges are of the opinion that, notwithstanding the general welfare clause of the Federal Constitution, we may not condemn

fetid, unhealthy and disgraceful buildings and erect in their place modern, comfortable dwellings for those in the lowest income groups.[69]

The Chicago Urban League was consistent in voicing its concerns over unsustainable communities for African Americans during the Depression era as a function of racial restrictions. League executive secretary A. L. Foster made numerous appearances before civic and political groups to voice the concerns of the organization. On April 5, 1937, Foster gave a speech before the City Club Forum about the conditions of African Americans in the Depression. He articulated in his speech "The Negro in Chicago and the Depression" that, although the main point of the presentation would center on the economic plight of African Americans, all of their problems were rooted in racism. Foster asserted before his all-white audience that the migration between 1910 and 1920 "of three-quarters of a million negroes . . . in 12 urban centers . . . was a problem, rendered more acute by the fact that negroes were segregated. Their dark skins marked them out. Instead of being absorbed as migrating groups sometimes are, they became communities within communities."[70]

These concerns were reiterated in a 1938 radio broadcast conducted by Mrs. Irene McCoy Gaines, president of the Chicago and Northern District Association of Colored Women, to mark the twenty-third year of service provided by the Chicago Urban League. The broadcast, titled "What the Urban League Movement Means to Chicago," was conducted with Earl B. Dickerson, attorney general of the state of Illinois and vice president of the Chicago Urban League, and with A. L. Foster, executive secretary of the league.[71] Dickerson and Foster both pointed to racial restrictions as the foundations for poor and unsafe African American communities in Chicago. Dickerson stated that "another contributing factor to our acute housing situation has been the restriction of adjacent property to Negro occupancy, thereby preventing the natural territorial expansion which always accompanies increasing populations." Concurring with Dickerson in the broadcast interview, Foster told the audience that "restrictive covenants not only prevail in adjacent property, but in other areas and in suburbs. The congestion in these communities accounts to a large extent for most of the social ills which beset the people in those communities, and the results are undesirable slum areas."[72] The broadcast interview was not meant to be confrontational but informative in hopes of invoking the sympathy of "their white friends" who could help them "approach the goal of a better and more inclusive democracy than we have hitherto envisioned."[73] According to Dickerson and Foster, the league's Civic Department had been formed to address the social ills that naturally accompanied racially segregated neighborhoods.

The Civic Department continued to be aggressive in executing its neighborhood improvement agenda in 1938. With the cooperation of the South Central Real Estate Board, the department launched what newspapers called "the most intensive community improvement campaigns ever attempted in Chicago."[74] This campaign, whose motto was "Your Neighborhood and Your Flat Are What You Make Them––Be Proud of Them," was clearly environmental in nature and objective. The organizers of the campaign distributed thousands of pamphlets throughout the African American community that informed residents that they could help improve the environmental quality of their communities if they would:

> Help beautify your building and your block by protecting trees, shrubs and grass.
> Prevent children from playing in halls and vestibules and from marking on walls and woodwork.
> Keep porches, windows and window sills free from bottles, rags, and other unsightly objects.
> Properly wrap and dispose of garbage to prevent rats.
> Prevent all kinds of insects by frequent cleaning of bedrooms, floors and sinks.

In 1938, the league created what would become one of its most critical community councils in the Urban Conservation Movement between 1945 and 1954, the South Parkway Council. The goal of this particular council, chaired by Dr. William H. Bhummit, was to make "South Parkway . . . again . . . the most beautiful boulevard in America." South Parkway Boulevard, formerly known as Grand Boulevard, had beautiful stone homes that became violently contested racial space beginning in 1919, when the home of famous African American Shakespearean actor Richard B. Harrison was bombed on May 19 of that year.[75] South Parkway Boulevard was also home to the Regal Theatre, "the largest motion-picture house for Negroes in Chicago" as well as a popular place for "Negro stage shows." It was also home to the Savoy Ballroom, the "largest dance hall for Negroes in America."[76]

Even though South Parkway Boulevard had, by the end of the Depression era, become the heart of the Black Belt, drawing thousands to its businesses and entertainment spots and affectionately known as Negro Heaven and the Ivory Coast, it was also fast becoming a slum. As art historian Maren Stange points out in her photographic history of Chicago's Black Belt, *Bronzeville: Black Chicago in Pictures, 1941–1943*, "even these ultra-respectable-looking house fronts in the 'best' area of the 'Black Belt' are merely shells enclosing slum living. The population density here is 70,000 per square mile compared to 34,000 per square mile in equivalent housing in the white district, a couple of blocks away, across Cottage Grove."[77] The South Parkway Council's formation was sponsored by the Civic Department and all of its organizational meetings were attended by the league's executive secretary, A. L. Foster, and by the chair of its Civic Department, Frayser T. Lane.

In January 1938, the Civic Department published a ten-page report that was clearly written to describe and advocate its own conservation efforts in Chicago's Black Belt, which it stated was physically declining from "zoning violations, crime and vice."[78] According to the report, the department was responsible for the grass planting, cultivation, and beautification in twenty-six blocks by 1937 in a half-square-mile area, a more than twelvefold increase from the previous two years, which had seen only two blocks planted in the same area.[79] The department also took responsibility for directly combating slum development by ensuring the reduction of abandoned cars left in the community: sixty-two cars in 1935, fifty-four cars in 1936, and eighteen cars in 1937.[80] In 1937, the league introduced the "Better Block Contest," the precursive conservation contests that motivated the African American communities to effectively launch the highly successful "Block Beautiful Contest" almost ten years later. The department stated that the Better Block Contest was "not an intensive effort but it was an opportunity for publicity in the local and daily newspapers in which other details of neighborhood improvement plans were set forth."[81] This was also the year that the department "promoted the first flower show and neighborhood fair which had ever been conducted in the Negro community in Chicago."[82] The fair was held for three days in May 1937 and according to the department was well attended. The fair's objectives were to show African Americans in Chicago "how to make flowers, gardens, and grass, and how to solve some of the problems which are conducive to the creation of slums."[83] The Civic Department used the fair to introduce members of the community to the concepts of neighborhood improvement clubs and gardening as a hobby, and to showcase "beautiful spots on the south side."[84] The skills learned from the fair made community members more competitive in the Block Beautiful contests.

In August 1939, construction began on the first federally funded public housing project for African Americans on Chicago's South Side, the Ida B. Wells Homes. This public housing project was supposed to be the model for sustainable housing for African Americans seeking to escape slum conditions. This legally racially segregated PWA (and eventually CHA) housing project was strongly supported by the Urban League in keeping with its advocacy for sustainable housing for African Americans. It proved to be a mixed blessing in the league's drive for sustainable living spaces in the city. The Ida B. Wells Homes encountered both technical and legal problems after the land for the property had begun to be acquired in 1936. Most of the legal problems came from "the adjacent covenant-protected white communities of Hyde Park, Kenwood and Oakland . . . who tried to stop condemnation proceedings by filing demurrers."[85] Urban historian Devereux Bowly Jr. notes in his book on subsidized housing in Chicago, *The Poorhouse,* that although the Ida B. Wells Homes was "the first housing project in Chicago that incorporated a city park with it," the land clearance of former tenement housing sites that was needed for its construction "caused additional overcrowding in the black community, and increased activity on the part of white neighborhoods to the south in adding restrictive covenants to property deeds."[86]

The director of the Chicago Urban League's Civic Department, Frayser T. Lane, understood the dilemma of land clearance for both private and public urban redevelopment occurring in the African American community. In 1940, his "Proposed Ten Year Plan for Chicago" lamented that as old buildings are being torn down––many good buildings are going to ruin for lack of proper care. Good properties are being sold for a song to profiteers. The influential dominant forces of the city are trying to root Negroes out of desirable sections. Since we have no other place to go, and since our children will also have to live here, we should purchase a foot hold and save the community from destruction, and from those who would get rid of us.[87]

Lane wanted the African American community to follow the examples of the successful ethnic groups who had found sustainable living spaces. He urged the community to "forget that we are black and remember only that we are American citizens and responsible for the present and future of the community in which we live in large numbers."[88]

Later that year, the Urban League issued a news release dated June 6, which described the accomplishments of its John R. Lynch Model Community Council identified at its June 4 meeting. The news release began by pointing out that the June 4 meeting had begun with an environmental presentation by a Mr. M. Ross of the Chicago Park District. Ross had come to the meeting to encourage citizens to cooperate with the Park District's Anti-Litter Campaign by "not littering the boulevards with newspapers, fruit skins and other debris." The news release also made it clear that the council, which had received strong support from League civic director Lane, had made considerable progress since its inception in April 1940. In keeping with the Urban League objectives of grassroots community pride and environmental preservation, not only had the organization developed a 200-person mailing list from residents in the area between 43rd, 47th, Michigan, and South Parkway Boulevard, it had also held a meeting attended "by representatives of the Health, Streets and Alleys and other public service officials from the City Hall and also representatives of city-wide protective agencies such as the Illinois Vigilance Association."[89] The news release identified eight improvements that the council had been instrumental in achieving for the impacted communities, including the removal of "hideous commercial signs on lawns," the closing down of police stations, the grassing of lawns by summer, and "an increase in the number of garbage receptacles."[90]

Along with other league-sponsored councils, the Model Community Council continued in 1941 to work at improving the living conditions of African Americans, just as the league's civic director, Frayser T. Lane, continued to emphasize the need to continue these conservation efforts because of unfair housing practices and policies that contributed to the creation of inequitable geographical spaces. In the league's February 1941 news release, "A Successful Experiment in Neighborhood Improvement," Lane decried that

> persistent efforts have been made to blame the present Negro residents for the 'blight' which characterizes the south central area but even a casual observer, if he wishes to be fair, will readily understand that this is not true. The area is blighted because restrictive covenants have made it a ghetto with no chance for normal expansion . . . apartment buildings have been converted into kitchenettes with the violations of every known building and sanitary code; streets and alleys have been allowed to go uncleaned; and gambling, especially policy, vice and crime have been tolerated by the law enforcing bodies.[91]

By the time the Ida B. Wells Homes public housing project opened on May 7, 1941, the stereotypical housing for African Americans living on Chicago's South Side was the kitchenette apartment. These apartments were created from larger old homes and apartments that were "cut up into smaller units, where a different family would occupy each room, which had a kitchenette installed in it . . . and a single bathroom shared by several families."[92] On December 7, 1941, the bombing of Pearl Harbor plunged the country into World War II. As the war progressed, the already unsustainable, overcrowded, and inadequate housing conditions were exacerbated with another mass migration of black Southern migrants to meet the demands of war and postwar economies. The African American population increased from 8 percent of the city's population (278,000) prior to the war years to 14 percent of the population (492,000) by 1950 and was "crowded into almost the same amount of space as in 1940."[93] The dismal housing conditions produced by this second migration fueled the emergence of the Urban Conservation Movement.

The Urban Conservation Movement, 1945–1954

Civil rights historians like Nancy J. Weiss have argued that the National Urban League was not a civil rights organization at its inception in 1910. Rather, Weiss feels that the league was a "social service agency dedicated to advancing the social and economic conditions of blacks in the cities" that "left the business of political and civil rights to its counterpart, the National Association for the Advancement of Colored People (NAACP)."[94] Much of the research for this book, however, contradicts Weiss's assertion, especially when one looks at the league's Urban Conservation Movement that occurred from 1945 to 1954.[95]

Through its various departments (such as the Civic Education Department) the league had always addressed what we refer to today as "sustainability" issues. In the face of the second migration, which in sheer numbers was much greater than the first, African Americans decided to make the best of what they perceived to be an exponentially deteriorating environmental geographical space. The Urban Conservation Movement was seen by African American leaders as a critical effort in the civil rights struggle for Chicago's African American community. Restrictive covenants and the resultant housing dilemmas were the primary civil rights issue of the time. As well, the continued existence of legal restrictive covenants immediately after the war fueled a new crisis as the concomitant environmental problems associated with crowded living conditions (tuberculosis, rat attacks, and house fires) reached crisis levels.

In a March 4, 1947, letter to National Urban League executive secretary Lester B. Granger, Sidney R. Williams, executive secretary of the Chicago Urban League, declared that "Chicago's most urgent immediate problem is housing" and urged a formal plan of action that would get "aldermen with all or large Negro constituents to have the city appropriate sufficient funds to subsidize the cleaning up of the buildings and alleys." In turn, that would "get the householders completely sold on the idea . . . to such a degree that they will become a political force of the first magnitude."[96] Williams also pointed out that Chicago's proposed civic program "would in no way detract from the current struggle against restrictive covenants. Rather it would support it. Moreover, pending the day when forced racial ghettos are a thing of the past in Chicago, it is desirable that Negro people live in healthier and more inspiring surroundings, if no other reason than for their children's sake."[97]

At the time that the Urban Conservation Movement began, racial tensions in Chicago were high. Housing demands had increased significantly due to the large number of returning war veterans. Restrictive covenants were in effect and were being legally and violently enforced. Chicago Mayor Dwight H. Green had appointed judge Leonard C. Reid, who openly supported and had signed restrictive covenants, to the circuit court.[98] The front headlines for the *Chicago Defender* on March 10, 1945, were "Hoodlums Attack Two Homes" and "Gov. Green Slaps Negroes, Names Race Hating Judge." The article about the race-based residential violence reported that white residents in the Englewood area had thrown a stench bomb into the home of a young African American couple and then, several hours later, had thrown bricks at the home of an African American war worker.

According to African American historian Arvarh Strickland, there were at least nine major riots in Chicago between 1945 and 1954 and between "1948 [and] 1951 there were 217 reported attacks against property."[99] This was, as Chicago historian Christopher Reed concludes, a period of "racial terrorism."[100]

The movement was initially driven by the Chicago Urban League's "Five Year Plan of 1945." The plan was in fact an expansion of the league's existing Civic Department made possible by financial support from the Community Fund.[101] The Five Year Plan was in essence a plan to help create sustainable (economically, socially, and environmentally) communities for Chicago's migrating rural African Americans. Each year of the Five Year Plan was to be focused on "some specific aspect of Negro life" like "household management, child rearing, civic responsibilities . . . and basic problems."[102]

The plan was developed by a seventeen-member interracial citizens' committee that included league president Earl B. Dickerson; Rabbi Louis Binstock; league vice president Theodore K. Lawless; Judge George L. Qullici; Sara Southall; A. A. Sprague; and Robert R. Taylor.[103] Its objectives were twofold: "first to educate the Negroes to their own rights as citizens, and second, to help them to make a better adjustment to city living."[104]

Public consciousness about the continuing struggle for equal access to viable housing was well developed when the Five Year Plan was published in local newspapers. Editorials by readers of the *Defender* included "Cleanliness Key to Better Housing" and "Urges Negroes to Help Themselves" and spoke to the need for African Americans to optimize their living spaces since they had little chance of escaping into better and cleaner spaces. In the spring of 1945, one *Defender* reader asked in an editorial, "Don't you think we could get or rent flats or homes in better neighborhoods if we were cleaner and more progressive in the homes we now live in?"[105] Within two weeks of that publicized question, on May 5, 1945, Bronzeville Mayor Dr. James M. Scott issued a "Clean Up Creed" that was published in the *Defender*.[106] The mayor's creed was clearly an environmental and public health proclamation "calling on all Southsides to aid in the 1945 Clean-Up drive sponsored jointly by the Board of Education, Park District, and the Association of Commerce."[107] The proclamation urged citizens to participate in the program because "the coming of spring will bring about the renewal of disease breeders, endangering community life . . . a few shabby, unsanitary properties (and rags) on the streets are conducive to disease, reduce adjacent property values and menace public health and safety . . . and rats and insect pests detrimental to the general safety and well-being of our children, must be completely exterminated."[108] Less than three months after the release of the Five Year Plan, the NAACP organized a 3,000-person protest and march "against restrictive covenants confining Negroes to present Southside boundaries."[109] The protest included speeches denouncing the problem from a diverse array of speakers that included Alderman William H. Harvey of the 2nd District (where the vast majority of African Americans lived); Bernice Fisher, the NAACP delegate who had recently represented the organization in a restrictive covenant hearing on a bill before the Illinois legislature; state representative A. E. Sykes; Oscar Brown, president of the Chicago NAACP branch; and Ishmael P. Flory, former CIO union organizer.[110]

The Urban Conservation Movement launched by the Five Year Plan was not simply an educational drive or awareness campaign. It was a well-organized action that consisted of letter-writing campaigns and town meetings for blocks, neighborhoods, and multiple communities that brought them together with public agencies and officials to protest the horrific conditions. It was also a grassroots movement that promoted and supported regular meetings of citizens. A more expansive definition of the plan was elucidated by the league in a "Hi Neighbor" leaflet that was distributed across African American communities in 1946. The leaflet detailed nine goals of the plan. The first was "to lead the people of the community to become conscious of the existence of their community as such and of the significance of the community as a basic unit of civilization, and to encourage them to feel that they are members of it."[111] This first objective, like the entire project, was aimed at re-enfranchising African Americans as members of communities so that they could create or sustain viable living environments as a unified neighborhood. These aims were clearly identified by the second through fourth stated aims of the plan:

2. To satisfy unmet needs, whether economic, cultural, or physical.
3. To incline the people of the community to plan and act together for common ends, and for development of common acquaintance and interests, so that there will be "all around participation in the thinking, the feeling, and the activities of the group."
4. To develop a community spirit and common community standards and to maintain them in a spirit of loyalty.[112]

Through its Civic Department and then the Community Organization Department, the Chicago Urban League held leadership training workshops that taught citizens how to demand city services and how to implement conservation programs for their communities. This effort was consistent with the Five Year Plan's goal to promote civic education and responsibility among African Americans in Chicago. By the end of 1945, the expanded Civic Education Department had secured the "signatures of 1,500 South Side citizens who pledged their support of and participation . . . in the Five Year Plan."[113] In its 1945 annual report, the league pointed out that the home and neighborhood problems identified by the communities were being solved by "the people themselves" and that community resources had also been organized for these communities.[114] The year 1945 also marked a change in the artwork used by the league in emphasizing its mission. For the first time, the cover page of the annual report showed contrasting pictures of poor living conditions and optimal housing under the banner

"For All—Regardless of Race, Creed or Color, Health Surroundings— Good Housing!"[115]

In 1946, exactly one year after the release of the Five Year Plan, the league provided summary reports about community efforts in its "Hi Neighbor" leaflet in the West Washington Park, DuSable, and Snowdenville areas and for the John R. Lynch Model Community project. The leaflet shared stories about grassroots and individual efforts to achieve sustainable living space like the "One Good Neighbor (in Washington Park), who had become weary of pleading with her landlord for a garbage can, piled the garbage on her third floor porch, until there was a big heap. Then she proceeded to call the Health Department. Enough said. Every flat in the building now enjoys garbage cans, furnished by the chastened landlord."[116] By the end of 1946, the league claimed that it was trying to meet the needs of between 350,000 to 400,000 African Americans in Chicago.[117] The Civic Education Department reported that it had received almost double the number of resident signatures in support of the plan (2,572 pledge cards signed in 1946 versus 1,500 in 1945). The Civic Department also stated in its 1946 report that it had made 341 agency visits, held 390 meetings divided between five African American neighborhoods on the South Side of Chicago, and had organized ninety-seven blocks to promote grassroots activities supporting sustainable communities, and that its neighborhood secretaries had conducted 5,773 personal interviews in the community.[118]

The Civic Department also reported its activities for the west side of Chicago in 1946. Although the African American population on the west side was smaller than that on the South Side, the department reported that it had conducted 678 personal interviews, received 1,932 telephone calls, and held 262 group meetings at the league's West Side Center. This was also the same year that "10 active blocks organized into a Neighborhood Improvement Council" on the west side and conducted seventy-five meetings in one year.[119] The league felt that the work of the Civic Department in 1946 was pivotal to the welfare of Chicago's African American communities because, according to league executive secretary A. L. Foster, the citizens were "overcrowded in areas which are neglected all too frequently by municipal services, denied many of the rights and privileges of American citizenship, frustrated and discouraged."[120]

In its 1947 annual report, the league published for the first time its philosophy and strategy. The league would state that in light of the enormous influx of African Americans into the city of Chicago it was its task to "assist the city in absorbing this huge post-war migration [of African Americans] and to aid the newcomers in becoming an integral part of the metropolitan area by minimizing the difficulties arising from race prejudice and by developing the best possible inter-relation of the white and colored population."[121] The three major program areas for the league featured on the front page of the 1946 report were: industrial, race relations, and civic education. In 1947 the Civic Department was renamed the Community Organization Department and articulated three areas of concern: race relations, social welfare, and community organization. Only the last two focus areas, however, were to be addressed by the department. Still emphasizing that the department and the league were dealing with abysmal living conditions produced by the crowding of "380,000 people . . . into areas planned to accommodate one third of that number," the 1947 annual report highlighted its activities with block organization and the progress of the "Block Beautiful Contest" it was promoting with the *Chicago Defender*.[122] Even with one less neighborhood secretary (from five in 1946 to four in 1947) the Community Organization Department reported that they had "interviewed or talked with 4,123 individuals to interest them in joining one of ninety-six block organizations or in forming a block unit in their own block."[123]

By the end of 1947 the department reported that it had three active Neighborhood Councils who were holding annual banquets with total attendance of three hundred people. It had also conducted a "Home Makers' Workshop" aimed at improving housekeeping practices as well as a "co-op food buying demonstration . . . to protest high prices."[124] The Community Organization Department made it clear that block units on the city's South Side were identified as such only after areas were divided into "natural sections" and then into blocks.[125] Once the block units were formed they were then "drawn into a neighborhood council for cooperative attack on common problems. It is in these small units that the citizen learns the responsibility of working toward the democratic ideal and improving his own usefulness to the community."[126] The department continued its work on the west side, where the African American population had grown to almost forty thousand. These efforts were directed toward meeting and supporting the largely environmental needs of that area's Community Improvement Council. The needs identified in the 1947 report for the west side were the "extermination of rats, elimination of storage boxes in windows, cleaned-up yards, porches, basements, and removal of old dilapidated billboards and prostitutes off the streets."[127]

The motto for the Chicago Urban League's 1948 annual report was "American Teamwork—Works." The cover page featured a photograph of two Cleveland Indians baseball players. Larry Doby (an African American player) and Steve Gromek (a white player) were hugging each other and had large, toothy smiles on their faces, epitomizing mutual acceptance. Using the analogy of team spirit and teamwork, the report began with an admonishment and a warning that interracial strife and dissension in Chicago and in America would cause both city and country to forfeit the game of democracy by striking out. On the second page of the report, the league pointed out that "the northern-type of exclusionism Negro citizen-players suffer in Chicago gives rise to a body of demoralizing attitudes among the badly coached elements of both our white and Negro rookies." The poor racial attitudes of "badly coached white rookies" according to the league had been absorbed by "altogether too many first-generation white citizen players which seems to cause them to believe that the acquisition of a strong anti-negro bias is the first base they must reach to qualify to become good respectable Americans."[128] The report gave a listing of negative racial attitudes that the league felt were contributing to the city's and the country's forfeiture of democracy. Among these were included the frequently opined "Let's run or burn them out else our property will lose its value!" from a white neighborhood protective association.[129]

The aggressiveness of the 1948 report was unprecedented and no doubt reflected the league's confidence to openly attack racial segregation based on that year's U.S. Supreme Court decision in *Shelly v. Kraemer*. The Supreme Court made at least two similar rulings that year which struck down spatial restriction based upon race. These decisions reinforced the moral authority of organizations like the league that were dealing with the unsustainable living conditions produced by these policies.[130] The league report for 1948 emphasized discrimination in both employment and housing and pointed out that housing discrimination problems had become so severe that it had temporarily added a housing secretary staff position. The Community Organization Department report continued to emphasize its block organization efforts and the Block Beautiful Contest, but instead of reporting statistics it now supplied only activities engaged in by the community (for example, the grass seeding activities along Calumet Avenue). The department proudly reported that "it took teamwork, interest and cooperation for neighbors in 52 city blocks to have loads of black dirt hauled into their areas; to plant grass seeds and flowers in spots long since void of any of these; and then to watch, nurture, and care for new grass and flowers from May to July."[131] The department also reported that community participation in the Block Beautiful Contest had almost tripled from the previous year––from twenty-two blocks participating in 1947 to fifty-six blocks participating in 1948.[132]

The pressing community issues for African Americans in 1948 were those related to the Chicago slum clearance program that was diminishing the already-limited available stock of housing. For many concerned about the geographical and spatial marginalization of African Americans, the city's plans for relocating African Americans to other African American neighborhoods through the slum clearance efforts seemed designed to achieve the same goals as restrictive covenants. In a *Chicago Tribune* newspaper article entitled "Race and Relocation," Homer A. Jack, executive secretary of the Chicago Council against Racial and Religious Discrimination, charged that many of the slum relocation sites selected for African Americans "perpetuate residential segregation" and that "the city administration is doing by site selection what the United States Supreme court ruled private individuals could not do by restrictive covenants."[133] The league demanded that slum clearance relocation sites selected for displaced African American communities be located "on vacant land, in new areas, on sizeable tracts, and with a non-segregated pattern."[134] Their demands were based on the reality that the African American communities they were serving (and who were the primary targets of slum clearance) were already being subjected to costly and unsustainable living conditions characterized by "excessively high rents and dismal kitchenettes . . . poor family health and . . . many other frightful situations."[135] At a 1948 meeting with another civic-minded group, F. T. Lane would publicly advocate the execution of a "Slum Prevention" campaign that would curtail the land lost to a national slum clearance movement that had begun in 1937 under the leadership of Franklin D. Roosevelt. Lane pointed out that "rehousing slum refugees is the bottleneck in slum redevelopment programs. There will be strenuous objections to Negroes moving to areas where there is vacant land. So, slum dwellers can't leave the slums. Vacant land within the slum must be built up and made available at a price within reach of the people who need housing most."[136]

Of the seven objectives stated for the league's "Plans for 1949," at least three centered around community organization and improvement——"to strengthen our Community Organization Department so that it may do an improved job, qualitatively and quantitatively."[137]

In direct contrast to and more cynical than the 1948 annual report, the 1949 report pictured a drawing of a fearful African American male worker looking over his shoulder at an angry white male worker with a curled lip and wrinkled brow. This visual image resonated the 1949 theme: "Freedom from Want, Freedom from Fear." As in 1948, the 1949 report describing activities for the league's Community Organization Department contained very little detailed statistical information about its activities. The report did, however, elucidate a "consumer" rights list that it had developed for and was communicating to African Americans in Chicago. The list included the rights:

1. To have free and equal access to and fully to participate in ALL community resources and facilities, especially public and private housing, public and private recreation, public and private health, and public and private welfare.
2. To develop a fuller sense of their responsibility for the maintenance, extension and improvement of the total community resources and facilities and
3. To overcome the special exploitation they now endure as a result of illegal residential segregation and unmoral racial discrimination.[138]

The only factual information presented in the league's annual report about the department focused on its work with a property located at 215-219 E. 31st Street. After interviewing 250 tenants, the Community Organization Department concluded that the structure was a public health threat to the occupants and that it should be demolished. According to the report, the property was in a similar condition to one at 56th and South Parkway, where "67 average size Americans lived in the basement next to the furnace, in the hallways and in the partitioned rooms of what was some forty-odd years ago a six family structure. It burned. Seven lives were lost, including two children, who never had a chance."[139]

The Community Organization Department's acting director pointed out that, with restrictive covenants declared illegal, racial violence was still a real and critical tool in maintaining deadly and overcrowded living conditions for the vast majority of African Americans in Chicago. The fear among the community and especially returning veterans was of a "'Molotov Cocktail' being thrown through their windows, their children being burned alive. . . . These vets of World War II also fear the thought of a red brick crashing through their windows."[140] Unlike the 1948 annual report's plans for the following year, the 1949 annual report's plans did not list community organization work as a primary objective. This may have been tied to the fact that the Community Organization Department at the beginning of that year had no permanent director and had experienced reduced funding.[141]

Despite the brevity of the Community Organization Department's report in the league's 1949 annual report, internal documentation revealed that the department was engaged in a well-organized and thriving movement of conservation across the city. In its own internal annual report, the department described itself as "the best grass root organization within the city of Chicago" and stated that its primary and fivefold emphasis in 1949 included the reactivation of block clubs and "alleviating inhibitions of block members." This internal report claimed the existence of thirty-five block clubs in the Parker Council and fifteen organizational committees in the Snowdenville Community Council. Of the eight "outstanding activities" identified for the year, six were environmental in scope and included securing and keeping better and brighter lighting; making street repairs on Princeton Street; buying and placing additional trash receptacles on the 700 block of 45th Street; and keeping vacant lots clean and planting flowers on 3900 Prairie Street.[142]

By the end of 1949, the Community Organization Department's acting director, Lillian Proctor, was submitting "how to" organizational packets to other Urban League affiliates across the country. These packets provided information on how to launch a conservation movement in their respective cities. They contained, at a minimum, the Chicago Urban League's "Five Year Plan Materials" packet consisting of five brochures and press releases, and seven items in their "Block Beautiful Contest" packet that included a judge's rating sheet, contest check sheet, "kick-off" letter, sponsor letter, and a "Block Beautiful" newsletter.[143] Proctor also began to seek out well-developed constitutions from other league affiliates to distribute to Chicago neighborhood councils.[144] All of the national leagues' Community Organization Departments were working collaboratively during this time to create structured and well-organized sustainable communities in urban centers.[145] Now well established and one year away from the completion of the Five Year Plan but constrained by a reduced budget, the Community Organization Department decided at the end of 1949 that its emphasis for 1950 would be to respond to the block clubs on an "as needed" and "as requested" basis and continue the "League Beautiful" program epitomized by the Block Beautiful Contest that had begun in 1945.

The department's goal to support its existing block organizations in 1950 was met with success. It almost doubled the number of active block units——from thirty-seven in May 1950 to sixty-nine in December 1950 (twenty-four of these were new block clubs).[146] Having active block units was critical to the conservation movement since most of them were engaged in improving their immediate neighborhoods. The year 1950 was also the fifth year of the league's "Block Beautiful" project and had the participation of "thirty-seven block clubs, one housing project, two neighborhood improvement associations and fifteen individuals."[147]

In early 1951, the department reported that its three major community projects for 1950, "The Block Beautiful Contest," "The Better Homes and Yards Contest," and "The Christmas Lighting Contest," involved 1,700 people. The greatest participation was in the Block Beautiful Contest (seventy-five city blocks and 500 people).[148]

The department continued to have internal problems through 1952 and reported that it had "a complete turnover in its staff with the exception of the Director . . . with all of the attendant problems of replacement and training new people."[149] Despite personnel problems the organization was able to almost triple the number of active block clubs by December 1952 (a total of ninety-seven). In addition to the "Block Beautiful" project, the block clubs were involved in multiple league-endorsed conservation efforts throughout the city, including the "Board of Education's Clean-Up Campaign" and the "Mayor's Cleaner Chicago Week."[150] The block clubs were still focused on "neighborhood improvement and conservation" in 1952; their activities ranged from working on children's play lots to "hiring gardeners and street cleaners."[151] The Chicago Urban League was proud of its environmental efforts––this was reflected in its 1952 "The Next Step" brochure, which asserted that "it was the league which created the 'block or council' type of community organization and the 'Block Beautiful' scheme, the forerunner of modern community conservation and planning."[152]

In 1953, the Community Organization Department's effort to recruit and maintain grassroots activism was successful, evidenced by the fact that, by the end of the year, it was "supervising a total of a hundred and forty-one block organizations."[153]

The momentum continued in 1953. The department reported that 163 blocks participated in the 1953 Block Beautiful Project, including five public housing projects and seventy suburban blocks––an increase of forty-six blocks from 1952.[154] As in previous years, the blocks continued conservation efforts. In 1953 the block units participated in a "Street Demonstration" conducted by the league in cooperation with the "Mayor's Committee on a Cleaner Chicago," the police department, and the Bureau of Streets and Sanitation.[155] The blocks themselves sponsored "Bubble Baths for Streets," had seeding parties, repaired streets, repaved sidewalks, secured better garbage collection services, and succeeded in forcing peddlers into alleys.[156]

The Chicago Urban League considered its Urban Conservation Movement as one of its greatest achievements. In 1954, they stated that they were the "first to organize and to use block groups as a medium to prevent physical decay of neighborhoods."[157] The environmental awareness and grassroots activism generated by the league was, in their eyes, manifested by the number of block clubs and the level of community participation in the annual Block Beautiful Contest. By 1954 there were 162 active block units in the city of Chicago; of these, 175 organized block units (active and non-active) participated in the annual Block Beautiful Contest.[158] The need for the league to claim this achievement was no doubt influenced by the recent and long overdue formal conservation efforts of the city of Chicago in 1953, which overshadowed the forty-year effort of the league.

The year 1953 was a watershed time for urban conservation efforts by the city government. In April 1953, a Neighborhood Conservation Commission was created by city ordinance and was made up of both public and elected officials. This commission was an advisory group established to help develop a "program of public education and information on neighborhood conservation to stimulate local citizen action" around four certified conservation areas that were slums.[159] On September 9, 1953, amendments to the city ordinance that established the Neighborhood Redevelopment Commission were passed. These amendments gave authority to the commission to approve redevelopment plans that impacted no more than two city blocks or 160 acres and specifically addressed the issues of power of eminent domain for slum clearance and conservation. A city ordinance was then passed on September 23, 1953, that established a Community Conservation Board authorized by the city's 1953 Urban Community Conservation Act. This nine-section act established and defined what was meant by the terms "conservation area" and "conservation plan" and the legal actions needed to achieve conservation aims in Chicago. Like the decades-long assessments of the Chicago Urban League, section two of the Act set forth the "Legislative Finding and Declarations," which declared that the already existing conservation areas were in danger of becoming slums and blighted and that some of the factors contributing to blight were "lack of physical maintenance, over-use of housing and other facilities and . . . progressive and advanced deterioration of structures."[160]

Ironically, when a lengthy article outlining the legal and institutionally supported conservation efforts spearheaded by Mayor Kennelley and other politicians, including former Governor Green, appeared in a 1953 issue of *Commerce* magazine, there was no mention of the decades-long conservation efforts of the interracial Chicago Urban League. Instead, the article—"Chicago Fights Slums before They Develop"—focused on the two-year community effort of the Southeast Chicago Commission, headed by the University of Chicago's chancellor, Lawrence A. Kempton, and the recent block movement by the racially controversial Hyde Park, Kenwood, and Oak Lawn neighborhood associations.[161]

Notes

1. Chicago's restrictive covenants only applied to those who were one-eighth or more African descent or known to be of African descent.

2. Chicago Urban League, "We Fight Blight" (1954), Chicago Urban League Papers, Vivian Harsh Collection, Chicago Public Library.

3. Arvarh E. Strickland, *History of the Chicago Urban League* (Columbia: University of Missouri Press, 1966, 2001), 179–80. Dickerson stepped down from office between 1948 and 1950 but served on the executive board. The board pressured him to return to office in 1951 and he finally left office in 1954.

4. "Earl Dickerson, a Chicago Leader," in The African American Registry, www.aaregistry.com/african_american_history/938/Earl_Dickerson_a_Chicago_leadership/

5. Christopher Robert Reed, *The Chicago NAACP and the Rise of Black Professional Leadership*, 1910–1966 (Bloomington: Indiana University Press, 1997). *Lee v. Hansberry* was the first restrictive covenant case successfully won by the NAACP and would lay the groundwork for the 1948 *Shelly v. Kraemer* case argued by national NAACP attorneys.

6. Jesse Thomas Moore Jr., A *Search for Equality: The National Urban League, 1910–1961* (University Park: Pennsylvania State University Press, 1981), 52. Other attorneys involved in the league included Matthew Washington Bullock, the Harvard-trained attorney and executive secretary of the Boston Urban League, and Sadie T. Mossell Alexander, University of Pennsylvania attorney who served on the boards of both the NAACP and the National Urban League.

7. "Earl Dickerson," http://www2.sis.pitt.edu/resources/diversity/naa/government.html, August 10, 2004. Dickerson was a graduate of the University of Illinois in 1914 and taught for a year at Tuskegee University in Alabama. He completed a law degree at the University of Chicago Law School in 1920.

8. "Block Clubs" (1950–51), Chicago Urban League Archives, Vivian Harsh Collection, Chicago Public Library.

9. Chicago Urban League, "We Fight Blight."

10. Chicago Urban League, "We Fight Blight."

11. Restrictive covenants in Chicago were only enforced upon darker blacks who were no more than one-eighth white or known to be of African descent.

12. Manning Marable, *Race, Reform and Rebellion: The Second Reconstruction in Black America, 1945–1990* (Jackson: University Press of Mississippi, 1991), 26.

13. Marable, *Race, Reform and Rebellion,* 27–28.

14. Chicago Urban League, *First Annual Report 1916,* Chicago Urban League Papers, Vivian Harsh Collection, Chicago Public Library.

15. Chicago Urban League, "Block Clubs," Chicago Urban League Papers, Vivian Harsh Collection, Chicago Public Library.

16. Chicago Urban League, "Block Clubs."

17. Chicago Urban League, *20th Annual Report* (1936), Chicago Urban League Papers, Vivian Harsh Collection, Chicago Public Library.

18. Chicago Urban League, *Brief Summary of Work of Chicago Urban League, March 1–August 1, 1917*, Chicago Urban League Papers, University of Illinois, Special Collections.

19. Chicago Urban League, *1st Annual Report*, 11.

20. Thomas L. Philpott, *The Slum and the Ghetto: Neighborhood Deterioration and Middle-Class Reform, Chicago 1880–1930* (New York: Oxford University Press, 1978). The Chicago Commission on Race Relations, *The Negro* in *Chicago: A Study of Race Relations and a Race Riot in 1919* (Chicago: University of Chicago Press, 1922), 214.

21. Chicago Urban League, *2nd Annual Report*, 10, 13. Addressing insanitary housing conditions was ranked second out of nine planning efforts for the forthcoming 1918–1919 year.

22. William Tuttle Jr., *Race Riot: Chicago in the Red Summer of 1919* (Chicago: University of Illinois Press, 1970), Philpott, *The Slum and the Ghetto*.

23. Chicago Urban League, *1919 3rd Annual Report*, Chicago Urban League Papers, Vivian Harsh Collection, Chicago Public Library.

24. Chicago Urban League, *1920 Annual Report*, Chicago Urban League Papers, Vivian Harsh Collection, Chicago Public Library.

25. E. Franklin Frazier, *Black Bourgeoisie* (New York: Simon and Schuster, 1957), 44.

26. Strickland, *History of the Chicago Urban League*, 82.

27. Chicago Urban League, *1920 Annual Report*.

28. James Grossman, *Land of Hope: Chicago, Black Southerners and the Great Migration* (Chicago: University of Chicago Press, 1989), 144.

29. Grossman, *Land of Hope*, 145.

30. Philpott, *The Slum and the* Ghetto, 166.

31. Chicago Urban League, *10th Annual Report, 1926*. Chicago Urban League Papers, Vivian Harsh Collection, Chicago Public Library.

32. Chicago Urban League, *10th Annual Report, 1926*.

33. Chicago Urban League, *10th Annual Report, 1926*.

34. Chicago Urban League, *10th Annual Report, 1926*.

35. Chicago Urban League, *1927 Annual Report*, Chicago Urban League Papers, Vivian Harsh Collection, Chicago Public Library.

36. There exists no quantifiable number of immigrants documented in the literature that came to the city of Chicago as a direct result of the flood.

37. Chicago Urban League, *1927 Annual Report*.

38. Chicago Urban League, *1927 Annual Report*.

39. National Negro Health Week was a national celebration that was initiated by Booker T. Washington.

40. Chicago Urban League, *1927 Annual Report.*

41. Chicago Urban League, *1927 Annual Report.*

42. Chicago Urban League, *1928 Annual Report.* Chicago Urban League Papers, Vivian Harsh Collection, Chicago Public Library.

43. Chicago Urban League, *1928 Annual Report.*

44. Chicago Urban League, *13th Annual Report, 1929.* Chicago Urban League Papers, Vivian Harsh Collection, Chicago Public Library.

45. Chicago Urban League, *13th Annual Report, 1929.*

46. Chicago Urban League, *Opportunity Magazine 77* (100), March 1929.

47. Arvarh E. Strickland, *History of the Chicago Urban League,* 107, 114. Chicago Urban League, "Welfare Council Report," 1936.

48. Chicago Urban League, 1935 *Annual Report.* Chicago Urban League Papers, Vivian Harsh Collection, Chicago Public Library.

49. Chicago Urban League, *Welfare Council Report 1936.* Chicago Urban League Papers, Vivian Harsh Collection, Chicago Public Library.

50. Chicago Urban League, *Welfare Council Report 1936,* 63.

51. Chicago Urban League, *20th Annual Report, 1936*, Chicago Urban League Papers, Vivian Harsh Collection.

52. Chicago Urban League, *1935 Annual Report,* Chicago Urban League Papers, Vivian Harsh Collection, Chicago Public Library.

53. Chicago Urban League, *1935 Annual Report.*

54. Chicago Urban League, *20th Annual Report.*

55. Chicago Urban League, *20th Annual Report.*

56. Chicago Urban League, *1935 Annual Report.*

57. Chicago Urban League, *1935 Annual Report.*

58. Chicago Urban League, "Community Cooperation for Neighborhood Improvement, Model Community Project," 1936. Chicago Urban League Papers, Vivian Harsh Collection, Chicago Public Library.

59. Chicago Urban League, "Community Cooperation," 1936.

60. Chicago Urban League, *1935 Annual Report.* Chicago Urban League Papers, Vivian Harsh Collection, Chicago Public Library.

61. Chicago Urban League, *1935 Annual Report.*

62. Chicago Urban League, *Welfare Council Report 1936,* 69, 71.

63. Chicago Urban League, *Welfare Council Report 1936,* 69.

64. Chicago Urban League, *Welfare Council Report 1936,* 70.

65. Chicago Urban League, *Welfare Council Report* 1936, 71.

66. Chicago Urban League, *Welfare Council Report* 1936, 72.

67. Press Release, Claude Barnett Papers, Folder 6, Chicago Historical Society, Chicago, Ill.

68. Ickes Address, 1936, Claude Barnett Papers, Chicago Historical Society, Chicago, Ill.

69. Ickes Address.

70. "The Negro in Chicago and the Depression," *The City Club Bulletin,* no. 15, April 12, 1937.

71. Broadcast Transcript with Foster, 1938, Irene Gaines Collection, Chicago Historical Society, Chicago, Ill.

72. "Broadcast Transcript with Foster, 1938."

73. "Broadcast Transcript with Foster, 1938."

74. "Urban League Stirs Tenants' Pride in Homes," *Chicago Tribune,* Nov. 6, 1938. Formed a year and a half before the campaign began, the South Central Real Estate Board, consisting of forty firms, was organized "for the purpose of cooperating in the rehabilitation of the south side."

75. Tuttle, *Race Riot,* 157–58.

76. Maren Stange, *Bronzeville: Black Chicago in Pictures, 1941–1943* (New York: New Press, W. W. Norton, 2003), 189.

77. Stange, *Bronzeville,* 3.

78. Chicago Urban League, Annual *Report of the Civic Department, 1938.* Chicago Urban League Papers, Vivian Harsh Collection, Chicago Public Library.

79. Chicago Urban League, *Annual Report of the Civic Department, 1938.*

80. Chicago Urban League, *Annual Report of the Civic Department, 1938.*

81. Chicago Urban League, *Annual Report of the Civic Department, 1938.*

82. Chicago Urban League, *Annual Report of the Civic Department, 1938.*

83. Chicago Urban League, *Annual Report of the Civic Department, 1938.*

84. Chicago Urban League, *Annual Report of the Civic Department, 1938.*

85. Strickland, *History of the Chicago Urban League,* 126.

86. Devereux Bowly Jr., *The Poorhouse: Subsidized Housing* in *Chicago, 1895–1976* (Carbondale: Southern Illinois University Press, 1978), 28, 30.

87. F. T. Lane, "Proposed Ten Year Plan for Chicago," Chicago Urban League, January 1, 1940. Chicago Urban League Papers, Vivian Harsh Collection, Chicago Public Library.

88. Lane, "Proposed Ten Year Plan for Chicago."

89. Chicago Urban League, "Model Community Makes Progress," News Release, June 6, 1940. UIC Special Collections.

90. Chicago Urban League, "Model Community Makes Progress."

91. Chicago Urban League, "A Successful Experiment in Neighborhood Improvement," News Release, February 1941. UIC Special Collections.

92. Bowly, *The Poorhouse,* 30.

93. Robert Mitton, "Commentary on Areas of Negro Residence Map, 1950, 1960 and 1964." Chicago Urban League Research Report, May 1965. Chicago Urban League Files, Chicago Urban League.

94. Nancy J. Weiss, *Whitney M. Young, Jr., and the Struggle for Civil Rights* (Princeton, NJ: Princeton University Press, 1989), 99.

95. Chicago Urban League, Annual Reports, 1940–1954. This movement emerged and thrived under the leadership of one of the most prominent civil rights attorneys of the time, Earl B. Dickerson, who was strongly affiliated with the Chicago NAACP.

96. Chicago Urban League, *1947 Prospectus,* UIC Special Collections.

97. Chicago Urban League, *1947 Prospectus.*

98. "Hoodlums Attack Two Homes" and "Gov. Green Slaps Negroes, Names Race Hating Judge," *Chicago Defender,* March 10, 1945.

99. Strickland, *History of the Chicago Urban League,* 160.

100. Christopher Robert Reed, *The Chicago NAACP,* 147.

101. Strickland, *History of the Chicago Urban League,* 115, 139. The Community Fund developed from the Governor's Commission on Unemployment and was a financial resource (providing funds) to social service agencies in Chicago.

102. Strickland, *History of the Chicago Urban League,* 139.

103. "5 Year Plan for Race Betterment, League Aim," *Chicago Defender,* April 21, 1945.

104. "5 Year Plan for Race Betterment."

105. "Cleanliness Key to Better Housing," *Chicago Defender,* April 28, 1945.

106. Nathan Thompson, "Short History of the Mayor of Bronzeville," in Palm Tavern website: http://palmtavern.bizland.com/palmtavern/Mayor_of_Bronzeville_story.htm, July 11, 2004. According to Thompson, the "mayor" idea came from James "Jimmy" Gentry, a *Chicago Bee* editor and then *Chicago Defender* writer who was also a club promoter who had "bankrolled the annual Miss Bronze American beauty pageants" since 1916. The Mayor of Bronzeville idea was launched in 1930 after Gentry went to the *Defender* with the support of Robert Abbott (the founding publisher of the *Defender*). According to the *Defender's* charter mission statement, "the Mayor of Bronzeville was conceived to elevate an outstanding citizen to heights beyond imagination and to make him a symbol for the city. The Mayor is the most important figure in the community, a person who has his hands on the pulse of every major development or situation affecting the area. He inspires his fellow citizens and elevates them as a mass. He is the servant of the community." The Mayor of Bronzeville was selected from a popular vote among African Americans in Chicago in an election conducted by the *Chicago Defender.* Thompson points out that "posters and ballot boxes were set up in every drug store, restaurant, boutique, barber shop, garage, church, grocery store, and newspaper stand in Bronzeville and nomination ballots ran in December. The campaign was all the rage." Even though the position was, according to Thompson, a "paper tiger" position, "when the Mayor of Bronzeville talked issues with outside business and

political leaders, his words were taken in a sense that this person truly spoke for the concerns of the community."

107. "Mayor of Bronzeville Issues Clean-Up Drive," *Chicago Defender*, May 5, 1945.

108. "Mayor of Bronzeville Issues Clean-Up Drive."

109. "3,000 Parade in Protest on Housing Ban," *Chicago Defender*, June 30, 1945.

110. "3,000 Parade in Protest on Housing Ban."

111. Chicago Urban League, "Hi Neighbor" (1946), UIC Special Collections.

112. Chicago Urban League, "Hi Neighbor."

113. Chicago Urban League, *1945 Annual Report*, UIC Special Collections.

114. Chicago Urban League, *1945 Annual Report*.

115. Chicago Urban League, *1945 Annual Report*.

116. Chicago Urban League, "Hi Neighbor."

117. Chicago Urban League, *1946 Annual Report*.

118. Chicago Urban League, *1946 Annual Report*.

119. Chicago Urban League, *1946 Annual Report*.

120. Chicago Urban League, *1945 Annual Report*.

121. Chicago Urban League, *Three Decades of Service, 1916–1946*. The motto for the 1946 report was "Not Alms, But Opportunity." Chicago Historical Society, Chicago, Ill.

122. Chicago Urban League, *1947 Annual Report*, UIC Special Collections.

123. Chicago Urban League, *1947 Annual Report*.

124. Chicago Urban League, *1947 Annual Report*.

125. Chicago Urban League, *1947 Annual Report*.

126. Chicago Urban League, *1947 Annual Report*.

127. Chicago Urban League, *1947 Annual Report*.

128. Chicago Urban League, *1948 Annual Report*, UIC Special Collections.

129. Chicago Urban League, *1948 Annual Report*.

130. "Supreme Court Strikes Anew at Racial Curbs," *Chicago Tribune*, May 10, 1948. On May 10, 1948, a week after *Shelly v. Kraemer*, the Court in a 6 to 0 ruling "overturned an Ohio court decision which limited use of a church property in Columbus to white persons. . . . An Ohio District Court of Appeals declared valid and enforceable an agreement intended to bar non-Caucasians from use of property in the neighborhood of 93 N. Ohio Ave." That same day and by the same vote (6 to 0), the Court returned for further finding to the California Supreme Court a case involving the purchase of homes by individuals of Chinese and Korean ancestry.

131. Chicago Urban League, *1948 Annual Report*.

132. Chicago Urban League, "The Urban League in Action," 1948.

133. "Race and Relocation," *Chicago Tribune*, August 21, 1948.

134. Chicago Urban League, *1948 Annual Report*.

135. Chicago Urban League, *1948 Annual Report.*

136. F. T. Lane, "Slum Clearance and Re-Housing," March 25, 1948. Chicago Urban League Papers, Vivian Harsh Collection, Chicago Public Library.

137. Chicago Urban League, *1948 Annual Report.*

138. Chicago Urban League, *1949* Annual *Report,* UIC Special Collections.

139. Chicago Urban League, *1949 Annual Report.*

140. Chicago Urban League, *1949 Annual Report.*

141. Chicago Urban League, "Suggested Program for the Community Organization Department of the Urban League, 1949–1950," UIC Special Collections.

142. Chicago Urban League, "1949 Community Organization Department Annual Report." Vivian Harsh Collection, Chicago Public Library.

143. Letter to Mrs. Inez. C. Evans, Dumbar Community League, August 30,1949, from Lillian Proctor, Director, Community Organization Department, Chicago Urban League. Vivian Harsh Collection, Chicago Public Library.

144. Letter to Mr. Henry von Avery, Director, Community Organization Dept., St. Louis Urban League, from Lillian Proctor, April 27, 1949. Vivian Harsh Collection, Chicago Public Library.

145. Evidence of this national collaboration is reflected in the National League's 1950 "Community Organization Council Minutes for Meetings at Annual Conference." Vivian Harsh Collection, Chicago Public Library.

146. Chicago Urban League, *34th Annual Report, 1950.*

147. Chicago Urban League, *34th* Annual *Report, 1950.*

148. A. B. Maxey, "Philosophy and Objective of Community Organization Department of Chicago Urban League," March 22, 1951.

149. Chicago Urban League, Community Organization Department, 1951 Annual Report.

150. Chicago Urban League, Community Organization Department, 1952 Annual Report.

151. Chicago Urban League, Community Organization Department, 1952 Annual Report.

152. "The Next Step," Chicago Urban League, 1952.

153. Compilation of the Community Organization Department's Work During 1953.

154. Compilation of the Community Organization Department's Work During 1953.

155. Compilation of the Community Organization Department's Work During 1953.

156. Compilation of the Community Organization Department's Work During 1953.

157. Chicago Urban League, "Scorecard," pamphlet, 1954.

158. "Scorecard," 154; Chicago Urban League Annual Report, 1954.

159. CUL Files on Block Beautiful. The four conservation areas were West Kenwood (39th–55th Streets); Normal Park (63rd–69th Streets); South East Area (39th–67th Streets, Cottage Grove–Lake); and Laketown (49th–55th Streets, Wallace–Racine).

160. City of Chicago, *Urban Community Conservation Act* (1953).

161. "Chicago Fights Slums before They Develop," *Commerce,* April 1953.

Raisins in the Sun:
Postmodern Environmental
Justice Struggles in Chicago

The title for the epilogue comes from the famous 1959 play A *Raisin in the Sun*, by African American playwright Lorraine Hansberry. It was chosen to reflect how elusive the dream of sustainable housing and communities became for the majority of African Americans in Chicago for most of the twentieth century because of their social construction as environmental lepers, regardless of class.[1] To much critical acclaim, Hansberry's play successfully portrayed the struggle of African Americans in Chicago in the mid-twentieth century to obtain sustainable living space, as well as the resistance they encountered both personally and publicly in trying to obtain that dream. Unlike Hansberry herself or her fictional Younger family, the majority of African American families found themselves unable to achieve the dream of living in a sustainable community until the 1970s. Large-scale movement of African American entry into white suburbia did not take place until after the passage of the 1968 Fair Housing Act, specifically directed at ending discrimination in lending and real estate practices. Prior to the 1968 Fair Housing Act, the vast majority of African Americans in Chicago packed into unsustainable and unhealthy racially segregated geographical spaces. A 1965 study by the Chicago Urban League on housing patterns for African Americans concluded, "By 1960,

96 percent of all Negroes in Cook County, and 76 percent of all Negroes in the State of Illinois lived in Chicago's huge Black Metropolis."[2] The dismal environmental state of these African American communities was reflected by the fact that two out of every five homes (41 percent) were "classified as dilapidated, deteriorating, or lacking plumbing facilities as compared to one out of five or 18 percent of all units occupied by white families."[3] Their dreams were thwarted by the city of Chicago's "Urban Community Conservation Movement," redlining, and federal policies that prevented the entry of African Americans into "white" suburban spaces, even after restrictive covenants were struck down in 1948 and legal racial segregation was found to be unconstitutional in the 1954 U.S. Supreme Court decision in *Brown v. Board of Education*.[4]

The city of Chicago's "Urban Community Conservation Movement" created in the early 1950s was, in actuality, a massive relaunching of the slum clearance and ensuing urban renewal program that had first begun in the Depression era with the passage of the Housing Act of 1937 and was further supported by the Housing Act of 1954.[5] This movement was the foundation of the city's urban renewal project, which could not proceed without the critical participation of the Chicago Housing Authority (CHA). The CHA was primarily tasked with relocating the African American population that lived in the targeted slum clearance and urban renewal areas into public housing. "Between 1954 and 1967, the Chicago Housing Authority constructed more than 10,300 public housing units" and "a mere 63 of them were built outside poor, racially segregated neighborhoods."[6] Chicago's slum clearance and its urban renewal programs were typical of those across the country that reconcentrated African Americans into even more racially concentrated geographical spaces.[7] In their seminal work *American Apartheid: Segregation and the Making of the Underclass*, urban scholars Douglass S. Massey and Nancy A. Denton concluded that "the razing of neighborhoods near [racially] threatened areas did check the spread of 'urban blight' and 'saved' many areas, but black critics complained that 'urban renewal' simply meant 'Negro removal' and the evidence largely bears them out."[8] According to Massey and Denton's study, "urban renewal . . . destroyed more housing than it created."[9] Planning scholar Sigmund C. Shipp concurs with Denton and Massey's conclusion in his essay "Winning Some Battles but Losing the Wars" and points out that "Negro removal" was synonymous with urban renewal and was also referred to as "a 'Negro clearance' program with its goal being the creation of a White middle-class neighborhood."[10] Research on this phenomenon has found that "between 1957 and 1961, almost two-thirds of those persons displaced by urban renewal projects nationwide were Black or Puerto Rican."[11]

The slum clearance and urban redevelopment activities in Chicago were typical of many similar efforts across the country and caused thousands of African American communities to be bulldozed and their residents packed into even more racially segregated public housing. The outcomes of Chicago's race-based resettlement policies implemented by the CHA in direct support of the city's urban renewal program were eventually found to be illegal on February 10, 1969, by federal judge Richard B. Austin. Austin's decision was based on the findings that the CHA had "imposed a racial quota in four predominantly white projects, Trumball Park, Lathrop, Lawndale Gardens, and Bridgeport," and that "CHA family housing was 99 percent occupied by blacks, and that 99.5 percent of its units were in black or racially changing neighborhoods."[12] This federal judicial decision emerged after Chicago African American community activist Dorothy Gautreaux and several other African Americans filed a legal complaint against the CHA in 1966. They felt that it was illegal and "unjust that CHA residents had no choice but to live in segregated high poverty neighborhoods."[13] They charged that the CHA and U.S. Department of Housing and Urban Development's action of concentrating more than 10,000 public housing units in isolated African American neighborhoods was a violation of the U.S. constitution that "guarantees all citizens equal protection of the laws and the 1964 Civil Rights Act, which outlaws racial discrimination in programs that receive federal funding."[14] In the legal decision of September 11, 1973, by the Court of Appeals of the Seventh Circuit, the judges stated that "anyone reading the various opinions of the District Court and of this Court quickly discovers a callousness on the part of the appellees [CHA and HUD] towards the rights of the black, underprivileged citizens of Chicago that is beyond comprehension."[15] The Gautreaux case eventually reached the Supreme Court, where the Court of Appeals decision was upheld by a vote of 8 to 0 on April 20, 1976.

The Gautreaux case was, unfortunately, the manifestation of the predicted fears that were articulated by African American leadership between the 1930s and early 1950s (especially those of Chicago Urban League president and NAACP attorney Earl B. Dickerson). The fears were that even more severely unsustainable communities would be created by more austere racial segregation from slum clearance programs. Many in the African American community and their interracial supporters failed to successfully act to alleviate these fears because (as discussed earlier in this book) public housing for African Americans was perceived as the optimal environmental solution to blighted slum conditions in Chicago. Planning scholar Sigmund C. Shipp points out that "some middle-class African Americans, as well as representatives of the local branches of the NAACP and National Urban League, spoke in favor of urban renewal because they saw them as ways to improve deteriorating Black neighborhoods."[16]

Interestingly, for many Chicago African Americans in the Great Depression, World War II, and the postwar era, the "American Dream" of a safe and healthy community was the public housing unit. This mentality was boosted by the development of public housing projects like the Ida B. Wells Homes and Altgeld Gardens in the 1940s. These public housing units were frequently portrayed as almost utopian environments for urban African Americans trapped in slum communities. African Americans desperately competed to gain entry into these housing units to escape the "blighted" conditions the new units were designed to replace.[17] The irony of this particular environmental solution (public housing) was that its implementation would result in African Americans (especially those who were unable to buy homes even after racial housing policies had been relaxed in the latter half of the twentieth century) being placed in less sustainable communities than those that had existed under slum conditions prior to the redevelopment movement. The public housing communities typically had "none of the stores, jobs, or amenities of their former neighborhoods."[18] These public housing communities became unsustainable in every sense. The entry into public housing was not a representation of a "dream deferred" but of a dream gone bad. The ensuing "exploding dream" was the unforeseen and disproportionate environmental health problems (many times deadly) eventually associated with public housing and the inner city because of dismal levels of indoor and outdoor pollution. These communities also became the geographical spaces that were saturated with gang violence, illegal drugs, and prostitution. Future deadly levels of asthma and lead poisoning, especially among children, were unimagined by residents who willingly packed themselves into public housing.[19] African American adults and children became the metaphorical "raisins in the sun" because their immune systems were compromised by the environmental conditions produced by the urban environment and infrastructure of the revitalized and redeveloped city.

Today, the African Americans living in these public housing units are those who are most environmentally impacted; the majority of them belong to the "underclass" as defined by sociologist William Julius Wilson. Unfortunately, today's class of African Americans has been unable to launch a city-wide environmental movement like that of the Urban League to address the environmental problems that plague the urban poor. Their impotence in addressing these issues of environmental justice is directly related to the fact that they do not have at their immediate disposal the community resources that once existed in the legally racially segregated era, which had a vertically integrated African American community (1915–1970). They do not have the same benefits or resources of an upper class and middle class African American community to help fight the environmental inequalities that they face in the new millennium.[20]

The most extreme example of this twist of environmental fate for African Americans living in public housing is Altgeld Gardens. The predominantly African American public housing community of Altgeld Gardens consists of approximately 10,000 residents and sits in the center of a "toxic doughnut." The term *toxic doughnut* is a metaphor for the environmental space that the public housing community occupies: it is like the hole of the doughnut, surrounded by heavy industry and waste dumps. My first visit to the community in April 2002 brought me south along I-94 into what seemed to be a highly isolated ecological and environmental paradox of forest preserve and a massive industrial complex. The leafy hills rising up next to the highway conceal a mammoth water-treatment plant with acres of sludge-drying beds. The industrial complex is massive and contains more than one hundred industrial plants and fifty active or closed waste dumps. The area contains 90 percent of the city of Chicago's landfills. Altgeld Gardens was itself built on the edge of an old industrial waste dump.

Although Altgeld Gardens was completed in 1944, prior to the launching of the city's 1950s Urban Community Conservation Movement, it was nonetheless invoked as the model of a sustainable African American community for at least a decade. The official opening ceremonies for Altgeld Gardens in late August 1945 lasted for more than a week and drew local and national political dignitaries like Temple McFayden, chairman of the Illinois State Housing Board; Congressman William A. Rowan; Judge George A. Quillici; Elizabeth Wood, executive secretary for the Chicago Housing Authority; Robert Sentman of the Federal Housing Authority; and Sydney P. Brown of the Metropolitan Housing Authority.[21] McFayden would declare at the dedication ceremonies that these "beautiful homes . . . were the fulfillment of the democratic ideals, one of which is the right of every American . . . to a decent home in which to live and raise his family."[22] The original residents of Altgeld Gardens arrived in this community almost sixty years ago during the second great migration period primarily as working class people––war workers in the World War II era. From its beginnings, Altgeld Gardens was a planned racially segregated community whose residents were primarily war worker migrants from the South in search of a promise of a better life for themselves and for their children. The development of the Altgeld Gardens was part of a national and local planning philosophy that believed in isolating and separating blacks from the "normal white community" and represented at that time the ideal solution to the housing shortage and overcrowding produced by the large influx of African American migrants from the South.

The community was originally intended to be 1,500 temporary housing units created by the federal government for war workers and their families. The Chicago Housing Authority, however, convinced the federal government to make the development a permanent site, and the construction that began in November 1943 would be completed in less than two years at a cost of $9.5 million dollars.[23] The original 1,500 units were built on a 157-acre tract in the Lake Calumet industrial area, on a vacant lot between 130th Street and Ellis Avenue. When it opened in 1945, 61 percent of its original 7,000 residents were children; the remaining 3,000 residents were adults.[24] The planners of Altgeld Gardens had hoped to achieve the public housing mission of providing affordable housing to people with insufficient funds. The majority of these families found well-built, fireproof, two-story row-houses designed by the architectural firm of Naess and Murphy; each of the homes had front and back yards. All of the original housing units were constructed of brick and had slate roofs, four-inch plastered interior walls, and concrete slab floors. Public housing historian Devereux Bowly points out that, because the community was built on the very outskirts of the city of Chicago, the planners had to make "provisions for many community facilities" that included "a Board of Health station, public library, six-room nursery school for 240 children . . . auditorium, clubrooms, teenagers' lounge . . . four one-story buildings for elementary and high school classes . . . shopping center which contained a cooperatively owned food store, drug and variety stores, doctors' offices, beauty and barber shops, a tavern . . . playgrounds, a community center and city park."[25]

Unfortunately, Altgeld Gardens was built on top of the former Pullman sewage farm (located on the southeast corner of Indiana Avenue and 130th Street) that was used to dispose of municipal and industrial sewage sludge. The land for the farm was originally prairie and was acquired by the Pullman Land Association. "Every industrial process generated during this period more than likely was sent to the farm where liquid wastes were deposited on the soil. The soil 'filtered' the wastes."[26] Construction of the sewage farm began in 1880 and its operation began in October 1881. "[Two hundred and eleven] million gallons of waste were transferred to the farm in 1882 with steadily increasing volumes until 1892 when 698 million gallons were handled. The waste consisted of both municipal sewage from the town of Pullman along with waste from the shops of the Pullman rail car manufactory."[27] The land used for sewage purification was also used for growing crops such as onions, potatoes, cabbages, celery, and beets. The sewage farm remained in operation until 1907, when the industrial waste streams were then sent, untreated, into the Little Calumet River.[28] According to an Illinois Department of Energy and Natural Resources 1985 study, the Pullman system also handled liquid waste from Sherwin Williams known to contain sulfuric acid, arsenic, copper, lead, zinc, chromium, iron, and sodium sulfide.[29]

The charges of health problems tied to environmental racism elucidated by Altgeld Gardens residents is specific and insidious. Residents have argued that their environmental health problems are directly linked to the original land use as a sewage farm and the more contemporary use of the site for the illegal disposal of PCBs by its landlord, the Chicago Housing Authority (CHA). Residents of Altgeld Gardens complained that rashes on children and unexplained illnesses in adults in the community were tied to chemical exposures from the sewage farm and local industries. In 1995, Altgeld Gardens residents discovered that a PCB contamination site was first identified in 1984 by the U.S. EPA and the CHA. This area of contamination was not disclosed to residents until 1995 in response to the request under the Freedom of Information Act submitted by People for Community Recovery through the Chicago Legal Clinic.[30]

The fight for environmental justice in Altgeld Gardens was spearheaded by an African American widow and resident of the community who had lost her husband to cancer, Hazel Johnson. Johnson's determination to find out why her husband and so many of her neighbors were dying from cancer led her to create the only public housing environmental justice organization in the country, People for Community Recovery (PCR), in June 1979 (later incorporated on October 25, 1982). Although PCR has failed to date to obtain a formal epidemiological study of the community, it has had independent health surveys taken for residents. One such survey was conducted in 1992 by Dr. Herbert White Jr., then regional medical director of Occupational and Environmental Medicine at St. James Hospital in Chicago Heights. Trained surveyors completed a health survey of two hundred randomly selected apartments with a total of 835 residents. Their results supported the historical beliefs of the residents regarding a community history of unusual health problems peculiar to their environment. The most disturbing findings in the report were that "50% of 270 pregnancies resulted in either miscarriage (25%), stillborn babies (7%), premature births (12%) or babies who require special medical care due to birth defects (7%)."[31] The survey also revealed a high incidence of chronic obstructive pulmonary disease among residents that included emphysema and/or chronic bronchitis. The 1992 survey indicated that 25.5 percent of the population surveyed reported having asthma––32 percent of the men and 20 percent of the women. The survey also reported that 68 percent of those surveyed indicated that their health problems disappeared when they left the community.

The health survey resulted in PCR's publishing a list of demands that was sent to local, state, and national government agencies. According to

PCR, the list of demands was developed "under the threat of artificially induced environmental destruction and the continued genocidal effects of people of color."[32] The demands included the implementation of a comprehensive health study for residents on the southeast side of Chicago and a permanent local, county, state, and federal ban on all waste facilities to be located within the Lake Calumet region of Illinois. PCR also created a "wall of death." This wall was the entire side of a building located near the offices of PCR. The objective of the wall from its inception until today was to commemorate those in their communities who had died from cancer and what they believed to be "environmental illnesses." PCR's twenty-five-year lament of being a poisoned community was partially resolved in August 2003 when the federal court decided in the community's favor against the landlord––the CHA––and awarded a judgment of $100 million dollars.

The modern environmental justice movement has done much to document the fact that communities of the poor and people of color are being marginalized because their geographical spaces are used as dumping grounds for toxic and hazardous wastes. These environmental policies and practices of putting wastes in black peoples' backyards ultimately have been linked to such environmental health problems as extremely high rates of mortality, infertility, cancer, and autoimmune diseases like lupus and asthma. The emphasis in much of this literature, however, has focused on contemporary problems faced primarily by Southern and rural African American communities and has failed to address the historical decisions that led to this phenomenon. Neither does this literature address the history of environmental racism faced by northern African American communities and the industrialized underclass like the Altgeld Gardens residents that arose directly from racist planning policies and practices to deal with the "Negro problem" as African Americans migrated north during the great migration periods.

More than half a century after its debut as a model African American community, Altgeld Gardens became one of the country's most recognized geographical spaces of environmental inequalities. Its creation and subsequent environmental problems were based on decades of documented racist planning decisions and policies over which the residents had no control. It is important for future planners and policy makers to understand and to take into consideration the history of geographical spaces that emerged from race-based policies. Knowing the history of a place like

Altgeld Gardens will contribute to a more honest and lucid discussion about remediating its current environmental dilemma. Knowing this history will also help planners and policy makers avoid future mistakes and resolve current problems that have evolved from historical planning decisions initially rooted in racist ideologies.

Notes

1. Lorraine Hansberry took her title from the famous poet Langston Hughes's poem "A Dream Deferred," because she felt that it embodied the plight of Chicago's African American community. Lorraine was the daughter of the successful real estate man Carl Hansberry, who owned and managed kitchenette properties in Chicago. Carl rose to even greater prominence with a legal case involving a restrictive covenant covering his personal residence in 1940, *Hansberry v. Lee.* This case was critical to the NAACP's eventual 1948 Supreme Court victory in overturning restrictive covenants in *Shelly v. Kraemer.* The Supreme Court ruled in favor of Hansberry in 1940 by striking down the validity of the restrictive covenant that was supposedly in force in the Washington Park neighborhood where he had moved in 1938. Lorraine, a small child at the time, would be victimized by violent attacks on her home by angry whites who objected to the family's presence.

2. Chicago Urban League Research Report, "Commentary on Areas of Negro Residence Map, 1950, 1960 and 1964," May 1965, Chicago Urban League Office.

3. Chicago Urban League Research Report, "Commentary on Areas of Negro Residence Map."

4. www.inresco.com/Glossary/REDLINING.html, March 10, 2004. "The illegal practice of a lending institution denying loans or restricting their number for certain areas of a community." For this study the term refers to the real estate industry and affiliated institutions like banks denying home loans to blacks who were trying to live in white areas.

5. Judith Manning Thomas and Marsha Ritzdorf, eds., *Urban Planning and the African American Community: In the Shadows* (Thousand Oaks, CA: Sage Publications, 1997), 187. Arnold R. Hirsch, *Making the Second Ghetto: Race and Housing in Chicago, 1940–1960* (Chicago: University of Chicago Press, 1983), 100–101.

6. "BPI Gautreaux," in Business and Professional People for the Public Interest. www.bpichicago.org/pht/gautreaux.html, July 11, 2004.

7. Michael H. Schill and Susan M. Wachter, "Housing Market Constraints and Spatial Stratification by Income and Race," in *Housing Policy Debate,* vol. 6, iss. 1.

8. Douglass S. Massey and Nancy A. Denton, *American Apartheid: Segregation and the Making of the Underclass* (Cambridge: Harvard University Press, 1993), 56.

9. Massey and Denton, *American Apartheid,* 56.

10. Sigmund C. Shipp, "Winning Some Battles but Losing the War," in *Urban Planning and the African American Community: In the Shadows,* ed. Judith Manning Thomas and Marsha Ritzdorf (Thousand Oaks, CA: Sage Publications, 1997), 188.

11. Shipp, "Winning Some Battles," 188.

12. Devereux Bowly Jr., *The Poorhouse: Subsidized Housing in Chicago, 1895–1976* (Carbondale: Southern Illinois University Press, 1978), 190.

13. Bowly, *The Poorhouse,* 190.

14. Bowly, *The Poorhouse,* 190.

15. Bowly, *The Poorhouse,* 193.

16. Shipp, "Winning Some Battles," 189.

17. Bowly, *The Poorhouse.*

18. Steinhorn and Diggs-Brown, *By the Color of Our Skin,* 99.

19. Sylvia Hood Washington and Dawn Nothwehr, *Struggles for Environmental Justice and Health in Chicago: An African American and Catholic Perspective* (Chicago: Depaul University, Egan Urban Center, 2004).

20. Massey and Denton, *American Apartheid.*

21. "Dedication Ceremonies at Altgeld Close Festive Week," *Chicago Defender,* September 1, 1945.

22. "Dedication Ceremonies at Altgeld Close Festive Week."

23. Bowly, *The Poorhouse,* 42–43.

24. Bowly, *The Poorhouse,* 42–45.

25. Bowly, *The Poorhouse,* 45.

26. Keith Harley, PCR Report, Chicago Environmental Law Center, 1993.

27. Illinois Department of Energy and Natural Resources, *Analysis of Pullman Farm,* 1985.

28. Illinois Department of Energy and Natural Resources, *Analysis of Pullman Farm,* 1985.

29. Illinois Department of Energy and Natural Resources, *Analysis of Pullman Farm,* 1985.

30. Hazel Johnson, People for Community Recovery (PCR) History. Self published, n.d.

31. PCR Health Survey Results, self published, 1993.

32. PCR office files, 1992.

Index

Printed in the United States
By Bookmasters